EXPEDITION
MEDICINE

THE ROYAL GEOGRAPHICAL SOCIETY
WITH THE INSTITUTE OF BRITISH GEOGRAPHERS

EXPEDITION
MEDICINE

EDITED BY
DAVID WARRELL AND SARAH ANDERSON

P

PROFILE BOOKS

First published in Great Britain in 1998 by
Profile Books Ltd
62 Queen Anne Street
London W1M 9LA

Copyright © 1998 Royal Geographical Society
(with the Institute of British Geographers)

The moral right of the author has been asserted.

Printed in Great Britain by Biddles Ltd

A CIP catalogue record for this book is available from the British Library.

ISBN 1 86197 040 4

CONTENTS

INTRODUCTION

Any expedition, being an organised journey with a purpose, will depend for its success on the health of its members. To achieve this it is necessary to identify and understand the medical issues that are essential for planning and undertaking an expedition. *Expedition Medicine* aims to provide information on both prevention and treatment of medical problems in challenging environments. Advanced planning is essential in preparing for potential medical problems in any expedition.

This book provides information for doctors, nurses and paramedics, as well as for people who are not medically qualified. Its aim is to be useful for people travelling to remote places, for people going on an expedition and particularly for people elected to be expedition medical officers. It will help readers to be better informed about medical hazards and their prevention. The early part of most chapters is general and requires little background knowledge of the subject discussed; more detailed medical and technical information follows.

Expedition Medicine is divided into three sections: Pre-expedition Planning; Field Medicine; and Medical Problems of Environmental Extremes. A glossary has been included to make the book more accessible to non-medical readers.

Section 1, Pre-expedition Planning, aims to prevent, as far as possible, problems arising in the field. There are chapters on immunisations necessary for travel, first-aid training and recommendations for expedition medical kits, medical insurance and risk assessment.

Section 2, Field Medicine, provides practical information for use during an expedition or journey to a remote area of the world. Chapter 7 covers the medical officer's role, Chapter 8 emphasises the importance of camp hygiene and includes practical information on latrines, kitchen cleanliness, food storage, rubbish disposal and camp safety. Chapter 9 provides details about how to provide a safe water supply for the expedition. Chapter 10 is mainly for non-medically qualified people to enable a safe assessment to be made of an injured or ill patient and so lead to appropriate management. Chapter 11 covers the basics of first aid and the management of minor injuries in the field. It should be useful for dealing with situations where medical help is not immediately available. Despite the best efforts at prevention, illness and injuries sometimes do occur. Chapters 12 and 13 contain details about communication if evacuation is necessary. Chapters 14, 15 and 16 provide medical information on diagnosis and treatment of common infections and the less common but important tropical diseases. Chapter 17 covers psychological problems that may arise during expeditions and Chapter 18 is a brief summary of dental problems and their management.

Section 3, Medical Problems of Environmental Extremes, deals with the specific problems created by tropical, desert, polar and high-altitude environments, mountaineering, underwater, caving and canoeing.

In short, *Expedition Medicine* aims to improve the confidence, enjoyment and achievement of people who go on expeditions by helping them to prevent or deal with medical problems.

SECTION 1

PRE-EXPEDITION PLANNING

1 WHAT IS EXPEDITION MEDICINE?

David Warrell

An expedition is an organised journey with a purpose. This purpose can be exploration, achieving a particular aim such as reaching the summit of a mountain, scientific research, surveying for minerals or a test of endurance. By their very nature, expeditions are likely to involve exposure to greater environmental extremes and hazards than other types of travel. However, the fact that they are organised implies that those who take part in them can anticipate and prepare for at least the predictable hazards. This book is about the branch of medicine concerned with maintaining health, physical and psychological, under the special stresses and challenges of an expedition. As expeditions are usually to areas remote from hospitals or even rural health centres and dispensaries, the responsibility for dealing with medical problems will fall on the members of the expedition. The explorer's worst nightmare may be to catch a dreaded tropical disease or to be attacked by a ferocious wild animal, but the documented causes of expedition illness and death are far more mundane. They include road traffic accidents, sometimes before or after the expedition proper, mountaineering disasters, drownings and attacks by people (Table 1.1).

TABLE 1.1 EXPEDITION MORTALITY

Perceived	Real
Exotic infections:	Road traffic accidents
viral haemorrhagic fevers – Lassa, Ebola, etc	Drowning
plague	Falls and other injuries
rabies	Altitude, heat stroke
sleeping sickness	Homicide
Attacks by large animals	Infections (malaria, HIV, etc)
Venomous bites and stings	
Cannibals	

Planning the medical provisions for an expedition should start well in advance (Table 1.2). Preventing or minimising risks is based on a careful analysis of the geographical area where the expedition will be carried out; its terrain, altitude and climate at the time of year chosen for the expedition. The aims and activities of the expedition may create special risks. In selecting members for an expedition experience, possession of the necessary skills (for example, diving, caving and mountaineering), physical fitness and a reputation for psychological stability under stress are among the most important criteria.

TABLE 1.2   **MEDICAL ASPECTS OF PLANNING AN EXPEDITION**
Assessment of risks
First aid training
Preventive medicine
Medical kit
Medical back-up

All expeditions should have a designated medical officer and as many members as possible should attend first aid training, which, ideally, should be aimed at the particular needs of the expedition. The minimum this training should cover is clearing the airway, controlling blood loss, treating shock, relieving pain and ensuring the safe evacuation of the injured. The design of first aid training and preventive medicine is based on the assessment and awareness of the particular risks of the expedition. Knowledge about local medical problems in the chosen geographical area will indicate appropriate vaccinations and prophylactic drugs. All members should have a pre-expedition dental check-up and, if possible, unresolved surgical and medical problems should be dealt with well in advance of the expedition. Medical hazards can often be prevented by sensible avoidance behaviour, although a cautious attitude may be considered out of keeping with the "macho" style of expeditions. Food and water hygiene is central to the prevention of time-, energy- and morale-wasting gastrointestinal (gut) infections. It is important to identify expedition members who may have special problems (Table 1.3).

Expedition medical kits need to be much more comprehensive than those carried by ordinary tourists. Lightweight emergency insulation must be taken if there is any risk of exposure in severe weather conditions, and an adequate water supply must be assured or taken if the expedition is to desert areas. A lightweight collapsible stretcher should be included for mountaineering and caving expeditions. A few instruments such as scissors and a generous supply of large triangular and crepe bandages and adhesive plasters are also important. Expeditions should take a small number of syringes, needles and intravenous drip sets in case members have to have blood tests, or emergency treatment, at hospitals which cannot afford disposable equipment. Such items and drugs may cause problems with customs officers at frontier posts. It may be helpful to have a covering letter on official notepaper signed by a doctor explaining the purpose of the medical equipment.

Local medical back-up must be arranged in advance through the expedition's local agent. The hospitals or medical stations nearest to the site of the expedition must be identified and, if possible, assessed in advance. An emergency plan must be drawn up for evacuation of severely ill or injured expedition members. In some areas, such as East Africa, organisations such as "Flying Doctor" services (AMREF) may agree to be responsible for evacuation of casualties. Medical insurance cover for the expedition must be generous and allow for medical care and, if need be, repatriation of injured persons.

TABLE 1.3 EXPEDITION MEMBERS' SPECIAL PROBLEMS
Pregnancy
Immunosuppression (by drugs or diseases)
Chronic illness (diabetes, epilepsy, asthma, ischaemic heart disease, etc)
Psychiatric problems
Physical/mental handicap
Alcohol/drug abuse

Correctly practised, expedition medicine should not constrain the enthusiasms and ambitions of an expedition but, by anticipating preventable medical problems, enhance the achievement and enjoyment of the expedition.

2 IMMUNISATIONS

David Warrell and Sarah Anderson

INTRODUCTION

The most common problems facing expedition members and travellers are accidents, diarrhoea and upper respiratory tract infections, which are not preventable by immunisation. However, immunisation can substantially reduce the risk of less common problems that may otherwise be difficult to avoid. Despite many peoples' fears, immunisations are extremely safe. The risk of complications is less than one in 10,000 and the only occasional adverse effects are pain or redness at the injection site.

Travel vaccinations can be obtained and given by your own general practitioner (GP) or a specialist travel clinic such as those run by British Airways. Before attending either of these it is important to find out what immunisations are currently recommended for the region to be visited. Details of how and where to obtain this information are given at the end of this chapter. To assess the likely risk you will be placing yourself under it is helpful to consider the region to which you are travelling, the duration of stay, the type of accommodation available and the purpose of your visit.

Immunisations can be divided into two main groups: first, those immunisations given routinely in childhood, which may need updating with a booster; and second, specific travel immunisations.

The course of vaccinations should start at least 6 weeks before travel commences as some of the travel vaccines require a number of doses to give full protection. Live vaccines, if not given together, must be given 3 weeks apart. There is no contraindication to giving more than one immunisation at once. The risk of encephalitis and other serious complications is remote. They occur no more commonly than if only a single immunisation is given.

If the traveller is immunosuppressed, it is advisable to be cautious about giving live vaccines (measles, mumps, rubella, polio and yellow fever are examples). Travellers who are on cytotoxic drugs, including corticosteroids, and those with HIV, must let their doctor know. Alternatives such as killed polio vaccine are available.

TABLE 2.1 PRE-TRAVEL IMMUNISATIONS

Vaccine	Type	Route[3]	Primary course	Booster
Routine				
Diphtheria	Adsorbed toxoid	i.m.	3 doses at monthly intervals	Single low dose if > 10 years
Haemophilus influenza b	Conjugated polysaccharide	i.m.	2–3 doses 2-monthly	Single dose
Influenza	Killed virus	i.m.	Single dose	Yearly
Pneumococcal	23-valent polysaccharide	i.m.	Single dose	Repeat in those at high risk
Polio (Sabin)	Live virus (attenuated)	p.o.	3 doses at monthly intervals	10 years
Polio (Salk)	Killed virus	i.m.	As above	10 years
Tetanus	Adsorbed toxoid	i.m.	3 doses at monthly intervals	10 years (max. 5 doses)
Travel				
Hepatitis A (Havrix Monodose)	Killed virus	i.m.	Single dose	6–12 months, then 10 yearly
(Gammagobulin)	Pooled immunoglobulins (mainly IgG)	i.m.	Single dose	6 monthly (while at risk)
Hepatitis B[1]	Adsorbed	i.m.	0, 1 and 6 months	3–5 yearly
Japanese (B) encephalitis	Killed virus	i.m.	3 doses on days 0, 7 and 28	1 year, then 4 yearly
Meningococcal	Polysaccharide types A, C (Y, W)	i.m. or s.c.	Single dose	3 yearly
Rabies[1,2]	Killed virus	i.m. or i.d.	3 doses on days 0, 7 and 28	2–3 yearly
Tick-borne encephalitis	Killed virus	i.m.	2 doses 1–3 months apart	1 year
Tuberculosis (BCG vaccine)	Attenuated	i.d.	Single dose	None
Typhoid	Killed bacteria	i.m.	2 doses 1 month apart	3 yearly
Typhoid	Live Ty21a strain (attenuated)	p.o.	4 doses on alternate days	5 yearly
Typhoid	Capsular Vi polysaccharide	i.m.	Single dose	3 yearly
Yellow fever	Live virus (attenuated)	s.c.	Single dose	10 yearly

1 Should not be given into buttock; deltoid or anterior thigh preferred.
2 Efficacy reduced if given with chloroquine antimalarial prophylaxis.
3 im = intramuscular, p.o. = by mouth, s.c. = subcutaneous, id = intradermal.

The immunisations given should be recorded in writing, ideally in an International Certificate of Vaccinations. This will include the required certificate of yellow fever vaccination, which should be kept safely with the traveller's passport and taken on the expedition.

PRE-TRAVEL IMMUNISATIONS

Cholera
Cholera vaccination is no longer required or recommended by the World Health Organisation (WHO). The vaccine is not very effective (although a new oral vaccine is promising) and whatever immunity is stimulated lasts only a few months. Because repeated injections may lead to hypersensitivity reactions, it should no longer routinely be given. However, in some countries, immigration officials may still demand to see proof of vaccination against cholera. Because of this, some authorities recommend immunisation purely to provide the basis for issuing a valid certificate (which is valid for only 6 months).

Diphtheria (Figure 2.1)
Although most people have been immunised at school, there is now evidence that the protection wanes with age so that some adults may need a booster if at risk. This is important as diphtheria is increasing in parts of the former Soviet Union. An initial course of diphtheria immunisation consists of 3 intramuscular doses of the toxoid a month apart with a booster at least 5 years later in children. Adults may need a primary course of immunisation (3 doses) or may require only a single booster if immunised as a child. In such circumstances (and in any person aged over 10), the adult

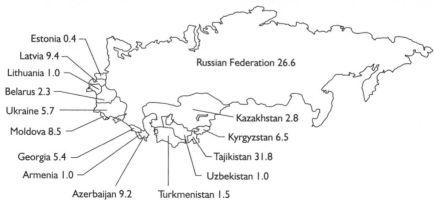

Estonia 0.4
Latvia 9.4
Lithuania 1.0
Belarus 2.3
Ukraine 5.7
Moldova 8.5
Georgia 5.4
Armenia 1.0
Azerbaijan 9.2
Turkmenistan 1.5
Russian Federation 26.6
Kazakhstan 2.8
Kyrgzstan 6.5
Tajikistan 31.8
Uzbekistan 1.0

Figure 2.1   *Reported incidence of diphtheria in the former Soviet Union (per 100,000 population)*

low-dose diphtheria vaccine should be used to avoid reactions in those who may already be immune.

European tick-borne encephalitis

This is a viral infection transmitted by the common wood tick, *Ixodes ricinus*. Most infections occur in the forested hills and mountains of eastern Europe in late spring and summer. The risk of infection can be reduced by wearing stout footwear and thick socks as well as by liberal use of insect repellent. For those who intend to walk or camp in high-risk areas there is a vaccine available but, in the UK, this can be obtained only on a "named patient" basis from Immuno Ltd (Arctic House, Rye Lane, Dunton Green, Nr Sevenoaks, Kent TN14 5HB, Tel. +44 1732 458101). Two doses of the vaccine are given a month apart, with a booster a year later.

Hepatitis A (Figure 2.2)

In the past the only protection against this food- and water-borne virus was by passive immunisation with intramuscular gammaglobulin obtained from pooled blood of persons known to be immune. Although this has been shown beyond doubt to be safe, it is inconvenient for long-term travellers because the largest possible dose (1,000mg) protects only for a maximum of 6 months.

There are now effective vaccines for active immunisation against hepatitis A. The most widely available, Havrix Monodose, is given as a course of 2 intramuscular injections. The first will provide protection for up to a year but, if boosted within 6–12 months, protection will extend for 5–10 years. Protection may last even longer but the

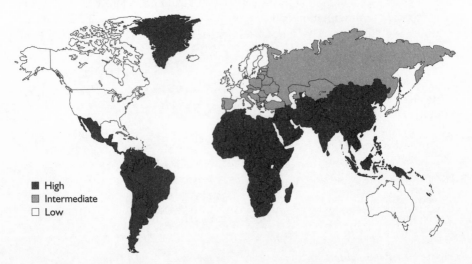

High
Intermediate
Low

Figure 2.2 *Endemicity patterns of hepatitis A virus infection*

vaccine is too new to be certain.

Currently, both forms of immunisation are available. Gammaglobulin is considerably cheaper and may be preferred for one-off trips lasting less than six months. The vaccine may be preferred for longer trips or for frequent travellers.

Hepatitis B (Figure 2.3)

This viral infection is like HIV in that it is transmitted by blood transfusion, sex and dirty needles. As well as causing hepatitis, the virus can persist in some people and may lead to chronic liver damage and, in some, to liver cancer. Vaccination against hepatitis B is available but expensive. It is not normally required for travellers or expedition members unless they are working with human blood (for example, taking blood samples) or are at high risk of injury and might need a blood transfusion abroad.

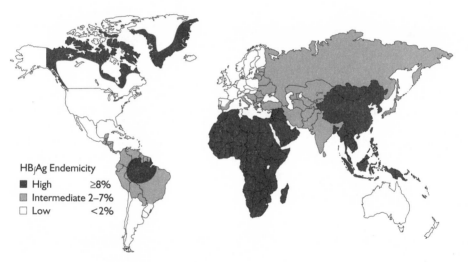

Figure 2.3 *Geographical distribution of hepatitis B prevalence*

Japanese B encephalitis (Figure 2.4)

This is still a comparatively rare problem for travellers, although it is a health problem in rural communities in Asia. The infection is caused by a virus which is transmitted by mosquitoes. The risk is mainly in rural areas of Asia, particularly where pig farming occurs, and is highest in those who reside there for prolonged periods. There is an effective vaccine for people at risk. It should be given subcutaneously in 3 doses on days 0, 7 and 28. A booster should be given 1 year later and 3 yearly after that.

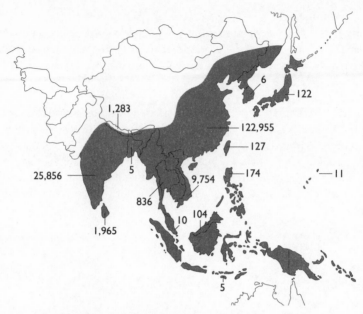

Figure 2.4   *Reported cases of proven or suspected Japanese encephalitis, by endemic countries and regions of South-east Asia, 1986–90*

Malaria

There is no vaccination for malaria. (See Chapter 15 for advice on prevention and chemoprophylaxis.)

Meningitis (Figure 2.5)

Meningitis, an infection of the nervous system, can be caused by a variety of bacteria and viruses. The usual risk to travellers is from the meningococcus, most commonly types A and C. There is now an effective vaccine against this organism. It is given intramuscularly and protection lasts for 3 years. Throughout the "meningitis belt" of sub-Saharan Africa there are dry season epidemics of meningococcal meningitis.

Plague

There are a few areas of the world where plague is endemic, notably Madagascar, Somalia and Indochina. However, the risk to humans is extremely low. Although a vaccine is available on a "named patient" basis, it is not fully effective and there is a significant risk of unpleasant side-effects. For those at risk or who might have been exposed, prophylaxis or presumptive treatment with a tetracycline may be more appropriate than the vaccine.

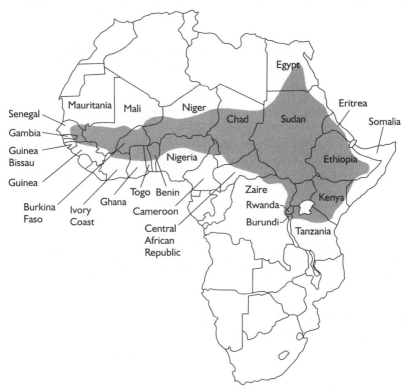

Figure 2.5   *Distribution of meningococcal meningitis in Africa*

Polio (Figure 2.6)
Paralytic polio is irreversible and fully preventable. The few cases of paralytic polio now seen in the UK are practically all imported from the developing world. The live vaccine is given orally as a drop either on the tongue or on a sugar cube. The initial course consists of 3 doses given at monthly intervals, with boosters every 10 years if required. There is a killed vaccine that is given by injection and is suitable for individuals with impaired immunity who cannot receive live vaccines.

Rabies (Figure 2.7)
Since the outlook for victims of rabies encephalitis is appalling, prevention is of paramount importance. People involved in high-risk occupations such as zoology, sledging with huskies, cave exploration, animal collecting and veterinary medicine can be protected by pre-exposure vaccination with a tissue culture vaccine such as human diploid cell strain vaccine (HDCV) or purified Vero cell vaccine (PVRV), both manufactured by Pasteur-Mérieux-Connaught; or purified chicken embryo cell vac-

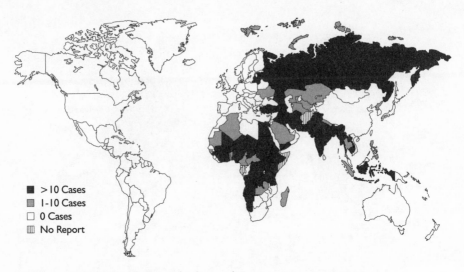

> ■ >10 Cases
> ■ 1-10 Cases
> □ 0 Cases
> ▥ No Report

Figure 2.6 *World distribution of polio myelitis, cases per year, 1995*

cine (PCEC), Behring; or purified duck embryo vaccine (PDEV), Berna. At least 3 injections, preferably on days 0, 7 and 28, are required. Immunisation may be less effective in people that are taking chloroquine tablets for malaria prophylaxis, so ideally the injections should be given before starting chloroquine.

Tetanus
Adsorbed antitetanus toxoid (ATT) is given as an intramuscular injection. The initial course is 3 injections given a month apart. Boosters are recommended at 10-year intervals. However, after 2 booster injections (5 doses of ATT in total) protection is probably life-long. Further boosters may cause unpleasant local reactions and are, therefore, not recommended except at the time of an injury.

Tuberculosis
Although tuberculosis (TB) is common, and in many parts of the world is increasing with the increase in HIV infection, most travellers are not at increased risk if they are otherwise fit and healthy. Vaccination offers only partial protection at best and is available in the form of BCG (Bacille-Calmette-Guerin) given intradermally. BCG is appropriate only for people who have a negative result on skin testing with tuberculin (Heaf test) and who are planning to live for a long period in a region where TB is common.

Typhoid
Two types of typhoid vaccine are commonly available. The Vi vaccine, consisting of part of the capsule of the typhoid bacillus, is given by a single intramuscular injection

Figure 2.7 *World distribution of rabies (rabies-free areas shown in white)*

(0.5ml). Repeat injections are required at 3-year intervals. The previous whole-cell vaccine is falling out of favour and is becoming more difficult to obtain. There is now an
oral typhoid vaccine (Ty 21a) which is given as 3 capsules on alternate days. This must
be repeated annually for those at risk. It is a live vaccine so it must not be given to people with impaired immunity. Its efficacy relies on the person taking all 3 capsules, so
compliance of the individual needs to be considered before choosing the oral vaccine.
Concurrent antibiotic administration may also lead to failure of the vaccine to take.

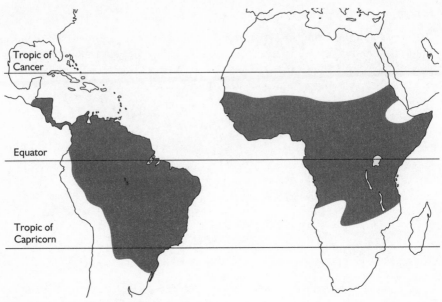

Figure 2.8 *World distribution of yellow fever*

Yellow fever (Figure 2.8)

This is now the only immunisation for which an international certificate is officially required. It is recommended by the WHO for visitors to some countries in tropical Africa and South America (there is no yellow fever in Asia). There have been a growing number of cases of yellow fever in recent years, mainly among tourists but also among local people, and this safe vaccination is very important. It is important to ensure that travellers are equipped with a valid vaccination certificate. People have been turned away from countries because they have arrived without a valid certificate.

This is a live vaccine given intramuscularly and should be renewed every 10 years. The vaccine can be obtained only from a recognised Yellow Fever Vaccination Centre. The addresses of these can be obtained from GPs or local health authorities.

Yellow fever vaccine should not be given to people with impaired immunity. In some cases such people may need to obtain waiver letters if they want to travel to endemic countries. It is best to check with the relevant embassies well before you travel. Nor should this vaccine be given to somebody who is pregnant. The risk may be small, but it would be unwise to go unprotected to an area where there is yellow fever, particularly in the first 3 months of pregnancy.

FURTHER INFORMATION

The WHO and the Centers for Disease Control in Atlanta, Georgia, USA, publish useful information as well as weekly reports on the incidence of illness in various parts of the world. The Communicable Disease Control Centre at Colindale, London, gives valuable advice. The following are also useful.

Published information

PHLS Communicable Disease Report (weekly)
Compiled at the PHLS Communicable Disease Surveillance Centre from confidential reports from PHLS and hospital laboratories in England, Wales and Ireland. Issued by PHLS Communicable Disease Surveillance Centre, 61 Colindale Avenue, London NW9 5EQ, tel. +44 181 2006868

WHO Weekly Epidemiological Record
Global Epidemiological Surveillance and Health Situation Assessment, World Health Organisation, 1211 Geneva 27, Switzerland

Morbidity and Mortality Weekly Report (MMWR) Supplement
Printed by the Adult Immunisation: Recommendations of the Immunisation Practices Advisory Committee (ACIP), US Department of Health and Human Services, Public Health Service, Centers for Disease Control, Atlanta, Georgia 30333, USA (for example, No. RR 12, September 6th 1996, Vol. 45)

Travel Medicine International, Mark Allen Publishing, Croxted Mews, 286a–288 Croxted Road, London SE24 9DA, tel. +44 181 6717521

Vaccination Certificate Requirements for International Travel and Health Advice to Travellers
Published annually by WHO, Geneva

Health Information for Overseas Travel, Lea, G. and Lease, J., HMSO, London, 1995

Information available by telephone
Hospital for Tropical Diseases
4 St Pancras Way
London NW1 0PE
Tel. +44 171 5303500
Travel Clinic: Tel. +44 171 3889600
Health Information Line: Tel. +44 839 337733

British Airways Travel Clinics Information Line
Tel. +44 1276 685040

Public Health Laboratory Health Centres
Birmingham: Tel. +44 121 7666611
Glasgow: Tel. +44 141 9467120
Liverpool: Tel. +44 151 7089393
London: Tel. +44 171 9272437
Oxford: Tel. +44 1865 225570

MASTA (Medical Advisory Service for Travellers Abroad)
Provides Health Briefs which give information about immunisations and malaria,
as well as any Foreign Office advice and the latest health news. To obtain a Health
Brief, telephone the number below and leave name, address and travel details. The
brief will be forwarded by first class post. It can then be taken to a doctor or any
British Airways Travel Clinic.
MASTA Health Line: Tel. +44 891 224100

Information sources on the Internet
World Health Organisation (WHO)
http://www.who.ch/

Centers for Disease Control (CDC) USA
http://www.cdc.gov/epo/mmwr/mmwr_wk.html

Communicable Diseases Surveillance Centre (CDSC) England and Wales
http://www.open.gov.uk/cdsc/cdschome.htm

Travel Health Online
http://www.tripprep.com

3 EXPEDITION MEDICAL KITS

Robin Illingworth

There may be some explorers who buy a bottle of aspirin and a tin of Elastoplast while waiting for their plane and bring them back unopened three months later. Most expeditions take rather more medical equipment but fortunately need very little of it. However, a few expeditions have major medical problems.

Organising the medical kits for an expedition takes a lot of time and effort if it is done properly. It is particularly difficult to know what to take on a small, light-weight expedition travelling in a remote area and carrying all its equipment. A large expedition can take more medical equipment, but however much is taken you cannot possibly deal with every conceivable accident and illness which might occur. Inevitably, you must try to compromise between taking so little equipment that you cannot deal with even the common medical problems, and taking so much that you are weighed down with an enormous medical kit which is never used. It is pointless to have a medical kit which is so big and heavy that it is left behind because you can't be bothered to carry it, or so comprehensive that nothing can be found when it is needed. However, with careful planning most common and minor medical problems can be treated during an expedition without outside help and first-aid treatment for more serious conditions can be given if necessary.

The commonest injuries on expeditions are blisters, small cuts and grazes. If cleaned and dressed properly these should heal without any problem but if treated badly they may cause considerable difficulties, especially if the person becomes unable to walk. Some sprains and minor fractures can also be treated quite adequately on an expedition. More serious injuries are fortunately rare; first aid treatment will be required before evacuation to hospital.

The common ailments are aches and pains, sunburn, insect bites and bowel disturbances. These usually get better without treatment but simple drugs provide symptomatic relief. These common conditions are the same wherever you go so the same basic medical kit can serve for many different expeditions. However, some expeditions will encounter particular medical problems, depending on their area and objectives, and so need extra drugs and medical equipment.

The amount of medical equipment which should be taken will depend on many factors, including the remoteness of the expedition from medical aid, the size and duration of the expedition, the mode of travel, the organisation of the expedition (in particular the number of camps and the travelling time between them) and the medical skills of the party.

Figure 3.1 *The medical kit used by a large vehicle-based expedition in the Savannahs of Northern Kenya (V. Southwell/RGS Kora Research Project)*

Remoteness of the expedition from medical aid

The time needed to get help is much more important than the distance to a doctor or hospital, and in a remote area the nearest hospital may be small and poorly equipped. If it is easy to get good medical attention you need take only basic medical equipment. If help is available, but difficult and expensive to reach, you should take more equipment and plan to deal with more of the possible accidents and illnesses without outside help. However, on some expeditions there is simply no help available and so the party must be completely self-sufficient, and also aware of the likely risks and consequences of any injury or illness.

The mode of travel

More equipment can be carried if yaks or lorries are available than if everything has to be carried in rucksacks. Weight is usually the most important factor, but the size and shape of the containers may also matter.

On some expeditions the party walks to base camp while the equipment is taken by lorry or helicopter. If this occurs the party must carry some medical equipment. There is no point in having a medical kit if it is not available when it is needed.

The organisation of the expedition
If camps are a long way apart each one must have a separate medical kit, since drugs and equipment for an emergency are useless if they are not available within a few hours. However, for non-emergency drugs and dressings it may be convenient to have small stocks at outlying camps with a larger reserve stock at base camp to replenish the other medical kits if necessary. Each group of people going away from camp should carry a small first aid kit, so that some basic first aid equipment is always available.

The medical skills of the party
There is no point in taking drugs and equipment if you do not know how to use them, since they may be ineffective or even dangerous. For every drug in the medical kit there should be specific instructions about when and when not to use it, the dose and the possible side-effects. A proper record must be kept when drugs are used. Many expeditions carry drugs which are normally available only on a doctor's prescription; this is reasonable if the drugs are carefully chosen and full instructions are provided, since the potential benefits outweigh the possible dangers. Sometimes medical advice may be obtained by telephone or radio, even from a remote area, and evacuation of the patient to a doctor or hospital may not be necessary if the necessary drugs are available.

Cost of medical equipment
If possible the cost of medical equipment should not determine how much is taken in the kit. Some drugs and equipment are expensive, but the cost is small compared with the cost and inconvenience of getting outside help for a condition which could have been adequately treated in camp.

Personal medical kit
Each expedition member should take some personal medical equipment, including Elastoplast or similar dressings, sun cream, lip salve, insect repellent and foot powder as required. For people who need to take a drug regularly it is best if they carry the main supply and someone else looks after the reserve stock. People who are allergic to Elastoplast should take a roll of Micropore tape which does not cause irritation.

Travel to the expedition area

While travelling to the expedition area the main medical kits may be packed and inaccessible, but some medical supplies must be kept available at all times. It is useful to have a small kit containing a few plasters, tablets for headaches, diarrhoea and travel sickness, and water purifying tablets (see also Chapter 9). If travelling outside Europe and North America a small pack of sterile needles, syringes and sutures must be available in case medical treatment is required.

EXPEDITION MEDICAL KITS

Recommendations for communal medical equipment are based on the kits which have been used on many Brathay expeditions. There are three standard kits: the field kit, the mobile camp kit and the base camp kit. A typical expedition of 20 people to south-east Iceland might have one base camp kit, one or two mobile camp kits and four field kits. Extra drugs can be added and special medical kits made if required for particular expeditions. For example, a Brathay expedition to Sabah (Borneo), involving 18 people as well as local guides and porters, took two base camp kits, one mobile camp kit, four field kits and four extra boxes of drugs, intravenous fluids and other items, a total of 27kg weight of medical kits.

Field first aid kit

The field kit contains basic first aid equipment for a small party away from camp for a day. It is in a plastic box 13cm × 11cm × 7cm and weighs about 350g. When items are used the kit can be replenished from the base camp kit.

TABLE 3.1   FIELD FIRST AID KIT

Item	Quantity
Plastic sandwich box and list of contents	1
Large plain wound dressing no. 15 BPC (note 1)	1
Crepe bandage 10cm x 4.5m	1
Triangular bandage	1
Release non-adherent dressing 10cm x 10cm	1
Elastoplast Airstrip and Fabric dressings	12
Zinc oxide plaster 1.25cm x 5m	1 roll
Antiseptic swabs (for cleaning small wounds)	6
Blood lancets (for blisters or splinters)	2
Safety pins	2
Scissors	1 pair
Paracetamol tablets 500mg	10
Emergency message form	1
Pencil (gardener's pencil with plastic cover to protect point)	1

See notes on pages 25–26

Mobile camp kit

The mobile camp kit is intended for a group of about six people away from base camp for a few days and carrying all their equipment. It is in a plastic box 23cm × 13cm × 8cm and weighs about 700g.

TABLE 3.2 MOBILE CAMP KIT

Item	Quantity
Plastic sandwich box and list of contents	1
Large plain wound dressing, no. 15 BPC (note 1)	1
Medium plain wound dressing, no. 14 BPC	1
Triangular bandage	1
Crepe bandage 10cm x 4.5m	1
Release non-adherent dressing 10cm x 10cm	2
Elastoplast Airstrip and Fabric dressings	12
Steristrip tapes 6.3mm x 10.2cm x 10 tapes (note 2)	1
Elastic adhesive plaster 2.5cm x 5m	1 roll
Hibicet or Savlon antiseptic concentrate (note 3)	20ml
Plastic dressing forceps, sterile	1 pair
Gauze swabs, 7.5cm x 7.5cm, packets of 5	3 pkts
Antiseptic swabs	10
Safety pins	4
Paper clip (note 14)	1
Blood lancets	2
Scissors	1 pair
Thermometer	1
Cotton-wool-tipped sticks (Q tips)	4
Paracetamol tablets 500mg	20
Ibuprofen tablets 400mg (note 4)	10
*Nalbuphine ampoules 20mg in 2ml (note 6)	2
*Tramadol 50mg tablets (note 5)	10
Syringe 2ml and needle 38mm x 0.8mm	2
Chlorpheniramine tablets 4mg	20
Loperamide capsules 2mg (note 7)	20
*Ciprofloxacin tablets 500mg (note 11)	10
*Erythromycin tablets 250mg (note 8)	20
*Amethocaine eye drops 1%, single dose units	2
*Chloramphenicol eye ointment	1 tube
Disposable gloves	2
Booklet First Aid on Mountains by Steve Bollen	1
Emergency message form, pencil, notebook	1
Instructions on use of drugs and dressings	

* Available on prescription only.

See notes on pages 25–26

Base camp kit

The base camp kit is designed as the main medical kit for an expedition of about 20 people for about four weeks in an area such as Iceland, where medical help is available within one day. The kit is in a fibre-board box 40cm × 25cm × 13cm and weighs 4kg. Part of the base camp kit is the accident kit, which contains equipment that might be useful at an accident away from camp. This should be kept intact at the top of the box where it may be found quickly in an emergency.

TABLE 3.3 BASE CAMP KIT

Item	Quantity
Accident kit (in polythene bag with list of contents)	
Large plain wound dressing, no. 15 BPC (note 1)	2
Medium plain wound dressing, no. 14 BPC	2
Small plain wound dressing, no. 13 BPC	2
Triangular bandage	4
Release non-adherent dressing 10cm x 10cm	4
Crepe bandage 10cm x 4.5m	2
Elastic adhesive plaster 2.5cm x 4.5m	1 roll
Safety pins	6
Scissors	1 pair
*Nalbuphine ampoules 20mg in 2ml (note 6)	5
*Tramadol 50mg tablets (note 5)	10
Instructions for using nalbuphine	
Syringe 2ml and needle 38mm x 0.8mm	5
Injection swabs	10
Disposable gloves	4
Luggage label (for labelling casualties)	2
Emergency message form and pencil	1
Documentation (in a polythene bag)	
Book *Medical Handbook for Mountaineers* by Peter Steele	
Instructions on use of drugs and dressings	
List of contents of medical kits	
Notebook and pencil	
Dressings and bandages (in polythene bag with list of contents)	
Antiseptic swabs	20
Hibicet or Savlon antiseptic concentrate (note 3)	100ml
Cotton wool balls, sterile, packets of 5	10 pkts
Gauze swabs 10cm x 10cm, packets of 5	10 pkts
Release non-adherent dressing 10cm x 10cm	10
Release non-adherent dressing 5cm x 5cm	10
Jelonet paraffin gauze dressing 10cm x 10cm	10
Elastoplast Airstrip and Fabric dressings (plasters)	60
Elastoplast dressing strip 3.8cm x 1m	1
Steristrips 6.3mm x 10.2cm x 10 tapes (note 2)	3 packs

Elastic adhesive bandage 7.5cm x 4.5m	I roll
Zinc oxide plaster 2.5cm x 5m	I roll
Tubigrip elastic tubular bandage, size C	Im
Tubigrip size D	Im
Conforming bandage (Krinx or Kling) 7.5cm	3
Eye bath	I
Cotton-wool-tipped sticks (for removing objects from eyes)	I0
Eye pad, sterile, no. I6 BPC	2
Disposable gloves	I0

Drugs and instruments (in a plastic box with list of contents)

Scissors	I pair
Splinter forceps	I pair
Plastic dressing forceps, sterile	2 pairs
Blood lancets	6
Disposable scalpel, no. I5 blade	I
Paper clip (note I4)	I
Safety pins	6
Thermometer	I
Buccastem 3mg (note I3)	50
Paracetamol tablets 500mg	I00
Ibuprofen tablets 400mg (note 4)	50
Chlorpheniramine tablets 4mg	50
Throat lozenges (eg Bradosol)	20
Antacid tablets (eg Alcin)	50
Loperamide capsules 2mg (note 7)	60
Senokot tablets	20
*Ciprofloxacin tablets 500mg (note I I)	50
*Erythromycin tablets 250mg (note 8)	60
*Co-amoxiclav (eg Augmentin) tablets 375mg (note I0)	60
*Metronidazole tablets 400mg (note I2)	60
*Flucloxacillin tablets (note 9)	60
Otrivine nasal spray 0.1%	I
*Otosporin eardrops	I
*Amethocaine eye drops I%, single dose units	3
*Chloramphenicol eye ointment	I tube
Calamine cream	2 tubes
Eurax (crotamiton) ointment (note I6)	2 tubes
Miconazole cream	I tube
Xyloproct ointment	2 tubes
Emergency dental kit (note I5)	I

* Available on prescription only.

Notes to Tables 3.1, 3.2, 3.3

1. The Standard Plain Wound Dressings are in 3 sizes: large (no. 15 BPC), medium (no. 14 BPC) and small (no. 13 BPC). Each consists of a sterile pad (20cm × 15cm in the large dressing) to cover the wound with a long bandage to hold the pad in place. These dressings can also be used

to fasten the legs together after a fracture, the soft pad being placed between the knees or ankles.

2. Steristrip tapes can be used to close some wounds which would otherwise need to be sutured. The wound must first be carefully cleaned and the skin dried. The tapes stick better if compound benzoin tincture (available in small vials for use with Steristrips) is applied around the wound. Steristrips should not be placed all around a finger since they may restrict the circulation.

3. Hibicet or Savlon contain chlorhexidine and cetrimide and are antiseptics for cleaning wounds. The concentrated solution is diluted with clean water and the wound is cleaned using cotton wool balls or gauze swabs held in the dressing forceps.

4. Ibuprofen is a non-steroidal anti-inflammatory analgesic drug which is useful for pain from sprains or other injuries. Ibuprofen should not be used in patients with peptic ulcers, nor in asthmatic patients who are allergic to aspirin or related drugs. It sometimes causes indigestion, vomiting and dizziness.

5. Tramadol is an analgesic for moderate to severe pain. It may cause side-effects such as nausea, vomiting, constipation and drowsiness.

6. Nalbuphine (trade name Nubain) is an injectable strong analgesic but is not subject to the legal restrictions covering drugs such as morphine and pethidine which make them impracticable for most expeditions.

7. Loperamide is for diarrhoea. Most cases of diarrhoea last only a few days and do not need drug treatment. Replacing fluids is more important. Loperamide may be particularly useful if diarrhoea occurs while travelling. (See Chapter 14 for more information about diarrhoea.)

8. Erythromycin is an antibiotic which is useful for throat and wound infections.

9. Flucloxacillin is an antibiotic which is useful for skin and wound infections.

10. Co-amoxiclav is an antibiotic useful for treating ear, chest, urinary and gynaecological infections.

11. Ciprofloxacin is an antibiotic which is especially useful for diarrhoea, chest and urinary infections.

12. Metronidazole is an antibiotic which is useful for gynaecological and dental infections and also some forms of diarrhoea (for example, amoebic dysentery and giardiasis).

13. Buccastem is a small tablet that should be placed high between upper lip and gum and left to dissolve. It is an anti-sickness medication, particularly useful after strong analgesia (for example, nalbuphine) or while sailing.

14. The paper clip is used for treating a subungual haematoma, a blood blister under the finger nail. If the finger tip is crushed blood may be visible through the nail and the finger throbs painfully. This can be treated by melting a hole through the nail using an opened paper clip heated to red heat in a flame. This is surprisingly painless and gives immediate relief.

15. A suitable emergency dental kit is the Lifesystems Dental First Aid kit, which includes equipment for providing a temporary filling or a dressing for a damaged tooth. (Lifesystems Limited, PO Box 1407, London SW3 6PL; available from Field & Trek and from YHA Adventure Shops.) Dental kits for expeditions can also be purchased from David Watt (see Chapter 18).

16. Eurax ointment is applied to itching insect bites.

Extra drugs and equipment

Many expeditions require extra drugs and equipment in addition to those listed above, and for a major expedition much more equipment will be needed. If there is a doctor or nurse in the party more drugs and equipment should be taken. However, he or she may not be available immediately when needed so it is best to have a basic medical kit which anyone can use if necessary and a separate kit for the doctor's use only.

Sterile equipment kits

Expeditions to areas outside Europe and North America should carry packs of needles, syringes and sutures and make sure that they are available if medical treatment is needed. In many developing countries medical equipment is often reused without sterilisation and there is a high risk of transmission of infection, especially hepatitis and HIV (the AIDS virus). Suitable kits for small expeditions are listed below. Large expeditions will need more equipment and should seek advice well in advance.

TABLE 3.4 SMALL KIT OF STERILE MEDICAL EQUIPMENT

Item	Type	Quantity
Disposable syringes	2ml	2
	5ml	2
	10ml	1
Injection needles	38mm x 0.8mm (green)	5
	25mm x 0.6mm (blue)	2
	24mm x 0.5mm (orange)	1
Disposable scalpel	–	1
Sutures with needles	monofilament 3/0	1
	monofilament 4/0	1
	(eg Novafil, made by Davis & Geck)	
	Catgut 3/0	1
	(eg Softgut, made by Davis & Geck)	

TABLE 3.5 LARGER KIT OF STERILE MEDICAL EQUIPMENT
(as above, in larger quantities, plus the following)

Item	Type	Quantity
Intravenous cannulae	18 G (eg Venflon)	3
Intravenous infusion sets	–	2
Intravenous fluids:	saline (sodium chloride 0.9%) 500ml	4
	gelatin (eg Gelofusine) 500ml	2

On any expedition *suturing equipment* and *local anaesthetic* (for example ligno-caine 1%, plain) may be needed for closing wounds, and could be used by non-medical people who have had suitable training.

Splints are fortunately rarely needed, and on most expeditions materials for making makeshift splints will be available. The most useful splint is a "long-leg" splint for fractures of the lower leg. Inflatable splints are easy to apply and are effective in some fractures, but may cause problems due to pressure on the skin if inflated too hard or for too long. They are also liable to punctures from changes in pressure due to temperature and altitude. Plaster of Paris is rarely needed on an expedition but could be useful to make "backslabs" for splinting fractures of the arm or leg. The most convenient form is the Gypsona "Emergency Splint Pack" made by Smith and Nephew (Healthcare House, Goulton Street, Hull HU3 4DJ).

A complete plaster cast should be applied only if equipment is available to remove it. It may occasionally be helpful to use a quick-setting synthetic cast, such as Baycast or ScotchCast, to allow a person to walk with a fractured ankle or strained knee, but these casts are very difficult to remove without a plaster saw or shears. Fibreglass repair kits for canoes can be used to make casts, but great care should be taken because the heat produced when the material sets may burn the skin.

Other items of medical equipment which could be useful if there is a doctor in the party are an oropharyngeal airway, stethoscope, auroscope and ophthalmoscope, urethral catheter, nasogastric tube, chest drainage catheter and Heimlich valve for pneumothorax, and dental forceps. Intravenous fluids are heavy but indispensable in the event of major trauma or severe illness. The most useful are saline (0.9% sodium chloride), dextrose (glucose 5%) and gelatin (Gelofusine or Haemaccel).

Extra drugs will be needed if members of the expedition are allergic to any drug in the medical kit or have pre-existing conditions such as asthma. Injectable antibiotics and ampoules of adrenaline, hydrocortisone, diazepam and an anti-emetic could occasionally be needed.

Some expedition doctors take enough surgical equipment for an emergency appendicectomy, but non-operative treatment of appendicitis with fluids, analgesics and antibiotics is much safer than emergency surgery outside a hospital. Fluids could be given rectally if intravenous fluids are not available. An appropriate choice of antibiotics would be gentamicin (by intramuscular injection) with metronidazole (rectal suppositories). If only oral drugs can be used the combination of ciprofloxacin and metronidazole may be effective.

It is unrealistic to plan for major surgery even if there is a surgeon in the party. Local anaesthesia is adequate for repairing most wounds and can also be useful for pain relief, especially femoral nerve block for fractures of the femur, using bupivacaine (Marcain). Ketamine is the most suitable drug in the rare cases when general anaesthesia is unavoidable.

Special hazards of particular areas and activities

Extra drugs should be taken if particular medical problems are likely. These are discussed in more detail in the relevant chapters.

Tropical areas

In the tropics infectious diseases are common, especially malaria and gut infections. Even if antimalarial prophylaxis is taken regularly drugs for treating malaria must be available (see Chapter 15). Tinidazole or metronidazole is useful for amoebiasis or giardiasis (see Chapter 14), chloramphenicol for typhoid and piperazine (Pripsen) for roundworms. Gastroenteritis is a major problem in hot countries. The large amounts of fluid lost from the gut may be replaced by oral glucose and electrolyte solution (for example Dioralyte) or by a solution of sugar and salt measured with a special plastic spoon (obtainable from Teaching Aids at Low Cost, PO Box 45, St Albans, Hertfordshire AL1 4AX, tel. +44 1727 853869; see also Chapter 14).

Wound infections are common on expeditions to hot, wet places such as tropical rain forests. Many people may need treatment with oral antibiotics such as erythromycin or flucloxacillin. The risk of infection can be reduced by cleaning wounds carefully and by using the antiseptic povidone-iodine. Fungal skin infections may require miconazole cream. Clotrimazole vaginal tablets are useful for women suffering from thrush. Snake bite is rare if sensible precautions are observed. Few expeditions need to carry antivenom but expert advice about this should be obtained in high-risk areas (see Chapter 16). For more information on medical problems in hot climates see Chapter 19.

Mountaineering

At high altitudes this activity carries risks of mountain sickness and frostbite (see Chapter 21), as well as the usual hazards of illness, injury and sunburn. Substantial quantities of medical supplies may be needed on a large expedition. The paper by A' Court, Stables and Travis lists the medical supplies taken on the 1992 winter Everest expedition (see References, Appendix 3).

Sailing

Members of sailing expeditions are liable to suffer from chapped hands, salt-water boils and excessive sun. Neutrogena hand cream may be needed in large quantities. Cinnarizine tablets often prevent sea-sickness, but occasionally injections of an antiemetic such as prochlorperazine (Stemetil) are required. Salt and water depletion is common while sailing in the tropics. Trauma may occur while sailing in bad weather. Falling overboard is likely to be fatal, so life jackets and safety harnesses must be used (see Chapter 24).

Diving

Diving expeditions share the same problems of exposure to the sun and water. Ear infections (*otitis externa*) are particularly common, especially if swimming near coral. Olive oil drops and antibiotic ear drops (such as Otosporin) should be taken. Further information is given in Chapter 22.

Where to get drugs and dressings

Many of the drugs recommended are available in the UK only on a doctor's prescription. A National Health Service prescription may not be used for drugs for use overseas, but a doctor may write a private prescription to enable travellers to purchase drugs.

Some of the dressings and equipment listed can be bought in ordinary shops, but some items are only available commercially in large quantities. It may be possible to buy small quantities of dressings, syringes, and so on for an expedition from a local hospital. A tactful enquiry to the hospital manager may be productive.

Packing and labelling drugs

Blister packs of tablets are convenient for expedition use, but they take up more space and are often more expensive than the same tablets in a bottle. Any bottles should be plastic with screw tops and clearly labelled with the official and trade names of the drug. The labels should be covered with waterproof tape. Instructions about the dose and the indications for using the drug may be included on the labels, but full information must also be available, especially about warnings and common side-effects. The most convenient source of information is the British National Formulary which is published twice a year and sent to every practising doctor.

The trade names of drugs often differ in different countries. Occasionally, the official names are also different; for example, paracetamol in the UK is the same drug as acetaminophen in the United States.

Drug export certificate

There are no restrictions on exporting medicinal products from the UK, except for controlled drugs such as morphine for which a Home Office certificate is needed, and for which there are special storage and prescription requirements. Special permission would also be needed to import such drugs into another country. Even with the relevant documents there is considerable risk of delays and legal difficulties if morphine or similar drugs are carried. It is therefore impracticable to take such drugs on an expedition.

Expeditions taking reasonable quantities of other drugs are unlikely to encounter problems at customs. However, a doctor's letter on official headed notepaper listing the drugs and stating their purpose can be extremely useful at border crossings

It may be helpful to check in advance with the embassy of the country concerned that there will be no restriction on importing the drugs. It is essential to make it clear that the drugs are for use by the expedition members and are not for sale or commercial supply. A detailed list of the medicines submitted to the relevant embassy for clearance is a great asset when importing the supplies. British drug export certificates are not needed for expeditions unless the host country specifically requests one. A certificate can then be obtained from the Department of Health (Medicines Division), Market Towers, 1 Nine Elms Lane, London SW1 5NQ, tel. +44 171 720 2188 ext. 3408.

During the expedition
During the expedition the medical officer should make sure that medical kits are actually available where they might be needed, rather than left behind in base camp. It is best if one person looks after the kits, but everyone should know what is available in case an emergency occurs. Notes must be kept if any drugs are used.

After the expedition
Any comments and suggestions for improving the medical kits should be recorded before they are forgotten. If most of the items are unused they may be kept for future expeditions, or possibly donated to a clinic or hospital in the expedition area. Some drugs have an expiry date printed on the container, and other drugs and dressings should be usable for at least three years if stored in reasonable conditions.

4 FIRST AID TRAINING

Bev Holt

K nowledge of basic first aid is essential for every member of the expedition team. This is best obtained by attending a first aid course. Never rely on having only one trained member on the team; it may be he or she who is injured. Importantly, it has been shown that people trained in first aid are more safety conscious and have fewer accidents than untrained people.

The aims of conventional first aid, as taught by such organisations as the St John Ambulance and the British Red Cross, are to prevent further injury and keep the patient alive and comfortable until skilled help arrives. On an expedition skilled help may take several days to arrive and, indeed, it is likely that the patient will need transporting to that skilled help. So a different philosophy is vital when considering "expedition" first aid.

TABLE 4.1   AIMS OF FIRST AID
• To preserve life • To prevent further injury • To promote recovery

The basic principles of first aid are more extensive when discussed in relation to an overseas expedition than basic first aid in an industrialised nation.

The basic principles sound simple. In first aid books it looks easy to place the unconscious patient on their side so that they do not obstruct their airway, but if the casualty is jammed upright in the front of a Land Rover it becomes apparent why training is so important. First aid in the field is very different from a book. It looks simple to apply pressure to a gaping wound to stop bleeding or to clear the airway of blood or vomit. Neither can be practised realistically but each must be anticipated.

Figure 4.1   *Practising a carry-out by stretcher*
(R. Turpin/RGS Oman Wahiba Sands Project)

TABLE 4.2   PRINCIPLES OF FIRST AID

- Assess the situation
- Make the area safe
- Assess the casualty
  - starting with the ABC of resuscitation
  - identify the injury or illness
- Give easy, appropriate and adequate treatment in a sensible order of priority
- Make and pass on a report
- Organise removal of casualty to secondary care where appropriate

Time spent in anticipating and preparing for such problems means that time is not wasted when seconds are vital and basic treatment can save a life.

The first rule of expedition first aid is to prevent further injury to the victim or injury to the rescuers. Expeditions are always at risk when people are tired, hungry, cold, wet, hot and frustrated. Good leadership is essential, and it is all too easy for people to become overextended trying to achieve an objective. It is also very easy when suffering deprivation to throw caution to the wind and rush into a raging torrent, remove your gloves in sub-zero temperatures or, more likely, dash on to an ill-lit road at night.

The best way to learn first aid is on a course. Below are listed some of the courses available, both basic and more advanced. All members of the expedition team should learn and practise basic first aid. The bare minimum of skills which can be expected of *all* expedition members should include:

- resuscitation;
- control of bleeding;
- relief of pain;
- safe movement of the injured patient.

The medical officer (MO) and as many of the other expedition members as possible would be advised to attend a specialist course. The advantages of such courses are that you will learn from experts and get hands-on experience. The disadvantages are that they are expensive and cover all aspects of emergency procedures when you may need to know only a few. The alternative is for the expedition doctor, if there is one, to select topics related to the environment to be visited, and to spend time with all team members explaining potential problems and getting everyone to practise specialised procedures.

Basic medical skills needed for expeditions include the following.

- Resuscitation (Chapter 11, pages 98–100)
- Care of head and spine injuries (Chapter 11, pages 100–103, 118–120)
- Recognition of coma and death (Chapter 11, pages 103–105)
- Assessment of the ill or injured patient (Chapter 10)
- Treatment of fractures (Chapter 11, pages 115–118)
- Treatment of burns and blisters (Chapter 11, pages 113–115)
- Management of venomous bites (Chapter 16)
- Wound care (Chapter 11, pages 106–113)
- Management of ear and eye complaints (Chapter 14, page 143–144)
- Management of dental emergencies (Chapter 18)

Each of the above skills is covered in detail in later chapters, which should be read carefully and understood before going into the field.

Having confidence to make the right decision is essential and will only come from attending courses and field experience. Do not rely on books and manuals alone.

For the MO other areas related to first aid and pre-expedition planning must be considered.

1. Before departure consider what risks you are likely to encounter depending on location, environment and activities. Do any members of the expedition have special medical needs, for example, diabetes or asthma? Ensure that pre-trip medical forms covering past medical history, regular medications, allergies, blood group and any details of a pre-trip medical performed by a GP (see Appendix 1) are completed.
2. Work out an evacuation strategy for ill or injured expedition members and ensure that your insurance covers this (see Chapter 5).
3. Know what skills your members already have. Will other members have access to these skills in the field? Check *again* that everyone has a knowledge of basic first aid.

With the above knowledge you can now plan for what you need. Decide what level of medical skills is required, then look carefully at the various courses available and find one to suit your needs. Ask the course tutors if they have particular experience of expeditions to the locality to be visited or activity to be undertaken.

FIRST AID COURSES

There are a number of organisations offering first aid courses in the UK. These range from basic first aid to courses tailored for expeditions and more advanced paramedic training. Please note that the following list is not exhaustive. If you know of any other suitable courses which are not listed here, or have more up-to-date information, the Expedition Advisory Centre (EAC) would be interested to receive details.

Basic first aid
This is best learnt by attending one of the many standard courses run by the St John Ambulance or the British Red Cross. The cost of such courses varies in different parts of the country. Information on course dates and times can be obtained by contacting the local branch offices. National offices can provide local branch telephone numbers.

British Red Cross +44 171 235 5454
St John Ambulance +44 171 235 5231

Many ambulance services also provide first aid instruction. Details of the ambulance service training units can be found in the First Aid section of Yellow Pages.

Advanced first aid training
Depending on how far from medical help expedition members will be operating, some will require more advanced training. The EAC has sent representatives on the

following courses and found them to be particularly relevant to expedition members and medics.

Wilderness Medical Training
This organisation offers advanced first aid training for expeditions operating in remote regions overseas, particularly for those expeditions without professional medical support. Residential courses include "Far From Help" (three days) and "Advanced Medicine for Remote Foreign Travel" (five days). The latter also includes the teaching of invasive techniques (suturing, injections, etc).

Contact: Dr Jon Dallimore or Barry Roberts
25 Beaconsfield Street
Royal Leamington Spa
Warwickshire CV31 1DT   Tel. & fax +44 1926 882763

Rescue Emergency Care
REC courses are modular, offering a practical progression from basic first aid skills to more advanced medical procedures. Different modules cater for non-medically qualified and medically qualified people. They aim to enhance individuals' own training, enabling them to work in particularly challenging environments. Modules last two days.

Contact: Peter Harvey
Wilderness Expertise Ltd
The Octagon
Wellington College
Crowthorne
Berkshire RG45 7PU   Tel. +44 7000 790217

British Red Cross
In addition to basic first aid courses the British Red Cross provides specialist courses for "Outdoor Activity" and "Expedition First Aid". These are modular courses with specialist elements, including casualty handling and specific modules on key environments, such as tropical and cold climates, and key activities, such as caving, mountaineering, water sports and pony trekking.

Contact: Lynne Covey
British Red Cross Society
9 Grosvenor Crescent
London SW1X 7EJ   Tel. +44 171 2355454

Life Support Training Services

LSTS provides modular courses for people going to remote areas. There is a basic course (two days) and a choice of advanced courses (three and five days). If there is sufficient demand, such as an entire expedition, courses can be arranged at a chosen venue and the cost is by arrangement, depending on the number of people and the venue. The courses concentrate on practical skills in as realistic a setting as possible.

Contact: Daryl Wight
Life Support Training Services
2 Underhill Cottages
The Hill, Millom
Cumbria LA18 5HA   Tel. & fax +44 1229 772708; mobile +44 1229 772708

Courses tailored to special requirements

The Ieuan Jones First Aid Course for Mountaineers
Contact: Dave Striver   Tel. +44 1248 600612

Mountaineering expeditions might like to attend courses specially run for members of mountain rescue teams (some of the best first aiders in the UK belong to mountain rescue teams).

British Association of Ski Patrols (BASP)
Contact: Fiona Gunn   Tel. +44 1855 2443

First aid and medical courses are also run by various outdoor adventure and training centres. These should be contacted individually to find out when and what sort of courses they offer. Centres that run first aid courses include the following:

Glenmore Lodge, Aviemore	Tel. +44 1479 861256
Brathay Hall, Ambleside	Tel. +44 1539 433041
Plas-y-Brenin, Capel Curig	Tel. +44 1690 720366
Outward Bound Schools	Tel. +44 990 134227 (Head Office)
Aberdovey	Tel. +44 1654 767464
Loch Eil	Tel. +44 13977 72866
Ullswater	Tel. +44 17684 86347

ESSENTIAL READING

Dunne, J. (ed.), *First Aid Manual. The Authorised Manual of St. John Ambulance, St. Andrews Ambulance Association and the British Red Cross*, Dorling Kindersley, 1997.

5 LEGAL LIABILITY AND MEDICAL INSURANCE

Charles Siderfin and Mark Whittingham

LEGAL LIABILITY

It is important to consider the issue of legal liability. Individuals are often concerned that giving medical care to an injured or ill person may expose them to the risk of legal action, if something goes wrong. This risk can be substantially reduced by a clear understanding of the issues involved and good preparation before the expedition departs.

Negligence

Medical legal actions usually revolve around the issue of negligence. For someone to prove negligence they must first establish a standard of medical care applicable to the given situation and show that the actual care received fell short of this standard. They must also show that *because of* this inadequate care demonstrable injury resulted. They can then sue for damages.

Consent

Consent is also an issue in liability. Without consent treatment is assault. Consent to emergency life-saving treatment is usually presumed by the law if the patient is unconscious or too ill to consent. The law presumes that a reasonable man would wish his life to be saved. In the case of a doctor or health-care professional acting within his sphere of clinical competence, consent is usually implied. That is, the patient does not resist the treatment and therefore is presumed to consent. In other situations where treatment carries considerable risk, or it is controversial, informed expressed consent should be obtained.

For consent to be informed the individual must understand the proposed treatment and the risks involved in accepting or refusing that treatment. This means that the patient should be made aware of material risks and common or serious side-effects, as well as the likely consequences should treatment be withheld. Verbal consent, especially in an expedition setting, is usually adequate. For an individual over 16 years of age, only that individual is able to give consent. Remember, patients have the right to refuse treatment.

Children under 16 can consent to medical treatment themselves if, in the opinion of the doctor, they are capable of understanding the nature and consequences of that treatment. However, when taking under 16s on an expedition it is wise to gain written permission from the parent or guardian that medical care can be given, if it is thought to be in the child's best interest. If written parental permission is not available, and a minor needs medical attention, treatment can be given if he or she is judged to be capable of consenting. If the child is *not* judged capable of consenting then actions taken will be judged against what a prudent and careful parent would consent to in the same situation. The child should, however, be given information that is relevant to his or her age and understanding.

Legal liability of different expedition members

For clarity it is helpful to examine the legal liability and responsibilities of different groups of people in turn.

Expedition organisers

When planning an expedition, the medical care provision needs to be consistent with the degree of risk that individuals are likely to be exposed to. It is the responsibility of the organisers to ensure that immediate medical care and plans for evacuation to medical facilities are adequate, or at least to a standard that could reasonably be expected in the given circumstances. Such provision should include adequate insurance and, depending on the level of anticipated risk, may require the presence of a doctor, or individual with training in simple or advanced first aid.

Members of the expedition should be informed of what medical facilities will be available and the hazards that they are likely to be exposed to. Once this has been done their continued participation in the expedition can usually be taken as consent to the risks and the degree of medical support available, and an acceptance that the standard of medical care in a remote area is likely to be inferior to that expected within the UK.

It is prudent to assess realistic levels of fitness and experience which expedition members will require. Those who do not match these criteria should be excluded. It is not reasonable to assess criteria and then not follow your own guidelines; this could be used as evidence of negligence.

Expedition leaders

The liability of the expedition leader will depend on the circumstances. If the expedition includes delegated trained health-care workers then his responsibility is probably limited to assisting with the management of a medical emergency. On expeditions run as business ventures the organisers maybe liable if the leader conforms to protocols which are negligently laid down in advance. If he deviates from standard procedures then he is likely to become personally liable. The leader is also responsible for ensuring that all necessary equipment is maintained throughout.

Medical doctors

A doctor who joins an expedition as an individual, and not as a doctor, has responsibilities no greater than any other person on the trip. Any emergency treatment that he gives would be judged as a "Good Samaritan" act. Beware of expeditions which give discounts to doctors who join them. By accepting remuneration, however small, the doctor forfeits his position of being an ordinary member of the expedition and may be judged to have taken on legal liability as an expedition doctor.

An expedition doctor would be expected to deal competently with medical problems. In planning the medical facilities he should anticipate likely problems and make contingency arrangements for these. He should screen expedition members, ensuring a standard of minimal fitness, and should make provision for the treatment of any existing medical conditions. He would be expected to provide immediate treatment to the standard of his peers in the same situation and to be competent in first aid. He also has responsibility to get a seriously ill individual to further continuing care and to anticipate and plan for complications en route.

If an expedition doctor is giving advice from a remote location, for example over the radio, he has a duty to ensure not only that his advice is correct but also that the individual giving the treatment has the necessary skills to carry out his instructions. Similarly, a doctor advising an expedition on equipment and drugs may give implicit consent to the equipment and drugs being used. Some courts may hold the doctor liable unless clear instructions and protocols are given for their use.

Other health-care professionals and lay people with medical responsibility

Many expeditions do not have a doctor. Individuals who take on the responsibility to provide medical care should remain within their level of knowledge and training. In addition to the criteria mentioned above, for consent to be informed, members of the expedition must know the level of training that individuals allocated the medical responsibility have received, both before departure and prior to specific treatment being given. If rendering emergency help to someone outside the expedition it is essential that they also understand the individual's level of training. It is an offence to pretend to be a medical doctor or imply registration under any of the Medical Acts.

The level and range of treatment that an individual in a remote situation can provide is largely dictated by training, patient consent and facilities and equipment. The care giver is, however, governed by a duty of care to exercise skills consistent with his training, experience and any procedures that may have been laid down. The patient still has the right to bring legal action for any breach of this duty of care.

The standard of care expected will vary in different circumstances. It will depend on the training and experience of the individual giving treatment, and the degree to which he follows advice given by more qualified personnel. His actions will be judged in comparison with what would reasonably be expected of another individual with the same expertise and in a similar situation. The greater the expertise and available advice, the greater will be the patient's expectations of adequate care, and the standard of care will be judged more rigorously by the Courts.

Confidentiality

Information gathered during a medical consultation should remain confidential. The need to get advice from a remote doctor may cause concern in respect of confidentiality, especially if medical cases have to be discussed over the radio. Breaches of confidentiality are sometimes unavoidable, especially in an emergency or if it is in the patient's best interest. If faced with such a problem be prepared to justify your actions. Consider whether it is possible to protect the patient's identity and especially ask the patient whether they mind the information being transmitted.

Professional indemnity

It is essential that health-care professionals ensure that their indemnity covers the country in which the expedition will operate and the activities they intend to pursue. If they are taken to court expert advice and representation will be required, even if the case is unfounded. Without indemnity the cost can be prohibitive and careers are at stake. The Royal College of Nursing will extend its cover to most countries, so long as it is informed. Similarly, most of the medical defence bodies will extend their cover to members. The important thing is to discuss the situation with the relevant organisations and gain their advice.

In summary, the fear of litigation should not prevent medical assistance being given on an expedition. Informed consent should be gained, if possible, and individuals should remain within the boundaries of their knowledge and skills. In planning an expedition it is essential that the level of medical cover and back-up facilities available are appropriate to the degree of likely risk.

Lastly, and perhaps most importantly, keep contemporary and thorough records of the history, examination findings, treatments and the monitoring of the patient's progress. If you should end up in court these will be your most important evidence.

The above is a medical practitioner's understanding of the law as it stands today. However, the reader should not rely on this chapter as a definitive or exhaustive review of this complex subject. It is designed to give a broad overview of the issues addressed. Readers requiring guidance on specific issues should obtain independent legal advice from their own solicitors or medical defence body before setting out.

MEDICAL INSURANCE

Expeditions, almost by definition, seem rarely to have sufficient funds for their true objectives, let alone the "luxury" of insurance. This can easily result in failure to insure adequately. Do not under-insure. Always bear in mind that if you cannot afford the premium, you are even less likely to be able to afford the potential loss.

Without doubt, the most important thing to remember when arranging insurance is that the law requires the person insuring to disclose all material facts to the insurers whether or not the information is sought by them. Failure to comply with this fundamental tenet of insurance (no matter how unfair it may appear) can have the effect of completely invalidating the insurance contract. For instance, if part of your expedition involves white-water rafting or mountaineering it is important to declare this.

What facets of insurance do expeditions need to consider when arranging expedition medical insurance?

There are four broad categories of insurance cover as follows.

1. Medical and additional expenses

This is a most important insurance cover. It usually covers medical and travel expenses for each member of the expedition following accidental bodily injury or illness. These expenses may vary from a doctor's visit through to major surgery and after-care. The UK has reciprocal National Health arrangements with some countries (see below). This category of insurance should include the following:

a) Emergency assistance and repatriation including air ambulance or air transport costs.
b) Emergency dental treatment.
c) Travel and accommodation expenses for people who have to travel to or remain with or escort an incapacitated insured person.
d) Local funeral expenses or transportation of the body to the UK.

- Medical conditions known to exist before the start of the expedition may not be covered. This exclusion may not apply provided the insured person has been without medical treatment or consultation during the previous 12 months. Expedition members who are in doubt about this exclusion should consult their insurance adviser before departure and/or obtain a medical certificate from their doctor stating that they are not travelling against medical advice. This may satisfy the insurance company's requirements.
- It is important if your travel policy has a 24-hour emergency telephone number for hospitalisation or repatriation that this number is used when an

accident or illness occurs. Professional advice may be available about hospitalisation, repatriation or alterations in any travel plan.

- If foreign nationals are on the expedition they may need to be repatriated back to their own country instead of the UK. Insurer agreement needs to be obtained to this *before* the expedition commences.
- Cover normally excludes claims associated with HIV-related illness. It is possible to obtain separate "Dread Disease" insurance for nurses, doctors and health workers where a benefit is payable should a person be tested HIV positive
- All travel insurance policies have geographical limits. Premiums are lower if cover is restricted to Europe instead of worldwide; however, careful consideration needs to be given to the insurer's definition of Europe.
- No limit less than £2,000,000 per person should be accepted for journeys to the United States.
- Travellers are recommended to carry proof of medical expenses cover at all times in the United States to avoid the authorities not providing treatment.

Any action taken by the expedition in the field without consultation with the emergency rescue company/insurers may have to be justified to the company afterwards. A diary of events should therefore be kept.

2. Personal accident

This covers death and disablement following accidental bodily injury. An amount is paid in the event of loss of use of an eye or limb, permanent total disablement, or death. Cover should include disappearance, and death or disablement by exposure. The amount paid will be additional to any other personal accident or life assurance that individual members of the expedition have arranged for themselves.

- Benefits should be payable for disability from *usual* occupation as opposed to *any* occupation.
- Note that cover should be accidental bodily injury; avoid insurance policies that restrict cover to violent visible or external means.
- Make sure cover is on a 24-hour basis and includes commuting to and from the expedition departure point and is not just restricted to certain activities.
- As expedition members can change, make sure cover is on an unnamed basis for all members, as opposed to named individuals.
- The lower age limit should be carefully checked, for the death benefit will be restricted to a nominal amount for minors below 16 years of age. Some insurers will try and apply the nominal amount to members aged 16 and 17.
- If your insurance policy is a group policy for all expedition members, the insurer may try and apply a limit of liability in respect of more than one

individual being injured on an aircraft or other conveyance. Larger expeditions should check the policy wording to make sure any aggregate conveyance limit is adequate.

3. Public/personal liability insurance

This is one of the most important elements of expedition insurance. All members must have adequate insurance against any legal liability in the event of an incident occurring, which would include liability to other members of the expedition.

The legal necessity for public or third party liability varies greatly from country to country (care should be taken to comply with local laws). This type of cover should include liability for bodily injury or illness caused to anyone. Cover should also include damage to other people's property, other than property in the care, custody or control of the expedition. *Warning:* do not admit liability in the event of an incident, as you may prejudice your rights.

Leaders have greater responsibilities than other members. Leaders of schools expeditions should ensure that the school's liability policy extends to include the teachers'/leaders' liability in full and in the region to be visited. If the school's insurance cannot be extended to provide this cover then some other form of liability insurance should be arranged. Check with your insurer that cover also extends to expedition organisers.

- If the expedition is being arranged by a company, special tour operators' liability may be necessary.
- Cover will exclude mechanically propelled vehicles – this includes waterborne craft and aircraft. Separate liability policies will be necessary for all waterborne craft and motor vehicles.
- If hiring a car in the United States or Canada, the indemnity limits will be low; separate top-up cover is normally necessary.

4. Replacement and rearrangement

You can insure additional travel and accommodation expenses for a replacement expedition member following the death or disablement of an insured person. In addition, this type of insurance would cover the cost of returning the originally insured person to complete the expedition following recovery.

Further points to consider when arranging insurance

1. If you hold insurance in your own name (for example, life, personal accident, all risks) you should notify the destination and details of your expedition activities to your insurers. If you do not, your policy could be invalidated.
2. When relying on an "umbrella" policy (for example, a school or association policy) check that the cover is adequate. Insurance provided by schools' policies

will not usually cover boys or girls who left school at the end of the term before the expedition.

3. If you hire local labour, make enquiries about your responsibilities before the expedition starts. In many countries something equivalent to the UK employers' liability insurance, normally known as workers' compensation, may be needed. In most cases, this can be arranged locally, before engaging local labour, and exact requirements can usually be confirmed from the host country's embassy. In addition, many expeditions work with local scientists and helpers who should be included in the expedition's liability insurance.

4. Read the insurance policy details carefully, and explain them to all members of the expedition.

5. Take some claim forms with the expedition to complete while the incident is still fresh in your mind. *It is absolutely essential that any claim is reported to the insurer immediately, as an insurance policy may time bar a claim if notified late.*

6. Be careful to declare separately to the insurer any holiday taken after the expedition has finished. Separate cover may need to be arranged as a separate risk from the rest of the expedition.

7. Check your policy will not expire if your expedition is delayed beyond the planned return date, due to circumstances beyond your control. It may be impossible to contact your insurer from the field.

8. Some insurers will try to exclude any cover arising from "war risks". This should be strongly resisted as expeditions often work in politically sensitive areas. A more acceptable wording is an exclusion of war risks by major powers only. If you are in any doubt about the stability of the area you are working in, check with the UK Foreign Office or equivalent body overseas and declare the facts to the insurer for written agreement.

Medical treatment abroad

There are over 40 countries outside the EU with which the UK has reciprocal health-care agreements that entitle British visitors to emergency medical treatment. A Department of Health leaflet *Health Advice for Travellers* provides vital information on obtaining emergency medical treatment abroad, and contains details of how to use Form E111, the passport to free or reduced-cost emergency medical treatment in most European countries. This is an important and complex process and the leaflet is essential reading. To order a copy, phone the Health Literature Line on +44 800 555777 anytime, free of charge. Orders for more than ten copies should be placed with the Department of Health, PO Box 410, Wetherby LS23 7LN.

Where to get insurance

Aon Risk Services Ltd has prepared a specialist Expedition Travel Insurance Scheme in consultation with the Expedition Advisory Centre of the Royal Geographical Society (with The Institute of British Geographers), which is designed to meet the specialised needs of scientific and educational expeditions. Details can be obtained from the Expedition Advisory Centre (tel. +44 171 5913030, fax +44 171 5913031), or contact: Emma Goddard, Aon Risk Services (UK) Ltd, Richmond House, College Street, Southampton SO14 3PS (tel. +44 1703 225616, fax +44 1703 631055).

Few insurance brokers are prepared to arrange expedition insurance, but the following are among those who have shown an interest in insuring expeditions:

Campbell Irvine Ltd, 48 Earls Court Road, London W8 6EJ (tel. +44 171 9376981, fax +44 171 9382250). In the first instance please submit brief details of the expedition in writing.

West Mercia Insurance Services & Des Roches, Witney Bay, Witney, Oxon, OX8 6BE (tel. +44 1993 700200, fax +44 1993 700502)

When obtaining quotations from other insurance intermediaries, make sure the insurance broker is a member of the Insurance Brokers Registration Council (IBRC).

For sporting expeditions

Many clubs and associations have special insurance schemes arranged for their members. These range from mountaineering and hang-gliding to canoeing and caving, and are designed to provide insurance cover for specialist high-risk activities.

Beware, some of these schemes have restricted cover, and others may not last because of either bad claims experience or lack of support.

For mountaineering expeditions

British Mountaineering Council, 177-179 Burton Road, Manchester M20 2BB (tel. +44 161 4454747, fax +44 161 4454500), contact: Ray Perry.

The BMC has a "comprehensive" scheme and welcomes new members requiring insurance.

For winter sports, trekking and rafting

The "Snowcard" was developed by SIS (Snowcard Insurance Services) through a demand for convenient and portable proof of insurance on the ski slopes. Popular with skiers, it has given them added security and peace of mind that help and assistance are only a phone call away should the worst happen. In any form of leisure activity, it is more practical to carry a "card" in your pocket than a piece of paper for proof of insurance. Therefore SIS now offers the same package to other holiday makers.

Assistance International 24-hour telephone service is provided for everyone insured under Snowcard's Flexi-Option Insurance in case of a serious medical problem. This policy has since been adapted for trekkers and river rafters.

For further information contact: Snowcard, Freepost 4135, Lower Boddington, Daventry, Northants NN11 6BR.

Insurance premium tax/VAT
When obtaining a quotation make sure the price you are quoted is inclusive of insurance premium tax or VAT. The present IPT rate is 4% when receiving a quotation from an insurance broker.

For general insurance
Endsleigh's ISIS insurance includes a range of policies designed for the specific needs of independent travellers, from the Backpacker right up to the Premier Worldwide policy. Benefits include: medical cover up to £5,000,000; luggage up to £1,500; cancellation up to £3,000; and personal liability up to £750,000.

For more information contact: Max Sengul, Endsleigh Insurance Services, 3 King Street, Watford WD1 8BT, tel. +44 1923 218438, fax +44 1923 218458, or one of the local offices to be found throughout the UK.

6 RISK ASSESSMENT AND CRISIS MANAGEMENT

Clive Barrow

Risk assessment is increasingly expected of organisers of expeditions and outdoor practitioners. It is now a legal requirement for commercially organised outdoor activities for under 18s in the UK. There is currently no law in this country governing the organisation of expeditions overseas. Many see this as a good thing. Fortunately, the number of accidents among participants in overseas expeditions is minute. However, the climate of opinion in the UK is changing in several ways. The public is more circumspect about safety and risk as a result of increased media coverage of expedition or outdoor activity accidents.

Planners and leaders of all overseas expeditions must carry out a systematic, careful and responsible safety management assessment. Risk assessment is the first and perhaps most important part of this. This chapter is intended to provide a practical guide to risk assessment coupled with the key considerations involved in crisis management planning for medical officers. Expedition leaders will use similar ideas to those outlined below but on a larger and more general scale.

RISK ASSESSMENT

Hazard and risk on overseas expeditions

Hazard and risk are inherent in everything we do. Much is governed by the environment in which we conduct a particular activity. In the UK the degree of risk is considerably less than that to which we expose ourselves overseas, particularly in developing countries where our knowledge of and our ability to control the environment are less. Risk assessment of overseas projects must therefore consider a wider array of hazards, and must always allow for the unexpected (see Table 6.1). The expedition organiser must always be prepared to adopt alternatives and/or completely abandon an activity if the risk assessment demonstrates that control measures cannot reduce the risk to an acceptable level.

In attempting to qualify and quantify risk, it is important not to worry unneces-

TABLE 6.1 HAZARD AND RISK ON OVERSEAS EXPEDITIONS

Hazard	Risk
1. The team	
Health and fitness (including previous/existing medical conditions)	Increased risk of health problems on expedition leading to serious illness/death
Attitude and behaviour	Increased risk of ignoring control measures resulting in illness/injury
Experience and training	Lack of increases risk in all activities
Personal equipment	Serious injury/illness due to inadequate equipment/equipment failure
2. The environment	
Mountains/sea/desert/jungle	Altitude sickness/drowning/heat problems
Climate and weather conditions	Heat and cold-related injury/death
Wildlife (including insects)	Attack/poisoning through bites/stings/disease
3. Health	
Endemic disease (Dengue fever/ Japanese encephalitis)	Serious illness or death
Malaria	Serious illness or death
AIDS/HIV	Serious illness or death
Polluted water	Serious illness
Contaminated food	Serious illness or death
4. Local population	
Political climate	Political instability/coup/kidnapping
Attitudes to foreigners/cultural differences	Attack/rape/theft/access to drugs
Hygiene/living conditions	Disease
5. Expedition activity	
Trekking/climbing/mountaineering	Altitude sickness/falls from height
River crossing	Serious injury/drowning
Water-based activities (diving/kayaking/sailing)	Drowning/embolism
Underground activities (caving/cave-diving)	Drowning/suffocation/starvation
Activity required for research/data	As above
Equipment failure/inappropriate use	Serious injury/death
Team-related hazards	See (1)
Games/sports activities	Injury/incapacitation
6. Travel and camp life	
Transport (public/private)	High risk of serious injury/death
Road/water conditions	Increased risk of accidents
Other road users	Increased risk of accidents
Camp hazards (stoves/fires/flooding/ avalanche/wildlife)	Burns/drowning/suffocation/mauling/injury/ death
Food and water	See (3)
Accommodation/hotels	Electrocution/serious injury/disease/mugging/ attack

Figure 6.1   *Fire and the danger of burns is an often underrated risk, especially when cooking on an open fire (V. Southwell/RGS Kora Research Project)*

sarily about trivia. A risk assessment which is too cluttered with minor concerns will be discarded in the field as a bureaucrat's folly, and will be of less value than not doing one at all. Any severe and persistent risk must appear in the risk assessment, together with appropriate control measures.

Acceptable risk
On an overseas expedition, risk can never be completely eliminated. Indeed, it is through the management of both perceived and real risk that expeditions of all types can be used to such beneficial effect to the participants. Most expedition organisers speak of reducing risk to an acceptable level. This is extremely difficult to define since opinions about acceptability may differ greatly among individuals. The experience, age, ability and technical competence of the participants on an expedition or overseas project must be considered, since this will affect the level of risk which is considered acceptable.

Control measures
Control measures are the backbone of the risk assessment process. They are what the expedition leader or medical officer (MO) initiates to reduce or eliminate a particular risk. Some examples would be as follows:

- providing first aid training before the expedition commences;
- getting immunised before exposure to disease;
- preventing bites by disease-transmitting insects.

In most cases, many control measures can be implemented before the expedition as part of the planning process. However, once the expedition or project actually starts there may be many more.

The five steps to risk assessment
The UK Health and Safety Executive refers to the process as one of five steps. These are as follows:

1. Identify the hazards and associated risks.
2. Identify who is potentially at risk and how.
3. Identify the precautions or control measures to minimise the risk, including any further action required to reduce the risk to an acceptable level.
4. Record (write down) your findings.
5. Review the risk assessment periodically.

This process is clear and straightforward and can be applied to any expedition overseas.

A convenient format for risk assessment is a table with each of the five steps as a column heading (see Table 6.2).

TABLE 6.2 RISK ASSESSMENT

Hazard	Risk level	Control measure	Additional action	Review mechanism
Data collection activities Trekking/river crossing	High	Careful route selection. Use of guides. Competent, experienced group leaders. Use of ropes/training in river crossing techniques. No activity after dark. Safety and medical kit carried at all times. Group risk assessment before each day's activity	Leader/staff approve activity or if necessary, halt progress if new risk arises rendering it unsafe to proceed	Post-expedition report with information about incidents and changes to risk assessment

Reviewing a risk assessment

Because of frequent changes in environment, risk assessment must be reviewed to remain effective. Risk assessments are useless if they are not properly communicated to staff and participants.

CRISIS MANAGEMENT

Crisis management comprises those *processes and systems developed to foresee, avoid and, in the worst case, manage a crisis on an overseas expedition.*

The principle adopted in crisis management planning should always concentrate on the worst case scenario. It is the expedition leader's role in planning an expedition to foresee and avoid a crisis in the making and to facilitate the handling of a crisis if it occurs.

An expedition crisis generally involves an accident, illness or injury to expedition members. The role of the MO in crisis management is to:

- organise adequate medical training for all expedition members;
- provide an appropriate medical kit;
- investigate the availability of local medical support (doctors/hospitals);
- investigate access to casualty evacuation locally, nationally and internationally;
- consider the use of an international assistance agency or emergency centre.

To be able to achieve the above, attention must be paid to the skills of the expedition members and accompanying staff. There must be sufficient first aid skills among the team to deal with the immediate care of a casualty. Several courses are now available, from organisations such as Wilderness Medical Training, which concentrate on more advanced medicine for remote foreign travel for competent first aiders.

Careful selection of the expedition medical kit is important. In the UK, a first aider is not permitted to administer tablets or antibiotics, but during an expedition this restriction may have to be relaxed.

The investigation and enlistment of locally and nationally available medical support forms another essential part of the MO's role. Embassies in the host country often have lists of recommended doctors and dentists in the capital city, but rarely have information about the further-flung outposts likely to be frequented by expedition teams. For this reason, detailed research is necessary to produce a support network of medical contacts in the areas in which the expedition will be operating. Support may come from local aid projects with medical back-up; clinics and dispensaries; local hospitals; or on a national basis the GPs and hospitals commonly used by the expatriate population of the country. It is important to identify a recommended dentist.

Communication is an important part of crisis management and the more options that are researched and made available, the greater is the chance of establishing and maintaining links with the outside world. Essentially, the expedition team relies either on its own communications brought in from overseas (radios, distress beacons, satellite telephones), or on local systems (telephone, runner, telex, local radio communications). In practice, some of both will be involved depending on the nature of the expedition and the size/budget of the organiser.

TABLE 6.3 EMERGENCY COMMUNICATION NETWORK
Casualty
•
Expedition leader
•
Local representative/doctor (contacted by runner, radio, local transport)
•
Assistance agency/national contact point (contacted by telephone/radio/telex/fax)
•
UK back-up link/emergency centre (contacted by satellite distress beacon/telephone/telex/fax/email)
•
Media/public/relatives (contacted by telephone)

Whatever the size of the expedition, it must have a 24-hour contact in the UK capable of responding and assisting in a crisis. For smaller or one-off trips abroad, this may be a family member or colleague who is fully conversant with the expedition medical and contacts network, as well as its itinerary and emergency procedures. This individual must have contact details for all next-of-kin/closest relatives of all expedition members (including staff). For larger organisations, this back-up may take the form of a duty officer and/or an assistance agency or emergency centre. Companies such as World Challenge Expeditions now offer the facilities of a round-the-clock emergency centre to any organiser of an overseas expedition, however large or small. The function of the UK back-up is to liaise with all the relevant parties in the UK. This may include relatives, sponsoring organisations, insurers, assistance agencies and the press. The potential scope and extent of this role in a crisis requires the UK back-up to be highly capable and responsible, and fully briefed by the expedition's organiser. Further information on communication and practical crisis management can be found in Chapter 12 on casualty evacuation.

SUMMARY

It is important to reiterate the small number of accidents recorded on expeditions overseas to date. Well-planned expeditions conducted by suitable and properly trained teams with the right back-up stand a very small chance of sustaining a tragedy. The potential benefits for participants and host country alike of overseas expeditions still far outweigh the risks of disaster. Through practical risk assessment and sensible crisis management planning, the balance can be continually weighted in the right direction.

SECTION 2

FIELD MEDICINE

7 THE ROLE OF THE MEDICAL OFFICER IN THE FIELD

Tom Davies

The medical officer (MO) is the guardian of the expedition's health. In the field your first function is to prevent people becoming ill, but if they do, you have to ensure the best possible outcome. This does not necessarily mean treating everything that is presented to you, but rather using your knowledge, authority and awareness of your capabilities to advise on the best course of action.

Prevention of ill health

Much of this must take place before the expedition goes into the field and should include:

- Advice on immunisations (see Chapter 2)
- Advice on malaria prophylaxis if needed (see Chapter 15)
- Organisation of first aid training (see Chapter 4)
- Provision of education on health and hygiene issues (see Chapter 8)
- Completion of a personal medical questionnaire by each expedition member (see Appendix 1)
- Encouraging members to have a pre-expedition dental check-up
- Preparing a communication network in case of evacuation (see Chapter 12)
- Organising medical insurance with full emergency evacuation cover (see Chapter 5)
- Preparing expedition medical kits (see Chapter 3)
- Improving your own knowledge of local medical problems

Once the expedition gets into the field the need to protect members remains, and if the expedition is to be happy and successful this must be done without causing antagonism.

In the field the MO should:
- Reiterate the rules of camp and personal hygiene
- Ensure a safe water supply
- Revise basic first aid and management of minor injuries
- Practise a mock evacuation
- Place expedition medical kits and communication network papers in a designated place
- Assess the risks posed by the natural environment
- Ensure the safety of expedition members

The risks which are most important are those of trauma, infection and exposure to physical risks, such as sunlight, low atmospheric pressures, cold and humidity.

Trauma
The risk of being exposed to injury is just as well assessed by the people who commonly encounter the hazard, such as climbers, cave divers and so on, and in these activities participants are usually well informed and are trained to advise beginners. Such risk can be minimised by the use of sensible precautions such as safety belts in vehicles and hard hats.

Infections
By following basic hygiene rules most ordinary infection risks can be reduced, but it is important to at least be aware of the more exotic ones. Yet common sense should be used, as trying to avoid every theoretical risk would quite possibly bring the expedition to a halt; the result would be that all your warnings would be ignored. For example, the risk of rabies should always be uppermost in your mind whereas treatable but unusual infections such as filiariasis should not impede the expedition. There is also the risk of becoming infected with STDs or hepatitis B through casual, unprotected sexual intercourse. There is a high prevalence of these, as well as HIV, in many countries.

The physical environment
One of the many roles of the MO is to be aware of the risks posed by the physical environment. There are, of course, many of these. Situations may arise in the field where the MO will either have to give an opinion about a proposed activity, or give unsolicited warnings when activities have already started. Assessment of risk by the MO once in the field is essential and a crisis management strategy should be prepared (see Chapter 6).

Inexperienced people are likely to underestimate risk, particularly where the hazard is not obvious. This is particularly true of cold, as was tragically illustrated by the deaths of boy scouts in Derbyshire many years ago. Their leader simply did not appreciate that the British climate could kill without a dramatic blizzard. Wet clothing, poor wind resistance and exhaustion is a lethal combination. The risk of sunburn is well known, although many Northern Europeans are not aware of how much more intense sunlight is at tropical latitudes and how heat exhaustion can kill.

Treatment

Most expedition MOs are not lavishly equipped, having had to bear in mind expense and mobility, and few diagnostic aids will be available. MOs should have supplies capable of treating minor illnesses and providing emergency care for serious conditions until a patient can be evacuated. The MO should set a specific, daily time to see patients with non-urgent problems. If a patient needs to be evacuated you are in an unusual position, the new considerations being:

a) the need to choose the safest option for the patient when diagnosis cannot be confirmed by colleagues or tests;
b) the often conflicting needs of the other expedition members;
c) the lack of privacy and confidentiality which is part of expedition life.

Most problems are straightforward and trivial and can be dealt with on the spot. The role of the MO is thus uncomplicated: to make a diagnosis and treat. Most doctors develop a sense of when something apparently trivial is actually a manifestation of something more serious, and in the usual urban surroundings help is available to confirm intuitive feelings or doubts. In the field this is not possible, and you therefore have to assume the worst possible scenario. This may mean causing a lot of inconvenience and concern, for example, by sending someone with stomach ache to hospital with possible appendicitis, or making someone with a headache descend 3,000 feet. You will arouse grumbling and hostility if the person recovers without intervention, but you really have no option than to take the safest course. If you are not reasonably sure that there is no serious disease you cannot gamble, and afterwards, even if the patient does get better without intervention, they may still have had the early stages of disease.

MOs are also there to offer reassurance. People come with genuine symptoms that do not reflect serious disease; hypochondria can affect the most heroic of explorers, although in most cases it is merely natural concern about real symptoms whose significance is not apparent to the sufferer. You will not know what the situation is until you have made a serious attempt to make a diagnosis, so never fail to take this step. If you think nothing is wrong, friendly reassurance is important. You should endeavour to treat even natural grumblers properly, because indifference or contempt will eventually leave them suffering in silence, and prevent them coming again when they really need to.

There is always the problem that illness in an expedition member may adversely affect the expedition as a whole, and members, not least the patient, may try to persuade you to allow activities to go on which would not be in the patient's best interests. It is important not to yield to this persuasion because it may harm the patient (and their persuasion will count for nothing afterwards) and it may also, in some circumstances, jeopardise the whole expedition.

People on expeditions tend to be self-sufficient people anyway, and the circumstances reinforce this. There is a tendency to overdo this and, where MOs are concerned, they sometimes attempt to solve all problems single-handedly, even when it is not necessary. Always ask yourself whether extra help and advice is available and if it would be useful.

All patients rightly expect that when they give the MO information, or a diagnosis is made or suspected, it will be confidential. People also have a right to refuse treatment, even if, in the MO's view, this will not be in their best interests. However, the General Medical Council has made it clear that doctors also have a duty to the public at large, and in expedition terms circumstances could arise where the leader would have to be told that someone should not be allowed to jeopardise the health or safety of other members by either concealing illness or refusing treatment.

Treating people not on the expedition

In many parts of the world expeditions are perceived by local people to be rich and endowed with clinical expertise and drugs. The apparently universal human desire to take medication may be stimulated by the arrival of the expedition, and the slightest hint that you will treat illness in the local population will produce a flood of people with no illness at all, minor illness and often serious chronic illness, all of whom request treatment. It is tempting to try to do good and establish goodwill by offering medicines to all of them, but before you do the potential harm should be considered:

1. You may not understand their problem.
2. You may endanger your own members by using drugs intended for them.
3. You may be blamed unreasonably for adverse outcomes.
4. You may offend local healers.
5. Treatment may be incomplete and thus ineffective or harmful.
6. You might be exploited for your novelty value.

Nevertheless, you cannot avoid doing what you can for other people, so the question is: what principles would help you decide whom to treat and what to do? People, particularly children, who are clearly and severely ill, should be treated, but not necessarily by you. Evacuate the patient if possible; your authority may help you to do this. Disease which, although severe, is obviously chronic, especially in adults, should not be treated by you; you will not have the resources and the time, and it would be better for everyone if the patient is treated by the local health service. The stream of people in whom you can see little wrong, and who mainly request medicine rather than presenting a problem, should be referred elsewhere.

8 BASE CAMP HYGIENE AND HEALTH

Hokey Bennett-Jones

Unstinting efforts to maintain a high standard of hygiene will contribute to a lower incidence of gastrointestinal problems and prevent losing working man-hours during an expedition. "Be obsessional about camp hygiene." Routine in camp life pays great dividends, and responsibility for the hygiene, cleaning and safety chores may have to be organised by a strict rota to ensure that standards are kept up throughout the project.

If you cannot help in the choice of a site for base camp, you should at least be aware of its characteristics and therefore any risks and hazards it presents. In planning the layout of the camp, particular attention should be given to the following:

- Water supply
- Latrines
- Areas for washing up, washing clothes, ablutions
- Drains
- Kitchen (smoke, smell, fire risk)
- Food storage
- Rubbish disposal
- Fuel dump and fire precautions
- Areas for eating, working, sleeping and relaxing
- Medical area tent/hut (on the edge of the camp for privacy)

Water supply

Be unremitting in your efforts to maintain a high standard of clean water (see Chapter 9). Find the best source of water. It may, for example, be possible to use rain water. Discuss with the leader before departure what safe water regime (rules) needs to be established. On a large expedition someone should be responsible for the water every day. This might be the responsibility of the medical officer (MO) throughout the project, or be organised in rotation, but everyone must be aware of how the system operates. Every member of the expedition must know the difference between safe and unpurified water containers: consider using a simple system of markers. They must also know which source to use for which purpose, for example, not to clean teeth with untreated water.

People use a lot of water. Water will be needed for drinking, washing (people, clothes, cutlery and crockery), cooking, vehicles and sometimes animals. Wherever your expedition is – in desert, tropical forest, tundra or at altitude – everyone should drink enough fluid every day to pass 1 litre of clear urine. This means that intake will change from day to day depending on workload and speed of acclimatisation.

- Do not underestimate the time it takes to purify water every day.
- Carrying water is hard work. Make sure that your containers are small enough to be carried without too much effort.
- Do not embarrass the local people by making unreasonable demands on limited supplies of water, or be seen to waste it.
- Do not allow members to pollute water supplies, your own or other people's, by being thoughtless.
- Have a back-up system for treating water. All too often the best made plans go wrong or break down in the field.

Latrines

Latrines are the subject of much interest, concern and a fair amount of embarrassed mirth. People's bowel habits change on expeditions, one way or the other, and often dramatically. Once again it is necessary to plan which latrine system is appropriate for your expedition. Mobile and short-stay sub-camps can use an earth pit or trench. Sub-camps should dig a trench at least 1.25 metres deep and about 30cm wide. It may be necessary to construct a grab rail and foot rests that can be repositioned. Each time the latrine is used, the user should shovel over a coverage of earth from the pile on the edge of the trench.

Long-drop latrines for static base camps should be at least 4 metres deep and have a seat and fly-proof cover placed over the top. In environments where the soil is unstable, such as sandy desert, consider using old oil drums (lid and base removed and perforated holes halfway up) to shore up the sides, adding a packing of sticks between the edges to stop loose sand filling the drums. Chemical toilets (Elsan type) are not often possible for the expedition camp, but if you are lucky enough to have them there must be adequate provision for the disposal of the contents in a sewage system or deep pit that can be covered. All latrines must be constructed more than 50 metres away from wells or other water supplies and kitchens.

It is difficult to calculate how many latrines you will need for a big group in a static camp, especially if there are both men and women on the expedition. The efficient working of any camp toilet is of course influenced by the environmental conditions

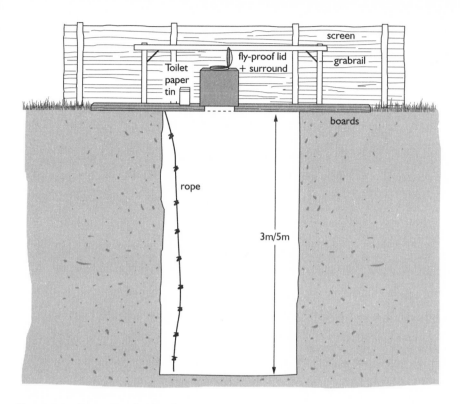

Figure 8.1   *Long-drop latrine for static camp*

of the camp – drainage, porosity of the soil and humidity – and by the number of people using it, so there can be no set formula to help calculate how many to construct. As a rough guide, one long drop for ten people should last two months. A large static camp of some duration may require new long drops during the project. If flies become a problem a covering of earth can be shovelled into the long drop after each use as for an earth trench. Storing toilet paper in a tin stops it blowing away, keeps it dry and keeps the ants out. Arrange hand-washing facilities near to the toilets (the bowl could be a different colour from the ones for kitchen use) and fix the soap on a string. You may need to establish procedures for the disposal of paper, tampons, and so on away from the latrine area. Be aware of any expedition members' religious requirements that need catering for when setting up latrines. If local people are to use your facility make sure that they understand how to do so. Problems arise if people try to use Western-style toilets in the local way.

The latrine area needs to be cleaned daily. A long-handled brush is useful for scrubbing the seat with disinfectant or soapy water. Pouring disinfectant down the

Figure 8.2   *Earth pit or Trench latrine for small, mobile camps*

long-drop does not significantly reduce infection but only delays decomposition. Try to keep the latrines as dry as possible to discourage flies. Spend time at the beginning of the expedition making sure that seats and lids fit and close properly, making them as fly-proof as possible. Whatever type of latrine you use you must understand its workings so that any malfunctions can be rectified. It is not a pleasant task to mend or reconstruct toilets when they are in operation. Check at regular intervals that the system is working and is safe. Boards can become slippery, rotten and damaged and long-drop sides cave in. It may be prudent to have a fixed rope down inside the long drop as a safety line. Mesh-covered duck boards around the toilet can be helpful, especially in muddy camps, as inevitably the area becomes squelchy. Snakes and other creatures are frequent visitors to latrines. Encourage everyone to use a torch at night to check, particularly under the seats.

If your expedition has built the latrines for your camps you must have a plan for dealing with the area after the expedition is over, leaving it safe and hygienic. This will require some thought and time if the camp has been of any size or duration. In areas of permanent frost, where natural biological breakdown of sewage is impossible, all camp excreta will have to be stored and then taken away.

TABLE 8.1   **CARDINAL RULES FOR LATRINE HYGIENE**
1. Clean seat daily; check operation and safety
2. Keep dry; do not pour down disinfectant
3. Ensure seats and cover are fly-proof
4. Beware of snakes; use a torch at night

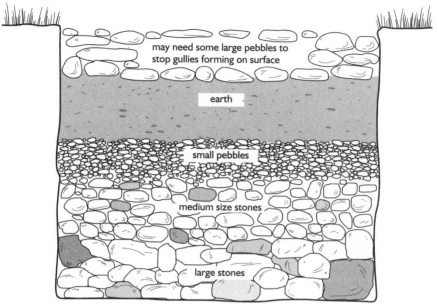

Figure 8.3 *A typical soak-away pit*

Drains

Even small mobile camps will need to dispose of dirty water somewhere. Without adequate drains your static camp will soon become smelly, and stagnant water is a breeding ground for mosquitoes and infectious diseases. Constructing drains is a time-consuming process. By their very nature they have a tendency to be regularly washed away or become clogged up. For camps which will be used for any length of time, building good kitchen drains and grease traps will pay great dividends in the long term, provided they are used and maintained properly.

Grease traps and soak-aways can get clogged up quickly by a surface layer of food particles, causing the whole system to break down. A good filter, which is small enough to hold back rice and other things and can easily be cleaned, is a great asset. Making a filter of plastic netting or mosquito screen over chicken wire is one possibility. Washing suds and toothpaste can cause problems as they form a slimy surface over soak-aways which then require regular maintenance to clear.

If you are constructing an improvised shower you will need a mesh-covered duck board to stand on and a drain and soak-away underneath.

Rubbish

Rubbish disposal should be tackled as a daily chore to prevent smell, flies and infectious diseases. Rubbish also attracts scavengers if not disposed of properly. It is ad-

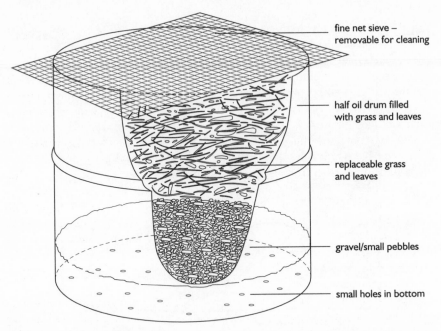

fine net sieve – removable for cleaning

half oil drum filled with grass and leaves

replaceable grass and leaves

gravel/small pebbles

small holes in bottom

Figure 8.4   *A typical grease trap*

visable to burn everything (including the top layer of grass or leaves from the grease trap) before burying it in a deep pit or taking it away for disposal. This includes tins and glass as even hungry expedition members leave unpleasant scraps in the corners of sardine tins. Flatten things like tins with a mallet. It can be useful to dig a rubbish pit on a slight gradient to promote drainage of rain water.

Kitchen

Expedition diarrhoea is usually caused by bad hygiene. Again, unremitting efforts to keep a high standard of hygiene in the kitchen will help cut down the man-hours wasted suffering from gut infections. It is imperative that hands are washed prior to all work in the kitchen. One person must be in charge of the catering, so that there is no doubt whose responsibility it is to cook each day, and who is to keep the kitchen area tidy and clean. Decide who will do the washing up, where it will be done, and how the cutlery and crockery are stored. Try, if possible, to wash up in hot water. Table tops and food preparation areas need to be scrubbed daily, aprons washed, cloths boiled and hung out in the sun to dry.

You will need to consider how to store food. Rodents quickly appear in camp and can severely damage stores as well as transmit disease to humans; for example, the multimammate rat *Mastomys natalenis* urinates on food supplies and transmits Lassa fever in West Africa. Hanging insect-proof larder cupboards are useful as they can be packed flat. Refrigerators in the field (whether gas, paraffin, or electrically operated) are seldom 100% reliable. They are usually unable to maintain the cold setting of a modern kitchen refrigerator, allowing disease organisms to multiply much faster. Scientific specimens may compete for space in the refrigerator with the food, beer and even the MO's drugs. This must be resisted at all costs. Scientific specimens must be kept in a separate refrigerator if they need to be kept at a low temperature. The camp kitchen refrigerator must be kept clean with raw meat at the bottom and cooked food above. It must not be overfilled and the door must not be opened and closed too often.

There must be firm rules about the cleaning and preparation of food, including the preparation of fresh fruit and salads; you may wish to ban lettuce, other broadleaf vegetables and shellfish completely. Raw food must be prepared, washed or peeled away from already cooked food, taking special care with raw meat. This should be prepared with a separate chopping board and knife kept for this purpose. Food must be properly cooked, served hot on clean plates and eaten promptly; it must not be left lying around or reheated. Make sure the other expedition members know the risks from milk, ice-cream, ice and so on, and which foods are unsafe if eaten away from camp.

If the expedition has the good fortune to have a cook, be vigilant about standards of hygiene. It is not safe to assume that your cook, whether local or expatriate, has any understanding of the principles of kitchen hygiene. Staphylococcal food poisoning usually results from contamination of, for example, chopping boards, by people harbouring bacteria in their noses. Always bear in mind the possibility that the cook may be a carrier of disease. Consider treating for worms and do not let someone who is ill do the cooking.

TABLE 8.2 CARDINAL RULES FOR KITCHEN HYGIENE

1. Wash hands and scrub nails with soap before starting any work in the kitchen
2. Keep fingernails short and cover wounds with a plaster
3. Wear clean clothes or an apron (available for kitchen use only)
4. Do not use the same chopping board or utensils for raw and cooked ingredients
5. Food should be eaten immediately after it is cooked or, if not, refrigerated or reheated to sterilising temperatures before being eaten

---

The cooks work long hard hours, getting up before the rest of the team and working late into the night. They are the heart of the expedition and it is a thankless task. On every expedition food will become the all-absorbing topic and higher on the agenda as time passes. However well you have planned to please everyone, there will always be complaints. The cooks can often become the whipping boys – they are moaned at if not actually abused – but an expedition cannot function without food. They need support, and a show of thanks from other members of the team will be much appreciated.

Camp safety
Spend time in camp removing hazards – marking guy ropes and washing lines, fixing handrails or holds and tying back branches where people regularly work or pass. Make sure everyone hangs and uses mosquito nets correctly. Be aware of anyone using or storing dangerous chemicals. Anaesthetic agents for small mammals and formaldehyde are commonly used on expeditions. If firearms are to be used, training and safe storage must be rigorous. Be especially aware of any scientist working with dangerous specimens (alive or dead). No one should handle venomous animals without previous training. If, for example, a venomous snake is to be handled, advise that it is done early in the day and not after the handler has drunk alcohol. If anything untoward happens, communications and, if necessary, evacuation, is far easier in daylight.

Everyone should know where the camp first aid kit is kept, but make sure all medical equipment and drugs are stored securely. Everything should be packed and labelled clearly with the name and batch numbers. There must be some system for the resupply of individuals' first aid kits. This will enable the MO to keep account of what minor problems members are suffering, and if necessary to check wounds, and to stop the medical stocks constantly being pilfered or bits of the evacuation kit (for example, spare torch batteries) being "borrowed". Consider having a book for recording every piece of equipment or dose of drug issued. Make sure that those who are on regular medication know where their spare supply is kept.

Think about the fire risks and what fire-fighting methods are available to you, especially in the kitchen. Store fuel safely away from the main camping area. Fuel (that is lamp fuel) should not be kept in people's tents nor in plastic containers. Money spent on clearly labelled metal cans is never wasted. In large camps the siting of the generator is important to reduce the effect of the noise and fumes. Make sure any electric cables and plugs are safe. Check these at regular intervals throughout the project.

TABLE 8.3 CARDINAL RULES FOR FIRE PREVENTION

1. Identify risks
2. Publicise extinguisher sites or sand buckets
3. Store fuel away from tents
4. Do not keep fuel in plastic containers
5. Regularly check plugs and cables

Remember that the risk assessment done during the planning stages of the expedition and the routine safety rules may need to be modified in the field (see further chapters). Keep a book at the base camp for people to record daily where they are going, with whom and their expected time of return. Try and make sure people have adequate clothing and kit for the environment and daily conditions.

Everyone should know the policy and procedure for a late or lost person.

Be aware of what first aid skills the rest of the team have. The acclimatisation period and time in base camp offers the opportunity to go over some basic first aid with expedition members, with special reference to local problems such as recognising and managing heat stroke or hypothermia. In the event of the MO having time away from camp for any reason, appoint a second in command.

Lastly, you should be aware of any local security risk, for example, driving after dark or whether it is safe to leave anyone alone in camp.

Camp life

A happy, relaxed atmosphere in camp can help support those who are feeling the loss of their usual social props or missing their homes and families. Base camp should be a place for rest and healing, but birthdays in the field are a good excuse for a party to boost morale. The MO can also help morale by taking an interest in, and spending time with, members working on their projects. This will be much easier to achieve if the MO is seen to be mucking in with general camp duties where possible. But the MO must remain available at all times for consultation and be seen to have an unquestionable standard of confidentiality.

Communication with the outside world by letter, radio or phone is very important. Do not underestimate the disappointment if this breaks down.

Meal times are important focal points for everyone and give the MO a chance to check that all are happy and well. The setting of the meal times can be critical and it is always difficult to please everyone and fit in with their work. It is frustrating to have meals consistently late, forcing people to wait around. Young people need food regularly and in large amounts. There will be accidents if they get hungry and tired. Try not to let people skip meals, and if possible make packed lunches for them if their work means they cannot get back for meals.

TABLE 8.4 MEAL TIMES

1. Meal times are an important focal point
2. The setting of meal times is important
3. Young people need food regularly
4. Make packed meals if away from base

It is often necessary, on a long expedition, to identify one day of the week (say a Sunday) which is slightly different from the rest in some way, perhaps with breakfast half an hour later. This Sabbath is also useful for those taking weekly antimalarial prophylaxis: "Sunday is antimalarial day". The MO can be responsible for putting out the appropriate pills and seeing that everyone remembers to take them. Do not forget that large numbers of people waiting around camp to see the MO can create a risk to the camp hygiene.

Records

Keep details of expedition members and records of all medical consultations. You should already have with you or have taken a detailed medical history of each expedition member, and be aware of what he/she wishes to happen in case of an accident, fatal or otherwise. Hold contact details of members' next of kin and the circumstances in which they should be contacted. Have a secure system for storing notes.

If there is an accident write down what happened in great detail as soon as you can. If you have planned how to cope when things go wrong and you stick to the rules you will not make matters worse. No one will blame you for the accident, but they will reproach you if you mishandle the situation afterwards, especially communicating with those at home. Clear and truthful information is vital. Make sure that the insurance companies are informed promptly. Never destroy any records.

Creating a happy camp life will help maintain the group through and during the aftermath of an accident, and keep it working together as a team for as long as is needed.

The end of the expedition

Lastly, remember to honour any commitment to sponsors and to thank all who have helped you in the host country and elsewhere. Make sure that all members know what to do if they fall ill after returning home, and the length of time for which this applies. Repeat antimalarial advice and check that everyone has enough first aid kit for the last few days in camp and journey home before everything is packed up. Make sure the campsite and the surrounding area are left clean and safe. The final days of the expedition are often one of the most dangerous times – people will be tired and with that end-of-term feeling rules are often broken. Be on your guard.

9 WATER PURIFICATION

Paul Goodyer and Larry Goodyer

A safe water supply is an essential part of camp hygiene. Water intake for adults in temperate conditions is around 3 litres per day, but this can rise to as much as 10 litres per day in hot climates because of loss in sweating. In addition, around 4 litres per person per day will be needed for cooking and washing up. Therefore considerable supplies may be required both at base camp and by field parties. In many cases, water obtained from rivers, lakes and ponds, as well as from taps and wells, carries a considerable risk of contamination. Spring water collected away from human habitation may be safer but it would be wise to treat even this water source.

Before treating the water to kill any organisms, organic matter and silt need to be removed. This can pose considerable problems if you are trying to obtain supplies for a large expedition, where sedimentation tanks and large ceramic filters would need to be employed.

Various methods for water purification will be described in this chapter. Some are more suitable for the base camp and others for field workers. Before deciding on the system used it is also important to consider the likely infective organisms and the risk posed by them to the expedition.

Transmission of disease by water
Numerous organisms and chemical pollutants which may be found in water can lead to human disease. The organisms include bacteria, viruses, protozoa and other parasites, which vary in the ease with which they can be killed (see Chapter 14). Water may be boiled or chemicals added for sterilisation, but if sediment is not first removed the sterilisation may be ineffective. If the expedition is close to mines or factories, chemical pollution must be foreseen and appropriate filtration used.

Removal of sediment and organic matter from water
If the water is cloudy or contains any suspended matter, this must be removed before further treatment. One method is to pass the water through a Millbank bag (see

Figure 9.1). This is a sock-shaped bag woven so that solids are retained but water flows by gravity through the weave. The bag can be left hanging over a receptacle with occasional top-ups to provide continuous production of filtered water ready for sterilisation. The bag is rugged and easy to clean. Millbank bags are available in two sizes: 2 litres for personal use and 9 litres for large quantities of water. Cloudy water can also be left to stand for some hours for solids to settle, either in a jerry can or in sedimentation tanks, depending on the volume to be treated. Very fine particles, such as "rock flour" in glacial outflow and mica flakes, are gastrointestinal irritants and must be removed by a ceramic filter (Table 9.1). Remember that simply clearing water does not sterilise it and that further treatment will be needed before it may be drunk.

TABLE 9.1 REMOVAL OF SEDIMENT AND ORGANIC MATERIAL

Filter/purifier	Litres	Filtration time/litre (minutes)	Purification time (minutes)	Chemical/filter employed
Pocket Travelwell	25	10	2	Filter/iodine
Millbank Bag	Unlimited	5	n/a	Cloth filtration
First Need Microlite	100	2	Instant	Microfilter
Trekker Travelwell	100	10	2	Filter/iodine
First Need Original	400	2	Instant	Microfilter
P U R traveller	400	2	3	Filter/iodine
The Pure Cup	500	25	5	Filter/iodine
P U R Scout	1,000	2	3	Filter/iodine
P U R Explorer	2,000	1	3	Filter/iodine
Katadyne Mini Filter	7,000	2	Instant	Ceramic filter/silver
Katadyne Pocket Filter	10,000+	1.5	Instant	Ceramic filter/silver

METHODS OF WATER PURIFICATION
Boiling
This is undoubtedly the best method, but it is often inconvenient and wasteful of fuel supplies or natural resources. Water should be kept at a rolling boil for 5 minutes, which is sufficient at any altitude. The water must be covered when cooling to prevent recontamination, and it will also taste better.

Iodine

This is the most effective chemical method. Its main disadvantage is that there are some people for whom it would not be suitable: those with a thyroid condition or iodine allergy, pregnant women and young children. There are also concerns, largely unfounded, about the long-term use of iodine treated water. A further drawback is that the cheapest method involves the use of iodine tincture, which must be carried in glass containers – there could be a disaster if they should break.

There is some discrepancy about the exact amount of iodine to use. Five drops of iodine tincture (2%) to 1 litre of water is most often used, increasing to 12 drops if giardia is suspected. It is always best to assume that giardia is present and add 12 drops to 1 litre when treating small amounts, or measure out 0.3–0.4ml/litre when treating large tanks.

An alternative to the tincture is to use water sterilising iodine tablets, but these are expensive and lose their potency after the bottle has been opened. Another method is to use iodine crystals (the Kahnn-Visscher method), but it is rather fiddly and not suitable for preparing large amounts of water.

The horrible taste of iodine-treated water can be reduced by adding small amounts of ascorbic acid (vitamin C) to neutralise the iodine. Again, clearly this should be done only at the point of use.

Chlorine

This is effective against a wide range of organisms, except for amoebic cysts, giardia and cryptosporidium. The effectiveness of chlorine is reduced by a number of factors which may not be easy to control, such as alkaline water, very cold water or in the presence of organic matter – hence the need for prior filtration.

Puritab tablets are the most widely available method of chlorination and one tablet of the maxi size will treat 25 litres. For very large tanks some expeditions prefer to use a substance called Chloramine T, where 5mg is added for each litre of water. Treated water should be left for at least half an hour before drinking and longer if it is very cold.

Taste can be removed with sodium thiosulphate. This will inactivate the chlorine so it should only be added by individuals at the point of use, that is to a drinking cup. It should never be added to a storage receptacle such as a canteen or jerry can.

Silver compounds

Micropure tablets contain a compound called Katadyne silver which is not effective against amoeba, giardia or viruses. It does not impart a bad taste and it is claimed to be able to prevent recontamination of water for many weeks. Micropure tablets should not be added to water previously treated with chlorine or iodine.

Figure 9.1   *A Millbank bag in use (Nomad Traveller's Store)*

Filters and pumps

There is now a plethora of devices available for purifying water (see Table 9.1), but care must be taken in choosing the right one for your expedition. Some devices employ a simple filtration method, whereby water is pumped through tiny holes through which organisms are unable to pass. Be careful to look at the pore size (measured in microns), as anything greater than 1 micron will not remove all organisms. Other devices employ both a filter and chemical treatment which strains and sterilises in one go. Choosing the right device is important, so here are some tips.

- Manufacturers often say how many litres of pure water a device will produce. However, this can be drastically reduced if the water is silty.
- If heavy use is expected make sure the purifier can be taken apart, cleaned and reassembled in the field to prevent blockages.
- Check the pump rate as some can take a lot of effort to produce a small amount of water.
- Many manufacturers of pumps go to great lengths to state what they will remove, while keeping quiet about what is not removed. For example, pumps will not remove chemical effluent, such as mercury in tributaries of the Amazon, without the addition of a carbon filter. For those visiting areas where there is mining or factories up-river this may be important.

• Storage is also important; ideally after sterilisation the water should be used within 24 hours.

CHOICE OF SYSTEM

This will depend on the size and circumstances of the expedition. If practicable a large pot should be put on to boil at the end of an evening meal to allow preparation of water for the following morning. In any case, all members should have some method of sterilising their own water. As a rough guide the choice of methods is as follows:

1. Large groups could consider chlorination, where the condition of the treatment tanks can be carefully monitored.
2. Smaller groups might use iodine, provided that everyone in the group can tolerate it.
3. For smaller groups, particularly if on the move, it would be acceptable to prepare water that has been strained through Millbank bags and provide each member with their own small bottle of iodine or chlorination tablets to treat water after drawing it off in their own canteens. The strained water could be used for boiling water, for example for beverages.

All field parties should be provided with small Millbank bags and some method of chemical sterilisation, or alternatively a portable filtration system.

Camp arrangements

Providing enough treated water from a natural source for a camp of 20 is time consuming but exceedingly important. The best approach is to incorporate a strict regimen from the start by appointing one person as "water chief" to supervise the sterilisation, safe storage and use of the water. The appointed person should also make sure that every member of the expedition is capable of sterilising their own water.

Rigid plastic containers with a tap and handle are the best for water. These come in 10 or 25 litre sizes, but the latter is heavy when full of water so keep in mind distances to water source and terrain. If you do not have a method of removing the taste of chemicals, water will taste better when cold. Storing water in special canvas bags will keep it cool through evaporation from the small pores of the canvas. If they can be obtained, army surplus ones are excellent in sizes suitable for storage of large volumes in camp or for tying to the back of a vehicle.

If a daily average of 6 litres per person is required for drinking and 4 litres for cooking/washing up, containers holding 10 litres per person per day will be required. Water treatment could be split into sessions if it is necessary to reduce the number of containers in use. To avoid confusion, have a good system of marking containers for the three different types of water treatment:

- untreated for storage, sedimentation or settling process;
- strained ready for treatment;
- fit for drinking.

Field parties

Always make sure that field workers carry their own water bottles, with a metal cup. Avoid plastic beakers as these often break. Each member should also have personal equipment for sterilising water; if a filter system is used a small Travelwell might be a good choice.

If travelling in a vehicle do not use one large container for storing water; a single puncture may have disastrous consequences. Jerry cans or the canvas bags previously mentioned are the best option, but try to adopt the same system of markings as employed in base camp.

10 ASSESSMENT OF THE INJURED OR ILL PATIENT

Charles Siderfin

This chapter aims to cover the assessment of the injured or ill patient in a way that is easily understood by non-medically qualified people. It can also be used as basic revision for people who are medically qualified. Please refer to the Medical Assessment Questionnaire (MAQ) in Appendix 2.

The assessment of a patient involves establishing what the problem is and monitoring the patient's progress. There are four components to assessment:

- History: the patient's account of events
- Examination of the patient
- Investigations
- Monitoring the patient's condition

INITIAL ASSESSMENT OF THE INJURED CASUALTY

In the injured casualty the initial priorities are:

- Airway
- Breathing
- Circulation
- Head to toe assessment

Airway, breathing and circulatory (ABC) assessment is covered in Chapter 11.

Head to toe assessment
The objective of the head to toe assessment is to make a quick, thorough examination of the casualty to gain an overview and plan the priorities for treatment. Mentally reconstruct the sequence of events to alert yourself to possible injuries. Start at the head and work down to the toes. The three basic tenets of examination

are *look*, *feel* and *listen*. You may need to remove clothing, but do not move the casualty unless it is absolutely necessary. Comparison of each side of the body will help you to decide what is abnormal. While making the examination talk to the casualty explaining what you are doing and give reassurance, even if the person is unconscious.

The head
Observe the colour, temperature and state of the face for signs of shock. Look at the face and head for deformity or bruising. Bruising just behind and below the ears may indicate a skull fracture, as does blood or clear fluid draining from the ears or nose. Blood in the whites of the eyes (subconjunctival haemorrhage) suggests a significant head injury. Check the pupils are equal in size and that there are no foreign bodies in the eyes. Run your fingers through the hair feeling the skull for blood, swellings or depressions.

The neck
Loosen any tight clothing around the neck. Look for bruising, bleeding or swelling and feel the back of the neck for swelling or steps between the spinal vertebrae. The line of the neck should be straight; any deviation from this should arouse suspicion of a fracture.

The chest
Look for regular chest movements and whether both sides are moving equally. Firmly feel the chest for wetness (blood), swelling, deformity, tenderness and chest movement. Remember to feel around the sides and back of the chest as far as possible without moving the patient. Listen to the breathing.

The abdomen
Feel the abdomen (see pages 88–91) for muscle tensing (guarding) or tenderness. With a hand on either side of the pelvis gently rock it (Figure 10.1). You are feeling for any movement or grating that would indicate a fracture. Place your hand in the small of the back and feel along the spine, as far as possible, for any irregularities.

The limbs
Lastly, examine the legs and arms; these are your lowest priority. Injuries to the head, spine, chest and abdomen can kill. Limb injuries, with the exception of severe bleeding, are rarely life-threatening. Look for deformity and bleeding. Feel each leg and arm to compare. Start at the top and work down. If the patient is conscious ask if he can feel you touching him and ask him to move the limbs. Any inability may indicate a spinal injury.

You now have a good idea of the state of the patient and are in a position to plan

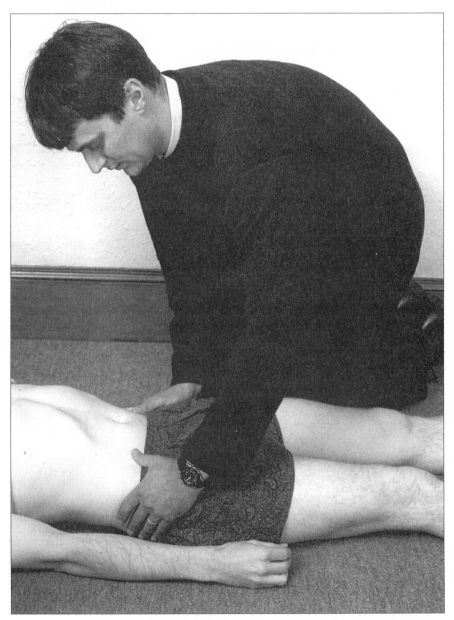

Figure 10.1 *Examination for a pelvic fracture*

his further treatment. Once the casualty's life-threatening injuries have been dealt with, or for the ill patient, a full assessment needs to be made.

ASSESSMENT OF THE INJURED OR ILL PATIENT USING THE MAQ FOR NON-MEDICAL PERSONNEL

The degree of assessment required depends on the circumstances. A sore throat with no other features requires little attention. A sore throat accompanied by fever, cough, breathlessness and chest pain requires more detailed assessment. Making an accurate diagnosis is not essential. Many medical conditions have similar features, especially early on, and it is not until later that specific features emerge.

An accurate and thorough description of a medical disorder is necessary to establish a comprehensive plan of care. The Medical Assessment Questionnaire (MAQ) was developed to help non-medical personnel achieve this. The MAQ (Appendix 2) leads you through a history and examination, ensuring that relevant information is not missed. It was originally developed to transfer information to a remote doctor via radio or fax so that medical advice could be given. For expeditions with medical back-up the MAQ may be a valuable additional tool for communication when the doctor and patient are separated. For expeditions without medical back-up the MAQ will help ensure that a full history and examination is performed.

This section guides you through an assessment using the MAQ. Remember, symptoms are the patients' description of how they feel; a sign is what you observe during the examination.

It is important to explain to the patient what you are about to do during the assessment.

The history

The history must give a clear picture of events. Time spent on gaining an accurate history is always time well spent. The history is about the events that led up to the illness and what *the patient* feels. It is not about what the examiner observes. *LISTEN TO THE PATIENT AND OTHER EYEWITNESSES.*

To make full sense of this chapter, please refer to the MAQ in Appendix 2. The alphabetical sections that follow correspond to the alphabetical subsections in the MAQ.

(B) PATIENT'S MAIN COMPLAINTS

This identifies the central problems. Later components of the history build upon this initial description. For example, a patient's main complaint might be:

1. abdominal pain
2. vomiting

(c) A SHORT DESCRIPTIVE HISTORY

Describe briefly the main features of the illness or injury. It is often useful to start with the question: "When were you last completely well?"; followed by: "What was the first thing you noticed wrong?"; and: "What happened next?". Specify the nature, location and duration of symptoms. Identify changes or additional symptoms that occur and factors that worsen or improve the symptoms. The information should be related to time. Do not use technical medical terms, they cause confusion unless their precise definition is known to the users; statements should be in the patient's own words. For example: Last completely well 2 days ago. Yesterday had no appetite, ate nothing and only small amount to drink. Woke at 4:00am today with pain in centre of abdomen, gripping in nature. Unable to sleep. About 8:00am pain more in the right, lower side of abdomen. Vomited twice at 9:00am and 9:40am.

SECTIONS (D) TO (K)

Apparently unrelated symptoms can help reach a diagnosis. It is therefore necessary to ask the patient all the questions from Section D onwards. The questions systematically cover the systems of the body and ensure that relevant information is not missed.

The examination

The examination questions need to be answered from your own observations. They are not questions to ask the patient. For example, "Is there pain on moving?" requires the patient to move and for the examiner to decide if this causes pain. Information is gained in three ways during the examination.

1. Look

Start by taking a good look at the patient and observing his general well-being and attitude. It may seem subjective to ask whether the patient looks well or unwell, but your gut feelings are valuable. When examining part of the body it should be fully exposed. Stand back and look.

2. Feel

A number of questions ask whether an area is tender and to answer you need to feel that area. You must watch the patient's face when examining as even small twinges of pain are usually registered on the face. Similarly, if an area is painful the patient usually tenses when it is touched.

To minimise discomfort be *gentle but firm* with your hands. Do not prod and poke, or be so cautious that you tickle the patient. Firmly apply pressure; you will learn nothing from prodding, poking and tickling.

3. Listen
Listen to the breath or bowel sounds either with a stethoscope or by putting your ear to the part you are examining.

SECTION (N)
These 12 questions are important because they provide a lot of information about the patient's overall condition. Each one must be answered.

Taking the temperature
The temperature can be taken from three places.

1. The mouth
Place the thermometer under the tongue and close the mouth. Leave for 3 minutes before reading. This method is unreliable if the patient has recently eaten, drunk or been exposed to cold or is breathing heavily through an open mouth.

2. The armpit
The thermometer is placed in the armpit and held in position for 3 minutes.

3. The rectum
This is the most accurate place to record the temperature and, despite its obvious disadvantages, is the best site. In a patient suspected of being hypothermic, the temperature must be taken with a low-reading thermometer in the rectum.

Lie the patient on his side and gently insert a lubricated thermometer about 6cm through the anus. Hold it in position for 3 minutes and do not let go. After taking the reading, clean the thermometer with gauze and an alcohol swab and identify it for rectal use only.

The normal temperature ranges between 36.5°C and 37.5°C.
Hypothermia is defined as 35°C or less.
A temperature greater than 37.5°C is elevated.

Taking the pulse
Blood is pumped from the heart to the arteries. The arteries transport the blood to the cells of the body. With each heart beat blood is injected into the arteries causing them to expand. This expansion is transmitted along the arteries, and can be felt as the pulse. The pulse rate is the number of pulses (or number of heart beats) per minute.

Normal adult pulse rate at rest is 60–90 per minute.

The pulse is easily felt, but it requires practise. Feel for it with the pulp at the end of your middle finger. The pulse can be felt at one of three sites.

1. The wrist
Press gently in the groove that runs between the lump on the thumb side of the wrist and the tendons.

2. The neck
The neck (carotid) pulse is sometimes the only pulse that can be felt in a very ill patient. Locate the Adam's apple with two fingertips. (The Adam's apple is the lump at the front of the windpipe that moves up and down when swallowing.) Run the fingers down the side of the neck towards you, until you reach an easily felt groove. This is the junction between the windpipe and the neck muscles. The carotid pulse can be felt with the fingertips in this groove (Figure 10.2). Press gently into the groove. Do not press hard as this will compress the artery, and do not press both sides as this will cut the circulation to the brain.

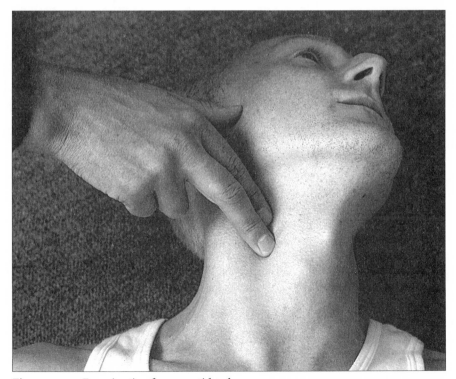

Figure 10.2 *Examination for a carotid pulse*

3. The groin

Press firmly into the skin crease at the top of the leg, at a point half-way between the mid-line and the prominent bony lump of the pelvis.

Once you have located a pulse, count the number of beats during a timed minute. This is the pulse rate. Exertion, fever, shock, pain, excitement and anxiety raise the pulse rate; it is slowed by hypothermia and fainting. You may also be able to evaluate the pulse strength and whether it is regular or irregular.

Taking the blood pressure

The blood pressure is the measurement of two pressures. The systolic pressure is the pressure of blood in the artery caused by the heart contracting. The diastolic pressure, which is lower, is the resting pressure in the artery when the heart is relaxed.

Blood pressure varies enormously between individuals. Interpretation needs to be made in conjunction with the clinical situation and other parameters such as pulse and breathing rate. Because of the wide variability, a normal range for blood pressure is not given. The blood pressure is extremely important in monitoring, as much can be learnt from whether it is stable, falling or rising.

- The blood pressure is taken with a sphygmomanometer.
- Ease any constricting clothing from the upper arm and firmly wrap the cuff above the elbow.
- With the palm upwards, straighten the patient's arm and locate the brachial pulse which lies just below the elbow, about one-third of the way across from the inner side. Continue to press gently on the pulse.
- Inflate the cuff and note the reading when the pulse disappears. Inflate the cuff for a further 20–30ml of mercury.
- Place the diaphragm of the stethoscope over the pulse and press gently to ensure good contact (Figure 10.3).
- Release the pressure in the cuff at a rate of 3–5ml of mercury per second by easing open the screw valve.
- Listen for the first pulse beat while watching the pressure fall. The pressure at which you hear the first thumping sound is the systolic pressure. (This is about the same level that the pulse was felt to disappear during inflation.)
- Continue to listen. The sounds will suddenly muffle and then disappear. The disappearance marks the diastolic pressure.

Mercury instruments should not be used on aircraft as spilled mercury can form an amalgam and weaken the integrity of the aircraft fuselage.

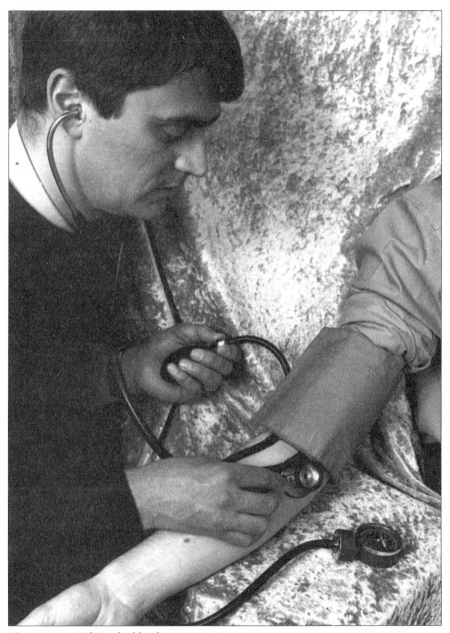

Figure 10.3   *Taking the blood pressure*

The blanching test

This can be a useful additional test of the circulation. It is unreliable if the patient is cold and needs to be interpreted in the context of other findings. There are two sites to perform the test:

1. Press your thumb on a fingernail or toenail. The nail bed will blanch immediately and the colour should return as soon as the thumb is removed. If the nail remains blanched for longer than 2 seconds then circulation is poor.
2. Press your thumb on the patient's chest for 3–4 seconds. This causes a white (blanched) area where the blood has been squeezed out of the capillaries. The colour should return in 3–4 seconds. If the circulation is poor it will take longer.

Measuring the breathing rate

Do this while pretending to count the pulse as the breathing may alter when the patient becomes aware of what you are doing.

Normal adult breathing rate at rest is 12–18 per minute.
The breaths should be quiet, regular, effortless and painless.

Use of the stethoscope

There are two points about using the stethoscope:

1. The earpieces are angled and should be placed in your ears angled forwards.
2. Most stethoscopes have a bell and diaphragm. They can be switched by spinning the end piece of the stethoscope. You should use the diaphragm.

(O) EXAMINATION OF THE CHEST

Much can be gained from looking at the chest as the patient breathes normally, but remember that the chest has a front and back. When examining the back, get the patient to sit forward with the arms crossed to pull the shoulder blades apart.

If one of the lungs collapses, the windpipe may be pulled to the side of the collapsed lung. The position of the windpipe can be assessed by feeling with two fingers in the mid-line at the base of the neck. You will feel a notch immediately above the breast bone, and by pushing your fingers gently into it you will feel the windpipe as it disappears into the chest cavity (Figure 10.4). It should be positioned centrally.

(P) EXAMINATION OF THE ABDOMEN

The patient should be as relaxed as possible, lying on his back, the head supported by one or two pillows. The whole of the abdomen needs to be exposed, including the groin. The male genitals are considered part of the abdomen.

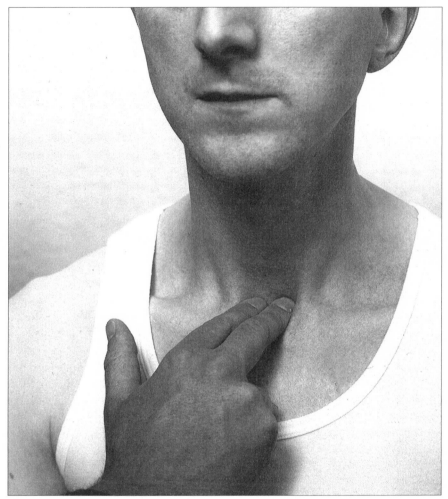

Figure 10.4   *Examining for the position of the trachea*

Look
Look at the abdomen and the male genitals. If there is any suggestion of a genital disorder, gently feel for the abnormality.

Feel
Ensure your hands are warm before touching the patient. If there is pain start feeling the abdomen away from the region of maximum pain and gradually work towards it. The following technique for feeling the abdomen is simple but essential to follow.

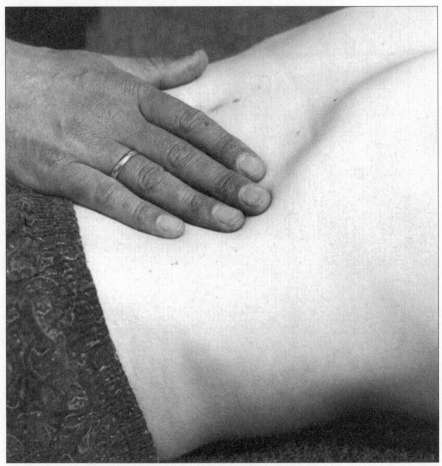

Figure 10.5   *Abdominal examination*

The flat of the hand is placed on the abdomen (Figure 10.5). The flat fingers are pressed *gently* into the abdomen by bending at the knuckles (Figure 10.6). Repeat this process over the entire abdomen. The abdomen is normally quite soft.

You are feeling for resistance (guarding) to your hand and pain. You need to know whether guarding is local or over the entire abdomen. At its most extreme the whole abdominal wall will be rigid, like a board. This results from peritonitis, general inflammation in the abdomen. An additional and useful sign is the "release sign", whereby gentle pressure from the flat of the fingers into the abdomen, followed by quick release of the fingers, causes more severe pain *on release* than on pressure. This again is used to detect peritonitis or evidence of abdominal irritation, for example

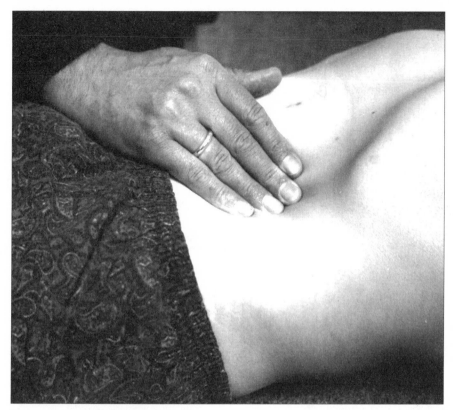

Figure 10.6   *Abdominal examination*

from a perforated bowel or blood in the abdominal cavity.

The signs of guarding and tenderness are important. The technique described is the only way they can be elicited accurately. Some patients have sensitive abdomens which guard at the first touch. Under these circumstances your examination can be helped by asking the patient to bend the knees and rest the heels on the ground. This helps relax the abdomen.

Listen for bowel sounds by placing the ear on the abdomen or placing a stethoscope firmly an inch below the belly button. The normal gut is moving all the time which is heard as quiet gurgles, a few times a minute. Sounds are increased when the bowel is overactive, as in diarrhoea, and absent in peritonitis, when the bowel is paralysed due to inflammation.

(Q) GENERAL EXAMINATION

Glands are found in the neck, the armpits and the groin. If there is an infection in the area that the glands serve, they will become enlarged up to the size of a marble. They will also be tender and can be felt with the fingertips. Normally glands cannot be felt (except in the groin) and they are not tender. The tonsils can be seen at the back of the throat and are an example of a gland. It is worth looking at the back of a friend's throat with a torch so that you are familiar with what a normal throat looks like.

In order to perform a good examination it is necessary to know what a normal body looks, feels and sounds like. To gain this knowledge you need to practise examining fit individuals and yourself. The skills are readily learnt and guidance from a doctor will be a great advantage.

TABLE 10.1 VITAL SIGNS CHART (WITH EXAMPLE DATA)

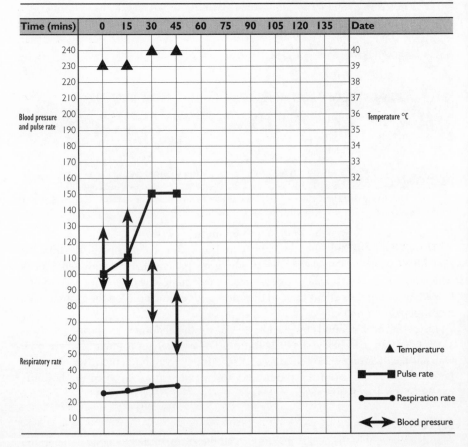

Investigations

One useful investigation is the testing of urine using a Dipstix, a multicoloured strip. The strip is dipped into the urine and examined for colour changes when compared with a range of standard colours on the side of the container. Changes indicate the presence of substances in the urine such as blood, sugar and protein.

Monitoring of progress

It is important that you should be able to determine whether a patient is getting better, deteriorating or remaining much the same. This information is gained by relating the initial assessment to ongoing assessments.

Always monitor the patient and record your findings.

Take notes on the patient's condition, remembering to include the date and time. Use a vital signs chart (Table 10.1) to record the pulse rate, temperature, breathing rate and blood pressure. The trends in these measurements are more important than isolated readings in determining how the patient is progressing.

THE ASSESSMENT OF THE UNCONSCIOUS PATIENT

Hourly head injury observations are needed if the patient:

- is unconscious, for however short a time;
- develops headache, vomiting, dizziness, or visual disturbance.

Observations should be made for a minimum of 24 hours after regaining consciousness or from the resolution of all symptoms and signs.

Head injury observations

The depth of unconsciousness can quickly be determined using the mnemonic AVPU:

- **A**wake and alert
- **V**erbal – the patient responds to verbal commands
- **P**ain – the patient responds to painful stimulus
- **U**nconscious – the patient does not respond

A more sensitive assessment can be made by examining three areas of basic brain function: eye opening, speech and movement. This is the basis of the Glasgow Coma Scale. When assessing these basic brain functions increase the stimulus until a response is elicited. If there is no response to speaking, squeeze the shoulder. If this gets

93

no response apply pain in one of the following ways. Take care not to aggravate any injury.

- Press the flat of a pencil firmly against a fingernail.
- Press the back edge of the jaw just below the ear with the thumb.
- Grind the knuckles on the breast bone.
- Squeeze the tendon at the back of the heel.

Each response is given a number and the total score (out of 15) reflects the patient's conscious level. Table 10.2 shows a chart for recording these responses.

- **Eye opening** is assessed by the question: "When does the patient open his eyes?" Scores are: spontaneously (4), when spoken to (3), when in pain (2), or not at all (1).
- **Speech** is assessed by how the patient responds to the stimulus. Scores are: orientated speech (5), confused speech (4), use of inappropriate words (3), muttering incomprehensible sounds (2) and no vocalisation (1).
- **Movement** is assessed by the patient's response to an external stimulus. Scores are: patient obeys commands to move limb (6), attempts to push away a painful stimulus (localises) (5), moves away from pain (withdraw) (4), the joints and back bend forward in response to pain (flexion) (3), limbs straighten and the back arches to pain (extension) (2), no movement to pain (1).

Deterioration is caused by bleeding, swelling or infection of the brain, and it will be picked up early only if regular observations are made. Deterioration is indicated by the following:

1. Deepening level of unconsciousness (a lower total score) on the Glasgow Coma Scale.
2. One pupil, possibly followed by the other, may become large and non-reactive to light (does not constrict). Fixed, dilated pupils are a characteristic and serious sign of the brain under pressure. The pupils should be round, equal in size and react with a brisk contraction when light is shone into the eye.
3. A slowing of the pulse rate, which follows a deepening unconscious level.
4. There is little change in the breathing pattern or blood pressure until very late. Deep rattling breathing and elevation of blood pressure are grave signs.
5. Rarely the temperature may become raised above 40°C.

Deterioration requires rapid evacuation and medical attention.

TABLE 10.2 **THE GLASGOW COMA SCALE (GCS) CHART**

Name		Time (mins)	0	15	30	45	60				
Eyes open	4	Spontaneous									
	3	To speech									
	2	To pain	✔	✔							
	1	None									
Best verbal response	5	Orientated									
	4	Confused		✔							
	3	Inappropriate words									
	2	Incomprehensible sounds	✔								
	1	None									
Best motor response	6	Obeys									
	5	Localises		✔							
	4	Withdraws	✔								
	3	Flexion									
	2	Extension									
	1	None									
GCS SCORE			8	11							

Acknowledgements

This chapter is based on a similar chapter in Milne, A.H. and Siderfin, C.D., *Kurafid: The British Antarctic Survey Medical Handbook*. It is reproduced here in a modified form with the kind permission of the British Antarctic Survey, High Cross, Madingley Road, Cambridge, CB3 0ET.

11 FIRST AID AND MANAGEMENT OF MINOR INJURIES

Jon Dallimore

Serious accidents and injuries on expeditions are rare. However, minor injuries of one kind or another are encountered on most expeditions. In some cases injured expedition members need to be evacuated to medical care, but most injuries can be managed adequately in the field. First aid books are of limited use to expeditions going overseas as they place great emphasis on getting medical help which in many parts of the world may be many days' travel away. This chapter will cover the following topics:

- Approach to the injured casualty
- Resuscitation
- Disorders of consciousness
- Wound care
- Wound infections
- Burns
- Bone and joint problems
- Pain management

APPROACH TO THE INJURED CASUALTY
When approaching any injured patient, stop and think. After an accident it is vital to avoid producing other casualties. Ask yourself the question: "Am I safe?" If it is safe to approach try to avoid moving the casualty. Occasionally you will need to "scoop and run", for example, if there is a danger of rock fall or avalanche. In these cases move the casualty to a safe place as carefully and quickly as possible. Particular care will be required if you suspect a back or neck injury. Using the principles of first aid assess the casualty.

TABLE 11.1 PRINCIPLES OF FIRST AID

- Assess the situation
- Make the area safe
- Assess the casualty
  - starting with the ABC of resuscitation
  - identify the injury or illness
- Give easy, appropriate and adequate treatment in a sensible order of priority
- Make and pass on a report
- Organise removal of casualty to secondary care where appropriate

First aiders will be familiar with the following system for assessing and examining any casualties.

TABLE 11.2 PRINCIPLES OF RESUSCITATION

A **A**ssessment of the scene
A **A**irway with neck control
B **B**reathing
C **C**irculation with control of bleeding
D **D**isability
E **E**xposure with environment control

BASIC RESUSCITATION

Basic life support is the maintenance of breathing and circulation without the use of equipment apart from a simple airway device or a shield to protect the person resuscitating from possible infection. A combination of mouth-to-mouth (expired air) resuscitation and heart massage (chest compression) is known as cardiopulmonary resuscitation. The best way to learn about resuscitation is to go on a first aid course (see Chapter 4). The main points are summarised here as a reminder.

Outcome of cardiopulmonary resuscitation

Survival from cardiac arrest is most likely when the collapse is witnessed, when early cardiopulmonary resuscitation is started and defibrillation (electric shock treatment of the heart) and advanced life support are started at an early stage. In an expedition setting it is unlikely that advanced life support will be available. If attempts at resuscitation are not successful after 30 minutes, the chances of success are extremely low.

There are two important exceptions: where a victim has been struck by lightning, or following cold water immersion. In these cases successful resuscitation has occurred after 2 hours or more.

Important note. If the pulse is absent (cardiac arrest) it is unlikely that the casualty will recover as a result of cardiopulmonary resuscitation alone. Once the heart has stopped beating the casualty is dead, and if your attempts to resuscitate are unsuccessful the casualty remains dead. It is important to remember this if the casualty does not recover.

Outline of resuscitation (revised guidelines 1997)
At the scene of an incident on an expedition where there appears to be an unresponsive patient:

- Stop, shout for help.
- Do NOT put yourself in danger – ask the question "am I safe?".
- Approach the casualty and assess the situation.
- Assess the casualty's response; say loudly: "What's happened? Open your eyes." *Gently* shake the shoulders.

If the casualty responds:

- Assess and treat any injuries or medical conditions (see Chapter 10).
- Consider placing the casualty in the recovery position (see Figure 11.1, page 105), but always remember that a spinal injury may be present.

If there is no response:

- Open the airway by lifting the jaw upwards (chin lift), but avoid extending the neck more than necessary (head tilt).
- Remove any obvious obstructions in the mouth but do not poke fingers blindly into the mouth.
- Look at the chest, listen and feel if the casualty is breathing out against your cheek for 10 seconds.

If there is no breathing:

- Give 2 breaths of expired air resuscitation. Pinch the casualty's nostrils, take a deep breath, place lips over the casualty's lips and breath out steadily into the casualty's chest. This should take about 2 seconds. Watch to ensure that the chest rises. Use a protective shield if available.

- After 2 breaths check the carotid pulse in the neck for 10 seconds and look for other signs of circulation: choking, coughing, return of colour.

If there is no pulse or sign of circulation commence chest compressions.

- First identify the site for chest compressions: run fingers along the rib margin until they meet below the breastbone.
- Place your index and middle fingers together at this point then slide the heel of the other hand to touch above your fingers. Ensure that only the heel of the hand is in contact with the casualty.
- Interlock the fingers and leaning well over the casualty with your arms straight, press down vertically at a rate of approximately 100 compressions per minute. In an adult the compressions should be about 4–5cms in depth. Compression and release phases should be equal in time.
- After 15 compressions give 2 breaths of expired air resuscitation and repeat. Two-person rescue is no longer recommended. Do not stop to check for a pulse – if resuscitation is successful the casualty will start to cough, swallow or choke.

Dangers of resuscitation
There is concern about the transmission of HIV and other diseases by mouth-to-mouth resuscitation. However, no case of HIV has yet been reported as a result of transfer of infection from the casualty to the rescuer (or vice versa). If available, a ventilation mask or filter device may be placed over the victim's mouth and nose; however, resuscitation must not be delayed while searching for a mask or resuscitation aid.

DISORDERS OF CONSCIOUSNESS

It is very worrying if someone cannot respond normally on an expedition because of an accident or illness. There are many reasons why someone may not be fully conscious; some of the commoner causes are discussed here:

- Head injuries
- Fainting
- Convulsions
- Recognition of death

Head injuries
Head injuries are a significant risk on expeditions, particularly in mountaineering accidents, motor vehicle accidents and on building project sites. Head injuries can result in changes in conscious level, bleeding, infection and disability.

It is very important to avoid injuring the neck when moving patients after head injuries as about 10% of individuals who receive a head injury resulting in unconsciousness will have an associated neck injury. Be suspicious of a neck injury in anyone who has a significant injury above the collarbones.

Minor head injuries may cause a transient loss of consciousness, but serious open head injuries are usually rapidly fatal. It is helpful to know a little more about head injuries so that decisions about the need for evacuation can be made. The following types of head injuries will be discussed:

- Closed head injuries
- Closed head injuries
  - with internal bleeding
  - with brain swelling
- Open head injuries
- Base of skull fractures

Closed head injuries
In closed head injuries the skull remains intact and there is no communication between the brain and the outside world. Bleeding or brain swelling may complicate closed head injuries.

Closed head injuries with internal bleeding
Any head injury may result in loss of consciousness. If the head injury is serious a patient may never regain consciousness; conversely, a minor injury may result in a brief loss of consciousness with mild concussion (a temporary loss of brain function). Where bleeding inside the skull complicates a head injury, the patient may be knocked out at the time of the injury, regain consciousness (the lucid interval) and then lose consciousness again. As blood collects inside the skull it exerts pressure on the brain tissue. Increasing pressure inside the skull results in increasing coma and eventually death. The Glasgow Coma Scale describes the changes as a patient becomes more deeply unconscious (see pages 103–104 and Chapter 10).

Closed head injuries with brain swelling
During a head injury, the brain moves inside the skull and may be damaged against the bony ridges inside the base of the skull or by the impact against the inside of the skull. The greater the degree of swelling, the deeper and longer coma is likely to be.

Open head injuries
These injuries are potentially serious because there is communication between the inside of the skull and the outside world and hence the main danger is the risk of infection. A common scenario might be a large scalp laceration with an underlying

skull fracture. If available, antibiotics should be given during evacuation. In severe open head injuries the skull is open with brain substance exposed. Great force is required to produce these injuries and the outcome is usually severe disability or death, even if the injury occurs near a properly equipped hospital.

Fractures of the base of the skull

These are open head injuries, because in fractures of the base of the skull, infection may spread from the nose, ears or sinuses. Features of base of skull fractures are as follows:

1. Racoon eyes – bruising around both eyes following a blow to the head.
2. Battle's sign – bruising behind the ear.
3. Cerebrospinal fluid leaking from the ears or nose.

Cerebrospinal fluid (CSF) is the straw-coloured fluid which bathes the brain and spinal cord and helps to protect them from injury. Bloodstained fluid from the ears or nose may contain blood and CSF. If the fluid is dripped on to a sheet or handkerchief, two concentric rings are formed if both blood and CSF are present. Because of the risk of infection, antibiotics should be given during evacuation.

Treatment of head injuries

All head injuries should be treated according to first aid principles:

A **Assessment of the scene.** Ensure that you do not endanger yourself.
A **Airway with neck control.** An unconscious casualty's airway is at risk as many people vomit following a head injury. The gag and cough reflexes may not function normally to clear the airway, depending on the level of unconsciousness, so it is important to place the casualty carefully in the recovery position. A chin lift and head tilt will normally open the airway. Remember the possibility of an associated neck injury, but the airway always takes priority. Try to avoid overextending the neck and stabilise the neck in a neutral position.
B **Breathing.** Once the airway is secure, check that breathing is adequate and measure the breathing rate.
C **Circulation with control of bleeding.** Look for any obvious external haemorrhage and control bleeding with direct pressure. Measure the pulse rate.
D **Disability.** Assess the response level using AVPU:

- Awake and alert
- Voice – responds to voice
- Pain – responds to pain
- Unresponsive

Look at the pupils and check that they constrict when a light is shone into the eye. Rising pressure inside the skull may mean that one or both pupils fail to respond to light and are fixed and dilated. This is a serious sign and means evacuation should be arranged immediately (see below).

The modified Glasgow Coma Scale (see below and Chapter 10) allows a more comprehensive assessment of unconsciousness.

E **Exposure with environment control.** Examine the casualty carefully from head to toe by undressing but always be aware of the risk of hypothermia. Do not move the casualty unnecessarily.

Head injuries and the need for evacuation

When a head injury occurs in a remote place, it is often difficult to know whether you should cancel your expedition plans and head off to the nearest hospital or whether it is safe to observe a casualty in a base camp or similar.

Three groups of patients always need to be evacuated for expert medical assessment:

1. Patients who remain unconscious.
2. Patients who have open or base of skull fractures.
3. Patients who have had a convulsion or fit.

It is more difficult to decide whether to evacuate a conscious patient following a head injury. The following pointers may be helpful in deciding who to evacuate:

1. Worsening headache
2. Vomiting
3. Drowsiness
4. Confusion
5. A dilated, unresponsive pupil on one or both sides
6. Convulsions
7. Blood or fluid seeping from the ears or nose
8. Deep scalp lacerations
9. Worsening Glasgow Coma Scale

It is always better to be overcautious where head injuries are concerned. If in doubt, make arrangements to evacuate the patient for assessment in a hospital.

Modified Glasgow Coma Scale

This scale (see Table 10.2, page 95) helps to assess the severity of head injury and when monitoring a casualty during evacuation. The patient's coma scale score is assessed in terms of eye opening and their verbal and motor responses.

Eyes. Do they: open spontaneously? open on command? open to a painful stimulus?
Movement. Does the casualty: obey commands? move in response to a painful stimulus? make no response?
Speech. Does the casualty: respond sensibly to questions? seem confused? use inappropriate words? make incomprehensible sounds? make no response?

Any patient should be closely observed on a regular basis, at least every hour, following a significant head injury. A decrease in the modified Glasgow Coma score should alert you to the need for immediate evacuation.

Fainting

Fainting is not usually a serious condition and may follow severe pain, exhaustion, dehydration (for example, following a bout of diarrhoea), lack of food or an emotional upset. Faints are caused by a temporary decrease in the flow of blood to the brain. The pulse becomes very slow during a faint, unlike in shock where the pulse is rapid.

Someone who is about to faint usually becomes very pale, starts to sweat and may feel nauseated. At the first signs, encourage the patient to sit down with their head between their legs or to lie flat. If the patient loses consciousness, lie them flat, loosen tight clothing and elevate the legs. Usually, unconsciousness lasts only a few minutes; sometimes there are convulsive movements during the faint. After regaining consciousness the casualty should be reassured and checked for any injury which may have been sustained during the fall to the ground.

Convulsions

A fit or a seizure is caused by abnormal electrical activity in one or more parts of the brain. Fits are most commonly seen in people with epilepsy but can occur with brain infections (meningitis and encephalitis) or following head injuries. People with diabetes may fit when their blood sugar level becomes low. Alcoholics and drug addicts may fit during withdrawal.

If there are people with epilepsy in your expedition team it would be wise to learn more about the management of their disease.

If a fit does occur it is important to note the following:

- How long did the fit last?
- Was there loss of consciousness?
- Were all limbs involved in the convulsion?
- Was there eye rolling, salivating and incontinence?
- Was there a period of sleepiness after the fit?

During a fit, teeth may be broken and the tongue may be bitten. Sometimes vomit is breathed into the lungs leading to pneumonia or asphyxia. Injuries may occur as a result of falling at the beginning of a seizure. Prolonged fits may deprive the brain of oxygen and result in brain damage, although this is rare.

Treatment of a fit
- Do not restrain the person unless injury is likely.
- Open the airway with head tilt and chin lift.
- Do NOT force things between the teeth – you may break teeth or get bitten.
- Place the casualty in the recovery position.
- If a fit occurs following a head injury, evacuate immediately.
- If meningitis appears likely treat with antibiotics and arrange evacuation. Meningitis should be suspected if a patient has a high fever, severe headache, vomiting, a stiff neck, is very sensitive to light and has a rash.

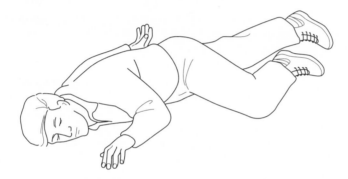

Figure 11.1   *The recovery position*

The diagnosis of death

Unfortunately, death is always a risk in a remote wilderness setting. It is therefore essential to diagnose death with certainty, particularly if a body is to be buried at sea or cremated in the mountains. Victims of hypothermia and cold water immersion injury should not be considered dead until they are warm and dead. In some cases where a body must be left behind it may be important to take photographs to establish the facts.

The signs of death are as follows:

- Unresponsiveness.
- Absent heart sounds (listen with a stethoscope or your ear against the chest for 2 minutes).
- No breathing effort.
- Pupils are fixed and dilated when a light is shone into them.
- Later signs include rigor mortis (stiffness) and clouding of the cornea of the eyes.

WOUND CARE

Minor cuts and grazes are common on expeditions. All wounds may be managed using the following principles:

- Stop bleeding.
- Decrease the risk of infection by cleaning.
- Dress the injury for comfort and to maintain cleanliness.
- Promote healing and restore function.

Stopping bleeding

All wounds bleed to a greater or lesser extent. In some cases, bleeding may be life-threatening. As always, use first aid principles:

- Apply *direct pressure* over the wound with any available clean material or dressing.
- Lie the casualty down.
- Raise the limb above the level of the heart.
- Apply further dressings to control the bleeding on top of any original pad.
- Bandage firmly to hold dressing in place.

When there are very deep wounds it may not be possible to control bleeding by applying pressure on the surface of the skin. The only way to stop severe, persistent bleeding from deep inside a wound may be to remove the dressings, open the wound, remove clots and debris and to pack the wound open with sterile gauze. The use of artery forceps should be avoided as they may damage important structures such as tendons and nerves.

Tourniquets should be reserved for injuries where a limb has been amputated or for uncontrollable bleeding. The tourniquet should be released every 20–30 minutes otherwise tissues beyond the tourniquet will die.

Preventing infection

- Clean all wounds with an antiseptic solution.
- Remove any foreign material.
- Cover wound with a non-stick dressing.
- Bandage to hold the dressing in place.

If foreign bodies are deeply embedded and cannot be removed easily, they should be left in place for removal by a surgeon. If an object remains embedded, the surrounding wound should still be cleaned carefully and then dressed. In the UK wounds are quickly seen by a doctor or nurse; however, during an expedition it may be necessary to care for wounds for days or even weeks. Every wound should be inspected at least daily and clean dressings applied. Any pus or exudate should be gently removed but damage to healing tissues must be avoided. If dressings do stick, soaking may allow easier removal. Infection with tetanus should not be a risk for expedition wounds if all expedition members are immunised correctly pre-travel (see Chapter 2), but always check on a casualty's tetanus immunisation status.

Dressings and bandaging

The principle of wound dressing is to apply layers to the wound:

1. Non-stick sterile dressing against the wound (such as Melonin or Jelonet).
2. Sterile gauze swabs to absorb any pus or exudate from the wound.
3. Crepe bandage, Tubinet or Tubigrip to hold dressing in place.

The bandage should hold the dressing in place without producing pressure or constriction. Bandaging techniques are taught on all first aid courses.

Promoting healing and restoration of function

Wound healing is aided by a healthy diet and rest. Any significant wound will heal more quickly with the increased oxygen at altitudes below 10,000 feet. Rest is needed initially but prolonged splinting leads to stiffness and muscle wasting. Joints adjacent to a wound or burn should be kept mobile.

Methods of wound closure

A gaping wound will heal better if the skin edges are brought together. This may be accomplished with Steristrips or sutures.

Steristrips

Steristrips are paper stitches which come in a variety of lengths and widths. They are placed across a laceration and, if left in place for a week or so, result in a clean, neat scar. Steristrips are not as effective near joints, on the palms of the hands and soles of the feet, or on the scalp. However, they are excellent for finger lacerations and facial wounds. Steristrips stick less effectively in humid or wet environments, such as the jungle or at sea. Applying Friar's Balsam to the skin may help to keep the Steristrips in place.

Suturing

Steristrips should be used where possible. If Steristrips will not close the wound, sutures will be necessary. Only clean wounds that are less than 6 hours old are suitable for suturing. Deep wounds may need to be closed in layers by a qualified surgeon. This is outside the skill of an expedition paramedic; in this case the wound should be cleaned, packed open and redressed daily. This may allow the wound to heal from the bottom upwards. Sutures should never be applied to animal or human bites, deep wounds or contaminated wounds.

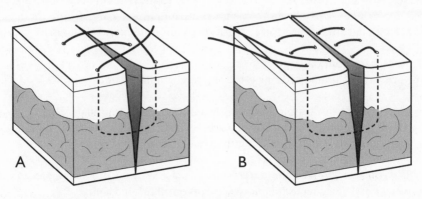

Figure 11.2   *Suturing of wounds: a Ordinary suturing*
b Eversion suturing

Types of wounds
Abrasions
These are grazing injuries where the top surface of the skin is removed. Abrasions should be cleaned and a non-stick dressing applied. Ingrained dirt, if not removed, will result in tattooing and makes wound infection more likely. Dressings may need to be changed once or twice daily depending on the environment. Dressings may stick and can be soaked off with clean water or saline.

Puncture wounds
Infection may occur at the base of deep, penetrating wounds. Tetanus is a risk, particularly with puncture wounds, and all expedition team members should be immunised. The skin surface should be prevented from sealing over by placing a small wick into the wound. This allows healing to occur from the bottom of a puncture wound upwards. Otherwise abscess formation may occur.

Blisters
Blisters are best prevented. All group members should be encouraged to stop walking and to cover hot spots before they develop into blisters. If a blister does develop, the fluid should be drained using a clean (sterile) needle and then the area covered with an adhesive plaster or Moleskin. Compeed and Spenco are alternative dressings. Blisters may become de-roofed; in this case treat as a graze with a non-adherent dressing. A thin application of Friar's Balsam at the edge of a blister may help the dressing to stay in place. Healing is rapid if friction at the blister site can be eliminated. Leaving

the blister uncovered, where possible, will assist healing by allowing the area to dry out.

Bruises
Contusions or bruises are usually caused by a direct blow to the skin surface. Bleeding under the skin gives the bruise its characteristic appearance. Rest, ice, compression and elevation (RICE) all help to reduce swelling and pain. Anti-inflammatory drugs such as ibuprofen or aspirin may also help. After a day or two the affected part should be mobilised to reduce stiffness. A subungual haematoma (a blood blister beneath the finger nail) can be easily treated by melting a hole through the nail using an opened paper clip heated to red heat in a flame. This is surprisingly painless and gives immediate relief.

Crush injuries
Large amounts of tissue may be damaged in crushing injuries and the potential for infection is high. The crushed part should be carefully cleaned and then elevated. Swelling in the affected part may cut off the blood supply to the limb beyond the injury. If the injury is severe there may be a risk of losing the limb and it is important to evacuate the casualty for medical assessment.

Amputation
A digit or limb may be replaced by microsurgery if the patient and the amputated part can be delivered to a surgeon in less than 6 hours. The amputated part should be kept cool, preferably in a container with ice, but not in direct contact with the ice. In an expedition setting it is highly unlikely that such surgical facilities will be available; in this case, treat the bleeding with direct pressure and elevation. The stump should be cleaned gently and then covered with a non-adherent dressing such as paraffin gauze. People with these injuries need to be evacuated to allow surgical treatment to shorten any bone ends and cover the stump with a flap of skin so that healing can take place.

Impalement
An impaled object protruding from a wound should be left in place. Removing an impaled object may cause further damage and therefore should be done in a suitably equipped hospital. Large objects, such as arrows or fence posts, may need to be stabilised and carefully cut to allow evacuation. Pain relief will be required.

Wounds causing particular problems
Deep wounds
In a deep wound underlying structures, for example arteries, nerves, tendons and muscles, may be damaged. It is important to assess:

- Movement: the patient should be asked to move the affected part through the full normal range.
- Circulation: check by feeling for pulses and look for capillary refill (see below).
- Sensation: check beyond the level of the injury.

To check for capillary refill press firmly over a fingernail or toenail to produce blanching. When the pressure is released the colour should return quickly (in less than 2 seconds), otherwise indicating the patient to be extremely cold, shocked or that the blood supply to the limb is interrupted. If the blood supply to a limb is completely interrupted it will be painful, pulseless, pale and cold. Surgical treatment is required within a few hours to salvage the limb.

Deep wounds are also prone to infection. They should be cleaned carefully and packed open so that the wound can heal from the bottom up. Dressings should be changed daily until the wound can be dealt with surgically.

Neck wounds

Injuries to the neck may be associated with damage to important underlying structures such as blood vessels, nerves and the airway. Neck wounds should be cleaned carefully but never probed. Unless the wound is clearly superficial it should be assessed medically. Bandages should never be placed around the neck as subsequent swelling may compromise the airway.

Flaps

Flap wounds are caused by slicing injuries, for example, with machetes on expeditions. Proximal structures are those near to the trunk; distal structures are those further away. In a proximal flap the point of attachment of the flap of skin is towards the trunk. Since arteries travel away from the heart, proximal flaps have a reasonable blood supply. Conversely, in a distal flap the point of attachment of the skin lies distal to the rest of the wound. The blood supply is therefore poor and so the skin overlying distal flaps often becomes infected and dies.

When managing a flap wound:

- Turn the skin flap back and clean underneath.
- Snip away small pieces of dead tissue with sterile scissors.
- Apply a non-stick dressing around the edges of the wound, under the flap. This stops the wound from sealing and allows exudate to drain away.

It is important to let a flap wound heal from its base to its tip. Distal flaps usually become dusky and either dry out and go black or become infected. Patients with such flaps need to be evacuated for surgical treatment and usually require skin grafting.

Treated properly, however, proximal flaps often heal well without infection. Flap wounds need to be re-dressed daily and a little less non-stick dressing applied each day so as to allow the flap to heal. Flap wounds should not be closed with sutures.

Contaminated wounds

Wounds are very likely to become contaminated in some environments such as the jungle. Wounds should be cleaned carefully to remove any foreign material which might form a focus for infection. Painkillers given half an hour before scrubbing out a wound may decrease pain during the procedure; alternatively, an injection of local anaesthetic may make the task of cleaning the wound easier if someone is available to administer it. Debris can be flushed out of the wound using sterile saline. Contaminated wounds should not be sutured closed. It is better to let the wound heal from the bottom upwards by packing the wound open and changing dressings daily. Oral antibiotics may be necessary if wounds are very deep or contaminated, particularly if there are signs of infection (see below). These wounds should heal but there may be scarring.

Hand and foot wounds

Wound complications in the hands or feet may result in crippling deformity. Any significant foot wound will not heal while an expedition member continues to walk around, so rest is imperative. Wounds should be treated by cleaning, careful assessment of movement, circulation and sensation, and then rest in the position of function. In the case of the hand, this means bandaging the hand around a sock or a crepe bandage initially, followed by gentle mobilisation. It should never be splinted with the hand and fingers straight, since if there is any stiffness after the injury the hand will be useless. Infections in the hands or feet can be devastating. If there is any suspicion of infection antibiotics should be started sooner rather than later (flucloxacillin or erythromycin).

Facial wounds

Facial wounds usually heal quickly and with little infection. They should be cleaned, closed using Steristrips rather than sutures where possible, and dressed as usual.

Bites

Animal and human bites almost invariably become infected. Wounds should be cleaned very carefully and any dead tissue snipped away with a pair of sterile scissors. As these wounds are so likely to become infected it is sensible to use antibiotics (Augmentin) prophylactically. (See also Chapter 16.)

Scalp wounds

The scalp has a very good blood supply and lacerations usually bleed copiously.

Bleeding should be stopped with direct pressure. The skin edges may be brought together by tying the hair together, by using surgical "superglue" (for example, Histoacryl) or by suturing the skin edges.

Foreign bodies
Foreign bodies in the eye
The patient is usually sure that something has gone into the eye. Check the surface of the eye carefully by asking the casualty to look in all directions. It may be possible to see the offending object and to remove it with a moistened cotton bud. However, often the foreign body is under the upper lid or there is too much spasm of the eyelid muscle to allow a good view. A couple of drops of local anaesthetic (amethocaine drops) will produce numbness after momentary stinging. It should then be possible to examine the eye more easily and evert the upper lid to check for a foreign body. To evert the lid ask the patient to look downwards. Grasp the upper eye lashes firmly while applying a cotton bud or match-stick to the skin crease of the upper lid. Push down with the cotton bud while lifting the eyelashes upwards with the other hand. This should provide a good view of the underside of the upper lid. Any foreign body can then be removed. If the foreign body cannot be removed simply the patient should be assessed by a doctor or nurse.

Foreign bodies in the ear
Insects and ticks may crawl into the ear on expeditions. This may be very frightening for the individual. Water or oil should be poured into the ear. This will kill the insect and may allow it to float out. Avoid using instruments to try to remove foreign bodies in the ear as they may cause damage.

Splinters
Splinters can usually be removed using a fine pair of tweezers (the ones on Swiss Army knives are good) or a sterile needle. For more stubborn splinters, soaking may help. Spines from sea urchins are easier to remove after a couple of days when the wound becomes inflamed, or after softening the skin with salicylic acid.

Wound infections
Any wound can become infected. However, certain wounds, particularly bites, contaminated wounds and deep wounds, are more likely to become infected. Signs and symptoms of a wound infection are: pain, redness, heat, swelling and loss of function. In the later stages, red lines may be seen running from a limb wound up towards the body. Lymph nodes in the armpit, groin or neck may become enlarged and fever may develop.

Abscesses

An abscess is a collection of pus. Even small collections of pus around the fingernails or toenails (whitlows) are extremely painful and debilitating. As pus accumulates, the skin over the abscess thins; this is referred to as pointing. Once the pus discharges through a breach in the thinned skin the pain, which is usually throbbing, rapidly resolves. If an abscess develops during an expedition local heat and oral antibiotics (for example, flucloxacillin) may help. However, once pus is present it may be quicker and kinder to drain it. The skin may be numbed by applying ice, and then a swift cross-shaped cut in the skin will produce a large enough hole to let the pus drain. A small piece of gauze soaked in saline inserted into the incision will act as a wick and stop the roof of the abscess healing over before all the pus has drained. In this way the abscess cavity will heal from the bottom upwards. The wick should be changed daily until the abscess has healed.

Cellulitis

Cellulitis means infection of the skin. There may not be an obvious focus of infection but the signs are the same as for a wound infection, that is, redness, heat, pain and swelling. Treatment with antibiotics will be necessary (ampicillin plus flucloxacillin, or erythromycin).

BURNS

Burns may be caused by dry heat, chemicals, friction or hot liquids. On expeditions open fires and fuel stoves commonly cause injuries, particularly when people refuel lighted stoves or burn rubbish with petrol.

Classification of burns

Burns may be divided into superficial, partial-thickness and full-thickness burns.

- Superficial burns: characterised by redness, swelling and tenderness; for example, mild sunburn or a scald from hot water.
- Partial thickness burns: characterised by painful red, raw skin and blisters.
- Full-thickness burns: characterised by pale, waxy and sometimes charred skin with a loss of sensation.

On an expedition it is important to differentiate between partial thickness and full-thickness burns. Full-thickness burns need skin grafting so evacuation to medical help is imperative.

Extent of burns

The "rule of nines", which divides the surface area of the body into areas of approximately 9%, is used to calculate the proportion of the body which is burned and so helps determine treatment (see Figure 11.3). However, the severity of burns is often underestimated, even by doctors and nurses, and extensive burns need specialist assessment and treatment.

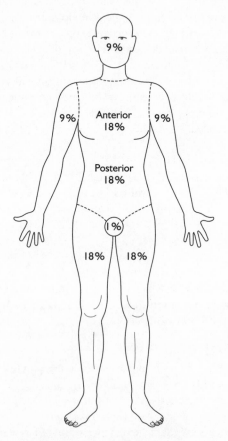

Figure 11.3   *"Rule of Nines", a method to help assess the percentage of body surface burnt (a patient's palm is approximately 1% of body surface area)*

Treatment of burns and scalds on an expedition
The usual first aid aims of caring for a burned patient are to:

- halt the burning process and relieve pain;
- resuscitate if necessary;
- treat associated injuries;

- minimise the risk of infection;
- arrange urgent removal to hospital.

In practical terms, to treat a burned patient:

- Resuscitate as appropriate, following ABC guidelines.
- Lie the casualty down.
- Douse the burn with copious amounts of cold water.
- Clean the burn carefully, leaving any adherent burnt clothing, etc, on the skin.
- Drain large blisters, as appropriate, by inserting a sterile needle at the edge of the blister, although the skin should not be removed.
- Apply flamazine cream (silver sulphadiazine) as an antiseptic.
- Dress with a protective layer, such as plastic kitchen cling film or a polythene glove for a hand burn.

Dressings should be changed every one or two days as necessary, remembering that each dressing change increases the likelihood of infection.

Sunburn
Sunburn, like blisters, should be avoided. Young people particularly try to get a suntan on the first day of an expedition and thus end up with sunburn. Graded exposure to the sun, high factor sun creams and sensible use of clothing should prevent sunburn. Once sunburn occurs, hydrocortisone or calamine creams may relieve the discomfort of mild conditions.

BONE AND JOINT PROBLEMS

Fractures
Fractures may be classified as follows:

- Simple fractures, where there is a single, clean, bony break.
- Comminuted fractures, where the bone is broken into more than one fragment.
- Open or closed fractures, depending on whether the skin is breached.
- Complicated fractures, if other tissues are involved.

Diagnosis of fracture
A fracture is suggested by pain and tenderness at the site of injury, swelling, bruising or discoloration, deformity and grating (crepitus). The last sign usually confirms a fracture. Pain, tenderness, bruising and swelling can also be seen in sprains and other soft tissue injuries. However, loss of limb function usually, but not always, suggests a

fracture. In an expedition setting where X-ray facilities are not available, treat as a fracture if uncertain. Evacuation can sometimes be delayed until the exact nature of the injury becomes more obvious.

Treatment of fractures

Alignment of the bone ends at a fracture site to enable healing requires *immobilisation*, which prevents further damage, reduces pain and decreases the risk of shock. This cannot always be obtained in the field.

Many things can be used to improvise splints for immobilisation:

- Rope or webbing
- Sleeping bags
- Inflatable splints
- Trekking poles
- Skis
- Triangular bandages
- Canoe paddles
- Purpose-built splints such as "Frakstraps"

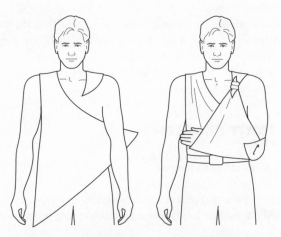

Figure 11.4a   *The broad arm sling for arm and forearm injuries*

When splinting any fracture, bony prominences must be padded and the joints above and below the fracture immobilised. It may be necessary to straighten the limb in order to apply a splint, to relieve pressure on a blood vessel or to allow transfer on to a stretcher. Straightening the limb (reduction) is painful but rarely causes increased damage. Reduction requires strong traction/counter-traction in the long axis of the limb and is more readily done soon after the injury before severe muscle spasm

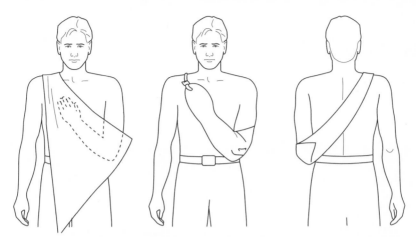

Figure 11.4b   *The high sling for hand injuries, infections and dislocated shoulders*

occurs. If there is no pulse beyond a fracture site the limb must be manipulated urgently into a position to restore the blood supply to the limb. Signs of an interrupted blood supply are absent pulses with pale, cold, numb skin and severe pain. Movement, circulation and sensation should be checked both before and after any manipulation or movement.

Bleeding

Bleeding occurs with all fractures and may result in shock or even death, particularly in fractures of the thigh or pelvis. Shock should be anticipated and treated appropriately.

Open fractures

In an open fracture the skin is breached and therefore there is a risk of infection. Infection involving the bone is called osteomyelitis. This can be difficult to treat and can lead to crippling deformity and even amputation. Open fractures should always be treated as for contaminated soft tissue injuries, by cleaning the wound to remove grit and foreign material and covering with sterile dressings. Co-amoxiclav (Augmentin) or erythromycin should be commenced to prevent infection and urgent evacuation should be arranged.

Pain relief

Pain caused by fractures is decreased by effective immobilisation. Painkillers should be given before attempting reduction and during evacuation.

Transportation
Fractures should be immobilised and other injuries attended to before evacuation, unless there are hazards in the immediate area. Always consider spinal injury, particularly if there is any injury above the level of the collar bones. Casualties with fractures of the upper limbs and ribs may be able to walk. Those with head injuries, back, neck or lower limb injuries have to be carried by stretcher.

TABLE 11.1 MANAGEMENT OF SPECIFIC FRACTURES

Hand and fingers	Bandage in a fist around a rolled up sock and elevate in a sling (ie splint the hand in the position of function)
Forearm	Splint the wrist straight and the elbow at 90°
Elbow/upper arm/shoulder	Use 2 slings or improvise with rope, tapes
Collar bone	Use a figure of eight, padded, to pull shoulders back or use a sling
Foot and toes	Often well-splinted in a boot. Watch for numbness and swelling. It may be necessary to cut the boot off if swelling occurs
Ankles	Immobilise the foot and knee. Assisted walking may be possible
Lower leg/knee	Immobilise foot, ankle and knee
Thigh/hip	Traction is desirable as the bone ends often override damaging the surrounding tissues. Splint both legs together or use a traction splint. In hip fractures there is characteristic shortening and external rotation on the affected side
Pelvis	Treat as for a fractured thigh. ***Pelvic fractures are associated with severe bleeding and damage to internal organs. Suspect if pressure on the pelvis leads to pain.*** Bind the legs together to prevent further movement of pelvic fragments

Spinal injuries
Damage to the spinal cord can result in significant disability and even death. The higher the level of spinal injury the greater is the degree of disability. Neck injury is associated with 5–10% of head injuries leading to unconsciousness and so all casualties with significant head injuries should be treated as if they have an unstable neck fracture. Spinal injury should be suspected if there is neck or back pain or pain radiating around to the front of the body. On examining the casualty there may be a

"step" or swelling along the vertebral column, or loss of sensation, weakness or paralysis. In males erection of the penis may occur (priapism). Remember the spinal cord may not be damaged initially even with a spinal fracture; however, moving an unstable spine may damage the spinal cord and result in permanent paralysis. All casualties at risk of spinal injury should therefore be moved with the spine "in line" as if they have an unstable spine. Movement, circulation and sensation should be assessed before moving the victim, unless the danger of further injury necessitates a scoop-and-run approach.

TABLE 11.3 TO STABILISE NECK INJURIES

- Reassure the casualty and tell them not to move.
- Steady and support the head in the neutral position by placing your hands over the patient's ears. Maintain this support.
- Add a hard neck collar if available (to immobilise the neck) but always continue to hold the head and neck.

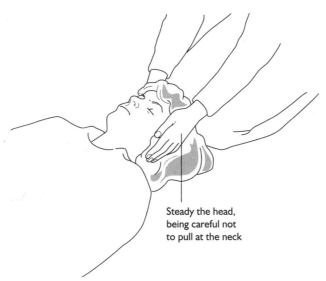

Steady the head, being careful not to pull at the neck

Figure 11.5   *Stabilisation of the neck*

TABLE 11.4 TO TURN/ROLL A PATIENT WITH A SUSPECTED SPINAL INJURY

- Stabilise the neck, as above.
- While maintaining support at the neck, ask ideally five people to help "log-roll" the patient, keeping head, trunk and legs in a straight line.

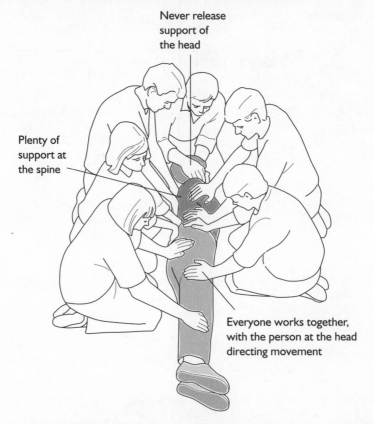

Never release
support of
the head

Plenty of
support at
the spine

Everyone works together,
with the person at the head
directing movement

Figure 11.6 *The "Log roll" method to turn or roll a casualty with a suspected spinal injury*

Patients with a suspected spinal injury should be evacuated by helicopter; however, if this is not possible every effort should be made to completely immobilise the neck and back. Patients who do not have normal sensation can quickly develop pressure sores so stretchers should be well padded. The patient will require regular and careful changes of position.

TABLE 11.5 SPECIFIC DISLOCATIONS

Fingers	Finger dislocations can usually be reduced easily. Splint to the next finger, ie "buddy strapping", after reduction.
Thumb	Often associated with a fracture, best management is immobilisation in the position of function.
Elbow	Reduce elbow dislocations as quickly as possible. As with all fractures and dislocations, check the pulse and sensation before and after reduction as nerves and blood vessels can easily be damaged. Considerable force may be required and if the pulse is not restored, try again. Splint the elbow at 90°.
Shoulder	Diagnosis is suggested by squaring of the shoulder joint, the arm is often rotated outwards and held away from the trunk. Reduction can be attempted by: 1. Lying the casualty prone with a 10–20lb weight hanging on the arm. 2. Pulling the arm downwards with a towel wrapped around the chest for counter-traction. 3. Placing a foot against the chest (not the armpit) and pulling down and out on the affected arm. Immobilise the arm in a sling for 2 weeks.
Knee	Major dislocations of the knee realign readily. Kneecap dislocations can be reduced by straightening the leg. Immobilise as for a fracture.
Jaw	If the jaw is locked open, it is dislocated. Wear gloves and pad the thumbs to avoid injury as the person will bite involuntarily. Place the thumbs over the victim's lower molars and press directly downwards. Considerable force is required.

Dislocations and other injuries

A dislocation interrupts the normal relationships of a joint. The bone may be forced out of its socket (for example, shoulder, hip and elbow dislocations) or the joint surfaces may simply be displaced (for example, finger dislocations). Fractures, nerve and blood vessel injuries may be associated with dislocations.

Dislocations cause pain aggravated by movement, tenderness, swelling, discoloration, limitation of movement and deformity. The injured limb should be compared with the non-injured limb. Correction of dislocations can be technically difficult as nerves and blood vessels can be damaged during reduction. However, attempts to correct the deformity are justified in certain circumstances, particularly in

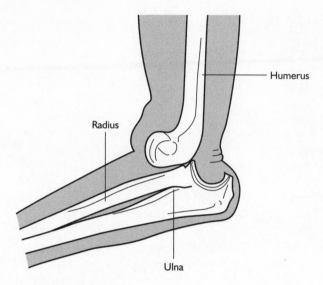

Figure 11.7   *Dislocation of the elbow*

remote areas. For example, if the blood supply to the distal part of the limb is compromised by a dislocation, reduction must be attempted. This should be done as soon as possible after the injury because of increasing muscle spasm.

- Steady, firm traction along the limb's long axis should be applied to attempt to correct the deformity and to improve the blood supply.
- After reduction the limb should be splinted as for a fracture.

Other injuries of bone and related injuries
Subperiosteal haematoma
A direct blow to a bone may damage the tissue, the periosteum, covering the bone. Bleeding underneath the periosteum produces a subperiosteal haematoma. This is a very painful injury, commonly seen on the shin; the area is often exquisitely tender with some swelling. Treatment consists of elevation, cold packs and anti-inflammatory drugs. If a fracture cannot be confidently excluded, treat the injury as a fracture.

Sprains and strains
These are tearing or stretching injuries of ligaments and tendons around a joint which can be associated with a great deal of swelling and bruising. The injury may impair function as seriously as a fracture or a dislocation. Treatment consists of elevation, rest and support bandages. Immobilisation with a plaster of Paris backslab or splinting will improve pain.

Muscle and tendon tears
Muscles may be torn from their attachments by a sudden, strong force or by penetrating injuries. A complete tear will result in loss of muscle function and a partial tear will produce weakness.

Common sites of muscle/tendon tears are:

- Fingertip (mallet finger)
- Shoulder
- Calf
- Thigh

Treatment consists of rest, ice and immobilisation. Evacuation for surgical repair may be necessary.

Tenosynovitis
Tenosynovitis is inflammation of the sheaths that surround tendons and is caused by overuse or penetrating injury. The diagnosis is made by eliciting pain on movement of the involved tendon. If the cause is overuse, treat with rest and anti-inflammatories (such as ibuprofen). If infection is suggested by a history of trauma and there is painful movement with redness and swelling, antibiotics and immediate evacuation may be necessary to save the function of the limb.

Joint effusion
Swelling around joints, particularly the knee and elbow, occurs commonly following trauma. Treatment consists of elevation, rest, support bandaging and anti-inflammatory drugs.

PAIN MANAGEMENT

A person's response to pain is subjective and is influenced by other factors such as fear, anxiety, fatigue, extreme cold or heat and the responses of those around them. Since these other factors are important in the perception of pain, much can be done to make a patient in pain more comfortable even if an expedition is carrying very few drugs. Reassurance, shelter, warmth, splinting of fractures, relief of skin pressure by careful turning, adequate food and fluids, and rest will all help to relieve pain.

Severe pain may be associated with nausea. The control of associated symptoms such as nausea and vomiting with anti-sickness drugs (such as prochlorperazine, Stemetil) will, in itself, promote rest and improve pain.

The treatment of pain
The treatment of pain requires an assessment by taking a history and doing a physi-

cal examination to ascertain the likely cause of the pain. The best therapy for pain is to treat the underlying cause. Where this is not possible, a simple stepwise approach using a limited number of drugs should control pain in the majority of cases.

The following features of the pain may be helpful in reaching a diagnosis:

- When did the pain start? Was there an injury?
- Where is the main site of the pain and does it move anywhere else?
- What makes the pain worse or better?
- Is it constant or intermittent?
- What is the character of the pain, for example, burning, crushing, dull, sharp, etc?
- Are there any other associated symptoms, for example, nausea, diarrhoea or vomiting?

Painkilling drugs

Painkillers can be divided into three groups: simple painkillers, moderate strength painkillers and strong painkillers. Expedition groups should have with them one or two simple painkillers, such as paracetamol or aspirin, and one or two moderate painkillers, such as dihydrocodeine or ibuprofen. Many groups choose not to carry strong painkillers, such as nalbuphine, tramadol and morphine.

Pain caused by an accident or injury should initially be treated with a simple painkiller given regularly, that is, given by the clock rather than waiting until the pain returns. However, for a headache, it is sufficient to take a dose of a painkiller and then wait and see if the pain returns. If pain caused by an injury is not controlled by a regular, simple painkiller, then a moderate painkiller should be taken, again regularly and at the recommended dose. Pain caused by severe injury may require strong painkillers. The same principles of regular administration apply, but the dose may also need to be increased until pain is controlled.

Simple painkillers
Paracetamol
This can be taken for mild to moderate pain and fever. Side-effects are rare and the dose is 2 tablets (1g) 4–6 hourly (no more than 8 tablets in 24 hours).

Aspirin
Aspirin is good for mild to moderate pain and fever. It is a good painkiller and an anti-inflammatory drug, but some people are allergic to it and it may cause stomach irritation. The dose is 1–3 tablets (300–900mg) 4–6 hourly (no more than 4g in 24 hours).

Ibuprofen (Nurofen, Brufen)
Ibuprofen is an anti-inflammatory drug which is useful in the treatment of muscle and joint pains, period pains and where pain is associated with inflammation. It can be taken in combination with paracetamol or weak or strong painkillers. However, it should not be given with aspirin or to patients with aspirin allergy or a history of peptic ulcers. Side-effects are indigestion, heartburn and nausea. In some individuals asthma may be made worse. It should be taken with food and the dose is 400mg every 8 hours.

Moderate strength painkillers
Dihydrocodeine (DF I I 8)
This can be taken for moderate pain. Side-effects are constipation, nausea and drowsiness. The dose is 1 tablet (30mg) 3–4 times a day.

Tramadol (Zydol)
Tramadol is used for moderate to severe pain. It can cause nausea, vomiting, dry mouth, drowsiness and a rash. It should not be taken with alcohol and should not be given after head injuries or to epileptics as it may precipitate fitting. The dose is 1–2 tablets (50–100mg) 4–6 hourly, maximum 8 tablets a day. It can also be given as an injection (50–100mg, 4–6 hourly).

Strong painkillers
Morphine
Morphine, an opiate, is a strong painkiller with potent sedative side-effects. Together these effects relieve pain and may help relieve anxiety following an accident or in serious illness. Morphine is a controlled drug and is difficult, but not impossible, to obtain and export for expedition use. As it causes sedation, it should not be given to any patient with a significant head injury. Morphine also depresses respiratory function and should be used with great caution in patients with chest injuries. It may cause nausea and vomiting and it is wise to give morphine with an anti-sickness drug, such as prochlorperazine, which can be given by mouth, by suppository or by injection. Morphine is very constipating. It should be given every 4 hours and the dose depends on the patient and the severity of the pain; however, a range of 5–15mg intramuscularly is usual. All opiates can cause drug dependence given over a prolonged period. This is not a problem for short-term use to relieve the pain of an injury. Morphine may also be given by mouth and by slow intravenous injection.

Nalbuphine (Nubain)
Nalbuphine is a strong painkiller but is not subject to the legal restrictions covering drugs such as morphine or pethidine. It is therefore more appropriate for most expeditions. Its side-effects are similar to morphine. Nalbuphine is given by injection

subcutaneously, intramuscularly or intravenously. The dose is 10–20mg for a 70kg patient every 3–6 hours.

Buprenorphine (Temgesic)
This drug is similar to morphine, although less potent, but is administered by placing a tablet under the tongue. It is also a controlled drug but the mode of administration may be easier in some cases. Other precautions and side-effects are as for morphine. Buprenorphine makes many individuals very nauseated and a drug such as prochlorperazine may need to be given with it. The dose is 1–2 tablets (200–400mcg) under the tongue 6–8 hourly.

If strong painkillers are necessary to relieve pain in an injured casualty the doses used and the time they were given should be recorded and this information handed on when the patient is evacuated. If a group decides not to carry strong painkillers, a severely injured casualty can still be managed with weak painkillers and the comfort measures noted above; information and the presence of a competent, reassuring companion will be particularly helpful.

SUMMARY

Minor accidents and injuries do occur on expeditions, but with knowledge and a reasonable medical kit most should be treatable in the field and should not impair the enjoyment of the expedition. The expedition medical officer has a responsibility to consider when an accident or injury requires more expert help and to arrange for the patient's evacuation to a place of safety and competent care.

The author is indebted to Dr Karen Forbes, Macmillan Consultant Senior Lecturer in Palliative Medicine at Bristol University, for her advice on pain control.

12 CASUALTY EVACUATION

Rod Stables

Thorough preparation and planning of all phases of an expedition are essential for a successful venture. This is particularly important in the handling of emergency evacuation. Casualty evacuation (casevac) procedures must be established and perhaps even rehearsed before deployment.

Expeditions vary in their destination, scale, complexity, duration, risk, isolation and levels of support. Beyond this each evacuation case will present its own problems, varying from the self-caring "walking wounded", to patients requiring continuous and intensive care.

The aim of this chapter is to provide a framework for sound planning. To do this the process of casualty evacuation has been broken down into several phases.

Preparation
⬇
Casualty event
⬇
Immediate rescue
⬇
Stabilisation
⬇
Call for help/move to help
⬇
In-county casevac
⬇
International recovery

Preparation

All phases of the casualty evacuation process must be considered. Seek information from all available sources, paying particular attention to local agencies and those

127

with recent experience of your expedition area. Reports from previous trips are often a useful reference. The Royal Geographical Society houses an extensive reference collection of past expedition reports in its map room, which is open to the public. It is also conducting a long-term survey of medical problems experienced by expeditions.

Establish contact by mail, fax, e-mail or telephone with relevant external agencies and aim to involve them in your planning process. On arrival in the country allow time for personal visits to ensure close liaison with groups or individuals that you may have to call on for support.

The evacuation chain usually involves a collaborative effort co-ordinated, in sequence, by three key individuals or agencies. (See Chapter 6.)

Expedition members
⬇
Local agent
(in-country but with international communications)
⬇
Home country contact

Consulate or other diplomatic officials have sometimes acted as local agents, but except in the case of dire emergency their availability should not be assumed and alternative arrangements must be secured.

Modern communications usually allow an effective link to be established between the home country contact and the local agent, but communications with the expedition group may be less secure and will vary from case to case. (See The call for or move to help, page 130).

Each element in this chain will require copies of some basic documentation. This should include but is certainly not limited to the following:

- A complete list of expedition members and their personal details, including nationality, passport number, full next-of-kin contact details, information about pre-existing medical problems and blood group information.
- Copies of all insurance policies relating to medical and evacuation cover.
- Contact details of involved travel and transport agencies, including international medical evacuation services.
- Contact details of local consulate or other diplomatic or home government officials for all nationalities represented on the expedition.
- Precise contact details of the other link agencies. This should include alternative contact individuals and fallback alternative telephone and fax numbers.

A similar but more personalised document pack should be produced for each expedition member. This should be kept readily available together with a passport and some cash, credit cards or other financial guarantee. An emergency casevac may separate an individual from the rest of the party and these documents should accompany the injured party. This "snatch bag" can be further enhanced by including a structured proforma to allow recording of the immediate medical history, clinical observations and treatment regimes.

Casualty event and immediate rescue
Expedition leaders and medical officers must consider the equipment that might be required in the immediate recovery of a casualty following an accident or sudden illness. Normal trauma packs are usually required, but steep rock, snow and ice, caves or the open sea may demand the procurement of specialist items. Improvisation and persistence can overcome most obstacles, but in difficult terrain there is no substitute for high-quality, purpose-built equipment.

Figure 12.1   *Stretcher casevac in the Khumbu Icefall on Everest in winter. The victim had bilateral compound fractures of tibia and fibula from a fall (R. Stables)*

Stabilisation
Once back in the base camp area an attempt can be made to stabilise the patient's condition. A decision on the need to evacuate and the timing of any such move must then be made. These can be difficult issues to resolve and involve a series of value

judgements based on the patient's condition, the level of care immediately available and the complexities and rigour of the casevac chain. Good communications with the local agent and hence with specialist professional advice can be of great value in this setting.

It is important to document clearly the details of the case and to record key clinical observations and treatments administered. This data should be sent back with the patient.

Ideally, an expedition member should accompany the patient, taking all the patient's personal equipment with them. This is rarely possible but should be considered if manpower and other circumstances permit.

The call for (or move to) help

Expeditions with no means of summoning outside help will have to move their casualty to the nearest human habitation or aid post. The most appropriate means for this move should be considered in the planning phase. Pack animals or stretcher carriers can be slow and present great problems for a severely injured patient.

Even large and well-equipped expeditions may face this problem if they are operating in remote or high-altitude areas, beyond the range of helicopter operations. Everest Base Camp, for example, is inaccessible to helicopters in the winter months and casualties must be moved to lower altitudes down the valley. It is important to remember in planning helicopter tasks that there is a complex relationship between range and payload (or freight). When the aircraft is operating at the limits of its range or altitude ceiling payload limitations may mean that the casualty has to move alone with minimal equipment.

The most usual means of summoning help is by radio communications, although local runners can provide a remarkable service in some areas. Traditional HF or VHF radio links to a local agent have previously been the mainstay of expedition communications, although in regions that are frequently overflown, such as the Denali National Park in Alaska, ground-to-air UHF systems can provide an effective alternative for emergency transmissions.

Satellite communication systems have revolutionised the potential for long-range communications, and secure voice and fax links across several continents are now readily available. This equipment is, however, expensive to hire or purchase and satellite air time is also charged at premium rates. For smaller expeditions, interested only in emergency communications, a number of companies now offer, for hire, a satellite emergency beacon transmitter device. This can be triggered to produce one of a number of coded signals to a central base. This central base will then notify the expedition's nominated agent that the expedition has, for example, transmitted "Message 2" logged as "Request immediate casevac at this location".

Figure 12.2 *Aeromedical evacuation (S.R. Anderson)*

In-country casevac and international recovery

The involvement of established agencies usually makes this the least problematical part of the process. Aeromedical evacuation is expensive and appropriate insurance cover should be established for all expedition members. Most insurance companies insist on being involved from the earliest stages of a claim and should be contacted at the first opportunity.

Companies that provide Air Ambulance services

Europe and Africa

Cega Air Ambulance Ltd, Goodwood Airfield, Chichester, West Sussex PO18 0PH, UK
Tel. +44 1243 538888, fax +44 1243 773169

Compagnie Générale de Secours, Paris, France
Tel. +33 1 47476666

East Africa Flying Doctors Society (AMREF), 11 Old Queen Street, London SW1H 9JA, UK
Tel. +44 171 2330066, fax +44 171 2330099

Europ Assistance, Sussex House, Perrymount Road, Haywards Heath, West Sussex RH16 1DN, UK
Tel. +44 1444 411999, fax +44 1444 415775

International Assistance Services, 32–42 High Street, Purley, Surrey CR8 2PP, UK
Tel. +44 181 7631550, fax +44 181 6681262

Swiss Air Ambulance, Zurich, Switzerland
Tel. +41 1 3831111

United States
Air Ambulance Network, Miami, FL
Tel. +1 800 3271966, +1 305 4470458

Air Ambulance International, San Francisco, CA
Tel. +1 800 2279996, +1 415 7861592

Air Response, Box 109, Fort Plain, NY 13339
Tel. +1 518 9934153

International SOS, Box 11568, Philadelphia, PA 19116
Tel. +1 800 5238930, +1 215 2441500

Life Flight Hermann Hospital, Houston, TX
Tel. +1 800 2314357

National Jets, Fort Lauderdale, FL
Tel. +1 305 3599900, +1 800 3273710

North American Air Ambulance, Blackwood, NJ
Tel. +1 800 2578180

Nationwide/Worldwide Emergency Ambulance Return (NEAR), 450 Prairie Avenue,
Calumet City, IL 60409
Tel. +1 800 6546700

13 MEDICAL ASPECTS OF SURVIVAL

Rod Stables

M any people will already be familiar with the demands of expedition travel to
wild and unfamiliar places. Fatigue, hunger, pain, thirst and even a measure of
fear are, to an extent, routine features of this type of endeavour. It is probably these
aspects of any venture that are the source of the best expedition anecdotes and the
most enduring, if least accurately framed, memories.

Few people, however, will ever experience a true survival situation when life and
death hang in a fine balance and all other concerns become secondary. Survival is the
art of staying alive. The human body, and perhaps more importantly the spirit, has
the capability to endure the most extreme hardship and privation under seemingly
impossible conditions. Examples of this tenacity can be found in an extensive literature recounting survival escapades.

Although a number of well-documented cases have involved a prolonged period
of isolation, the "Robinson Crusoe" scenario is rare and most survival situations are
played out in the course of hours and days rather than weeks and months. In all cases,
however, it is usually possible to identify a number of core issues that determine the
eventual outcome.

The pyramid of survival
Survival skills can be described in terms of a pyramid. The most important elements
form the broad base and are the factors that distinguish the survivor from the victim.
The relative importance of the other components varies in different situations and
with different personalities.

Equipment

Physical state
Health   Fitness   Reserves
Acclimatisation

Knowledge and skills
Adapt   Improvise   Overcome

Will to survive
Courage   Determination   Stamina   Resourcefulness
Tenacity   Team spirit   Humour   Faith

The will to survive

Qualities of character and resolve usually dictate the chances of survival. Physically unprepared individuals with no equipment or specialist skills have survived against all odds by refusing to surrender to death. The survivor will cling to the last threads of life, however desperate the circumstances. Escape or rescue, followed by treatment and rehabilitation, allows a return to normal life in almost all cases, but once the threshold of death is crossed all is lost.

When disaster strikes initial feelings of panic and self-pity must be controlled. Positive action even in a most rudimentary form will improve self-confidence. Courage, determination and tenacity are important qualities, but it is also important to maintain individual and group morale. Humour and faith (in all its forms) are important in this regard.

For groups, survival situations present new challenges for the leader or leaders. Often a very different style of leadership is required and the demands of the new circumstances can bring previously unrecognised strengths of certain individuals to the fore. The case of the Argentinian rugby team isolated in the high Andes following an aircraft crash is an interesting example (see the film *Alive*, available on video).

Knowledge and skills

Self-confidence can be enhanced by good training and sound knowledge. Much of this will be of a general nature but basic skills in the essentials of survival should be practised by all who venture any distance off the beaten track. A number of books and training courses are available to provide an introduction to this subject.

For any specific trip or expedition, thorough research and planning are essential.

The demands of the environment or other possible threats should be identified and studied. Contingency plans and reserves should be in place to cope with likely problems, and a means of summoning help or evacuation should be established. Throughout the venture all team members should be kept fully informed of key data, such as local terrain, key locations, personnel distribution, weather patterns and communication plans.

Knowledge dispels fear and is an important weapon in the fight for survival. This must be coupled with resourcefulness and a will to adapt, improvise and overcome.

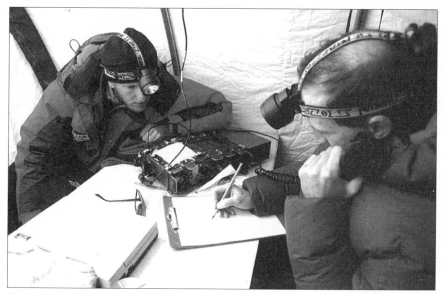

Figure 13.1   *High-frequency radio communication between Everest Base Camp and Kathmandu (R. Stables)*

Physical preparation

Medical and dental health should be checked before departure on any venture. Personal health issues, such as the need for medication (even the contraceptive pill), should be considered and an emergency stock carried on the person at all times.

Physical fitness is a key factor in a survival situation and will allow the individual to cope better with not only physical exertion but also sleep deprivation and climatic extremes. In some environments and for prolonged expeditions it can, however, be a mistake to be too lean. Adipose (fat) tissue is laid down to act as a food reserve in times of need and can provide important thermal insulation.

A period of thorough acclimatisation to extremes of temperature, altitude or other environmental factors should be allowed before expedition members are subjected to the risks of isolation from support.

Equipment

Well-chosen equipment is obviously important but it is critical to ensure that key items are available when needed. Each expedition or individual should have a clear concept of what should be carried:

- on the person;
- in the pack or on the belt when away from base camp;
- at the base camp.

Survival situations often start with the loss of equipment. Key items such as map, compass, torch and whistle should be carried on the person and secured by lanyards at all times. Other equipment choices and standard procedures will be governed by the nature of the trip and personal preferences.

Summary

It is impossible in this short chapter to offer anything more than basic guidelines. More detailed information, perhaps specific to the expedition aims, will have to be sought in appropriate texts and appropriate skills acquired and practised.

14 TRAVELLER'S DIARRHOEA AND OTHER COMMON INFECTIONS

Richard Dawood

Many people worry about exotic infections, such as Lassa fever, when they con template travel to less developed areas of the world. The reality is that exotic infections are just that and are rarely encountered. This section outlines some of the more common infections not described in other chapters that may affect expedition members. Most of these problems can also occur at home but there is an increased risk when travelling.

DIARRHOEA

Traveller's diarrhoea is one of the commonest afflictions of expedition members, surpassed in frequency perhaps only by sunburn and insect bites. Estimates of its incidence range from 25–40% in travellers to southern Europe to as high as 80% in tropical developing countries. It is such a common condition that many people believe it to be inextricably linked to the experience of travel. Changes of diet, spicy foods and the stresses of travel are sometimes blamed for it. All of these are fallacies: traveller's diarrhoea is the result of infection with one or more of a variety of organisms. In most cases, the illness that results is "self-limiting" – it gets better with no treatment, usually within 48 hours. Infection is the result of consuming food or water that has been contaminated with faeces.

Causes and mechanisms

The following is a brief guide to the commonest infecting organisms.

1. Enterotoxigenic Escherichia coli (ETEC)

ETEC is a variant strain of *E. coli*, a normal bacterial inhabitant of the large intestine, which produces a toxin that acts in the same manner as cholera: it causes a direct increase in the net secretion of water and electrolytes into the bowel lumen, without causing inflammatory changes. The reabsorptive capacity of the colon is overloaded,

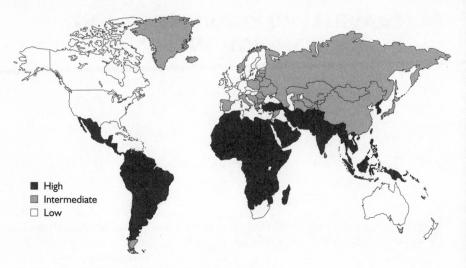

Figure 14.1   *Worldwide risk of traveller's diarrhoea*

and profuse watery diarrhoea results. It is responsible for between 10% and 40% of cases of traveller's diarrhoea. An oral vaccine against ETEC has been developed and marketing is being considered.

2. Shigella
Shigella is the main cause of bacterial dysentery, and may be responsible for up to 20% of diarrhoea episodes in travellers. There may be a transient phase of small intestinal secretory diarrhoea but the main impact is on the colon, which is acutely inflamed; the stools contain blood and pus in severe cases. Milder illnesses, however, cannot be distinguished clinically from non-dysenteric diarrhoeal illnesses.

3. Salmonella and campylobacter
Both these organisms produce inflammation of the terminal small bowel and the colon, so the clinical picture varies between non-specific diarrhoea and a much more dysentery-like illness. Salmonella causes around 4% of cases, and campylobacter may cause up to 15%. Several other bacterial species can cause traveller's diarrhoea, such as the non-cholera vibrios and even *Vibrio cholerae* itself, and other organisms are still being identified.

4. Viruses
Viruses, particularly Norwalk virus and rotavirus, together account for about 10% of diarrhoea cases. The practical result is that these infections are not treatable by antibiotics, and must simply take their course. Rotavirus is easily transmitted by droplet

spread, and large outbreaks may follow; scrupulous hygiene is necessary to contain outbreaks.

5. Amoebic dysentery and giardiasis
These parasitic diseases account for about 5% of cases in travellers. They can be difficult to diagnose and treat, and account for a much higher proportion of cases in travellers who are left with persisting symptoms after their return home. Amoebic dysentery is characterised by blood in the stool; giardiasis causes flatulence with foul-smelling stools that are difficult to flush.

In 10–15% of cases more than one organism is responsible. In about the same number, no cause can be found. However, new causes of diarrhoea are being discovered all the time. Recent newcomers to the scene include cryptosporidium and coccidia, the latter apparently being responsible for large numbers of cases among travellers to Nepal.

Prevention
Almost all of these organisms are transmitted in the same way: by contaminated food and water. Infective material must be swallowed in order to contract the illness. One result is that this entire class of infections can be prevented by devoting rigorous attention to hygienic food preparation and handling, and to water sterilisation.

In many ways, an expedition setting enables a much greater degree of control over these factors than is possible for travellers who depend on hotels and restaurants for their food, or who live in close contact with local communities in developing countries.

The following foods are risky, and are best avoided:

- Shellfish and seafood. Molluscs and crustaceans are filter feeders, and accumulate whichever organisms happen to be present in the local sewage system. They need a minimum of 8 minutes' vigorous boiling to be rendered safe.
- Salads, raw fruit and vegetables. These have the reputation of being healthy and nutritious at home, but human and animal excreta are widely used as fertiliser in most developing countries. They require careful sterilisation and preparation.
- Rare meat (including undercooked chicken), raw fish. There may be a high risk of parasitic infestation.
- Buffets, food left out in warm temperatures. Bacteria multiply fast at warm temperatures, and trivial contamination can rapidly turn into a serious risk.
- Food on which flies have settled.
- Food stored and reheated after cooking.
- Spicy sauces and salsa, left out on the table.

- Food handled with dirty fingers.
- Milk products and ice cream.
- Foods containing raw egg (for example, mayonnaise).
- Fruit juices from street vendors.
- Ice.
- Tap water, even for brushing teeth.
- Hospitality. If you are offered food that is not safe make an excuse and refuse it.

The following foods are usually safe:

- Freshly, thoroughly cooked food, served hot.
- Fruit easily peeled or sliced open (bananas, melons, papaya, avocado).
- Freshly baked bread (find the bakery).
- Packaged or canned food.
- Bottled drinks opened in your presence; the safest are carbonated.
- Boiled water, tea.
- If nothing else looks safe, ask for chips, omelettes, boiled eggs, or other dishes that must be cooked to order.

Drugs for prevention

Many drugs have been proposed for prevention, but none is entirely suitable. Advocates of such treatment argue that precautions can be difficult to follow, and do not always work. The contrary view is that drugs can cause harm without offering complete protection, and make travellers more likely to expose themselves to risk in the mistaken belief that they are protected against all ills.

Bismuth subsalicylate (Pepto-Bismol) is one drug that is believed to reduce the incidence of traveller's diarrhoea, and has some popularity in the United States. It needs to be taken in substantial doses, and may cause a black, furred tongue and black stools.

Another approach is to use the quinolone group of antibiotics. However, these drugs are expensive, are not without risk, and may make it more difficult to diagnose and treat any illness that does occur despite the treatment.

Treatment

Remember that most cases of diarrhoea improve without treatment.

Rehydration

The most important aspect of treatment is to correct dehydration, particularly in a tropical environment, and particularly if the sufferer has not yet acclimatised to the heat; in such circumstances, fluid losses can be considerable. Children and the elderly are most at risk from the consequences of dehydration; for them rehydration must be an urgent priority. Healthy adults only rarely become severely dehydrated as the result of diarrhoea, but rehydration is nonetheless worthwhile, making sufferers feel rapidly better.

The fastest and most effective way to replace fluid is to use oral rehydration solutions. These are available as sachets of powder to be made up in clean water. Well-known brands include:

• Sodium Chloride and Glucose oral powder (BNF)
• Oralyte (UNICEF)
• Dioralyte (Armour)
• Rehidrat (Searle)
• Electrolade (Eastern)

Alternatively, add 8 level or 4 heaped teaspoons of sugar (white, brown, or honey), plus 2 teaspoons of salt, to 1 litre of clean water. A double-ended measuring spoon is available from Teaching Aids at Low Cost (TALC), PO Box 45, St Albans, Hertfordshire AL1 4AX, tel. +44 1727 53869.

Drugs for the treatment of diarrhoeal symptoms
The most effective and fast-acting drug for controlling the symptoms of diarrhoea is loperamide (Imodium, Arret). It should be remembered, however, that this does not treat the underlying infection. Loperamide should not be used in children; it is otherwise widely considered to be a safe drug. Concern has been expressed on theoretical grounds that such medication might have the effect of prolonging infection, but several studies have shown such fears to be unfounded. The dose of loperamide is 2 2mg capsules at once, followed by 1 capsule with each loose stool.

Other drugs used in the treatment of diarrhoeal symptoms include: Lomotil, which is a combination of diphenoxylate (a morphine-like drug) with atropine (the atropine component of this combination is included only to prevent Lomotil from being abused and results in symptoms such as a dry mouth and headache); and codeine phosphate. Both of these drugs have constipating effects. None has any advantage over loperamide, which is the drug of first choice for symptomatic treatment of traveller's diarrhoea.

Drugs for the treatment of infection
If symptoms do not improve, and diarrhoea persists after 2–3 days, antibiotic treatment may be necessary. In the absence of a laboratory diagnosis, the safest and most suitable antibiotic is ciprofloxacin at a dose of 500mg twice a day for 3 days, which is particularly active against salmonella, shigella, campylobacter and typhoid fever. (It is also effective against respiratory and urinary infections.) Ciprofloxacin should be used with caution in patients with a history of epilepsy, in patients with liver or kid-

ney impairment, in pregnancy, and in children. It can also cause tendon damage, and the drug should be discontinued at the first sign of limb pain or inflammation.

If amoebic dysentery is suspected, the drug of choice is tinidazole (500mg, 4 tablets every morning for 3 days) followed by diloxanide furoate (Furamide, 500mg, 3 times a day for 10 days). This will also deal effectively with giardiasis. If tinidazole is not available, metronidazole (Flagyl, 400mg, 2 tablets 3 times a day for 5 days) is a not quite so effective alternative. Note that no alcohol should be drunk while tinidazole or metronidazole are being taken.

Devising a strategy

Experts differ in their attitudes to the use of anti-diarrhoeal drugs and antibiotics.

A conservative approach would be simply to maintain hydration with sips of water initially, followed by oral rehydration solution if symptoms are severe, or continue for more than 24 hours. Unless nausea and vomiting are a problem, food intake should be maintained in small quantities, keeping to simple, easily digested foods and avoiding alcohol and heavy, fatty meals.

The authors' approach is to use oral rehydration *and* anti-diarrhoeal treatment from the first symptom.

A more aggressive approach, advocated by some experts, would be to begin treatment with a quinolone antibiotic (ciprofloxacin 500mg twice a day) from the first symptom, instead of or in addition to anti-diarrhoeal treatment. The authors prefer to reserve antibiotic treatment for cases that do not clear up easily with anti-diarrhoeal drugs alone, or for circumstances where it is crucial for the sufferer to be rendered symptom-free as quickly as possible.

When to seek medical attention

Symptoms that justify getting skilled advice and follow-up are: a temperature above 40°C; significant fever lasting longer than 48 hours; diarrhoea lasting longer than 4 days; severe diarrhoea with difficulty keeping up with fluid and salt replacement; and diarrhoea with blood. Laboratory tests may also be necessary.

Persistent diarrhoea

The commonest cause of diarrhoea persisting after returning home is giardiasis. Laboratory tests are worthwhile and essential to exclude other possible causes. However, a negative laboratory result may not completely rule out the possibility of giardiasis, and if the symptoms are convincing, presumptive treatment (such as with tinidazole, as described above, preferably taken under medical supervision) may be worthwhile.

Another important cause of persistent diarrhoea is lactose intolerance. This is not an infection, but a problem that frequently follows damage to the lining of the small intestine following one or more episodes of severe gastroenteritis. In this condition, lactose – the sugar present in milk and all milk products (yoghurt, cheese, and so on)

– is poorly digested and instead undergoes a fermentation process. This results in symptoms that are similar to those of giardiasis. There is no easy way of confirming the diagnosis, other than by excluding infective causes and completely eliminating lactose from the diet. It is usually necessary to avoid lactose for about 6 months.

OTHER COMMON INFECTIONS

Respiratory infections

Viral *upper respiratory tract infections* are more common in travellers, partly because of increased exposure to other people in crowded airports, aircraft, buses, and so on, and partly because of exposure to new strains of viruses from other regions to which the traveller has not previously developed immunity. Coughs and colds and 'flu are unpleasant but rarely life-threatening. These infections are self-limiting but symptomatic treatment with paracetamol or aspirin may help. Most sore throats are viral in origin and also get better with time. However, some may be bacterial. If there is evidence of pus (white spots) on the tonsils (*tonsillitis)* or at the back of the throat, it may be prudent to take antibiotics. Penicillin V or erythromycin (500mg, 4 times a day for a week) would be reasonable choices. Ampicillin should be avoided in these circumstances as it may lead to a nasty rash if the sore throat is due to glandular fever (infectious mononucleosis).

If an expedition member develops a cough with a fever and brings up purulent (yellow/green) sputum they may have *bronchitis* or *pneumonia*. The latter is more serious and is often accompanied by breathlessness and chest pain that is made worse by deep breathing. In these circumstances, antibiotic therapy with erythromycin (500mg, 4 times a day for a week) is appropriate.

Sinus infections can sometimes be a problem, presenting with nasal stuffiness, discomfort overlying the sinuses and sometimes a fever and headache. Although occasionally caused by viruses, most are bacterial in origin and complicate viral colds and 'flu. If 'flu or cold symptoms persist for longer than a week with new symptoms suggestive of *sinusitis*, an antibiotic such as Augmentin (375mg, 3 times a day for a week) should be considered.

Ear infections

These may be a particular problem for expeditions involving diving or caving. Sometimes the lining of the ear canal becomes infected (*otitis externa)* and is red and painful. This can usually be treated with antibiotic ear drops, such as Otosporin (2 drops, 3 times a day), and careful attention to keeping the ears as dry as possible. Rarely in adults the middle ear can become infected (*otitis media*). Again, pain is the main symptom and, if observed, the eardrum appears red. Oral antibiotics should settle this down, co-amoxiclav (Augmentin 375mg, 3 times a day for 5 days) being first choice.

Eye infections

Sometimes the small glands in the eyelash follicles in the eyelids become blocked and infected, producing a painful swelling called a *stye*. This will usually settle with topical antibiotics, such as chloramphenicol ointment. Warm compresses may also help the symptoms.

Conjunctivitis is not uncommon and is normally bacterial in origin. The best treatment is usually chloramphenicol ointment. Put a little snake of cream on the turned down lower eyelid. Pull the upper eyelid over it and massage gently. This should clear the infection in the course of a couple of days. It should be remembered that this condition is highly infectious so an affected person should not share face flannels or towels with others. Other eye infections are rare in otherwise healthy people, but trauma to the eye may lead to secondary infection. If trauma does occur urgent help should be sought, but if none is readily available it is appropriate to use chloramphenicol eye ointment prophylactically.

People who wear contact lenses, especially soft ones, are at increased risk of infection and need to be scrupulous with their hygiene. A widely present amoeba can occasionally infect the cornea, which can lead to serious scarring. It is important to discuss the situation with a contact lens practitioner before leaving home. If it is not possible to guarantee good hygiene, contact lens wearers should revert to spectacles.

Urinary tract infections

Women are at more risk of urinary infections than men mainly because of their comparatively short urethra. However, men over the age of 40 have an increasing chance of infection, often originating in the prostate gland. Infections of the urinary tract are usually limited to the bladder and produce a variety of possible symptoms including urinary frequency, pain or discomfort passing urine, and urgency. Sometimes the urine appears cloudy or smells offensive. If the infection ascends the urinary tract to the kidneys, the patient is usually more unwell with the above symptoms and has loin pain, fever and, sometimes, rigors (shivering). Most simple urinary tract infections can be treated with oral antibiotics. Co-amoxiclav (Augmentin 375mg, 3 times a day for 3 days) or ciprofloxacin (250mg, twice a day for 3 days) are all reasonable choices for empiric therapy. A good fluid intake is also important and proper hydration is good prophylaxis against urinary infection.

Women may sometimes be troubled by thrush, a vaginal yeast infection. Thrush occurs more commonly in tropical conditions and may also be triggered by taking antibiotics. Thrush can be treated using local clotrimazole (Canesten) cream and pessaries. Frequent sufferers should discuss the problem with their doctor before leaving home, and ensure that they travel with a suitable supply of medication.

Soft tissue infections

Infections of the skin and subcutaneous tissues are not uncommon in expedition members, sometimes complicating superficial wounds and sometimes newly arising. *Boils* are really small abscesses in the skin, often starting in an infected hair follicle, and are usually caused by staphylococci. When small they respond to antibiotics such as flucloxacillin (250–500mg tablets, 4 times a day for 5 days). If they are large and painful, or if the person is unwell, incision and drainage of the boil will lead to quicker resolution. *Insect bites* may also become infected, often with localised redness and sometimes with pustule formation. Again, flucloxacillin will help settle things down quickly.

Athlete's foot, or *tinea pedis*, is a fungal infection of the skin between the toes. This can be particularly tiresome for people with sweaty feet. Wash the feet thoroughly, and dust the feet and socks with Mycil or some similar antifungal dusting powder, or apply ointment, such as Canesten.

Sometimes large areas of skin on the legs become infected, usually with streptococci or staphylococci, and cause the leg to become painful, usually swollen, with the skin pink or red. Sometimes blisters appear in the skin. This condition is called *cellulitis* and requires antibiotics. If not treated quickly, the infection may spread further, necessitating intravenous or intramuscular antibiotics. Initially large oral doses of flucloxacillin (250–500mg, 4 times a day) or Augmentin (375mg, 3 times a day for 5 days) are the best treatments.

Minor wounds may become infected, particularly in hot and humid climates. Wounds should be cleaned with an antiseptic and kept covered. If they begin to look infected, flucloxacillin should be given.

Antihistamines can be used to suppress *allergic reactions* of various sorts and are useful in suppressing nettle-rash, itchy skin conditions, hay fever and the itch associated with insect bites. Remember that antihistamines all, to a varying extent, cause drowsiness. People who are at all drowsy should not drive. Loratradine (Clarityn), available over the counter, is very effective and only needs to be taken once a day at a dose of 10mg. Chlorpheniramine (Piriton) is a slightly sedating antihistamine but again is very effective taken as 4mg up to 6 times a day. People who are driving should not use this.

HIV and AIDS

HIV1 and HIV2 are retroviruses that invade certain human white blood cells (CD4 positive T lymphocytes) where they multiply, eventually destroying the cells. This leads to suppression of the body's immune system, rendering patients susceptible to a range of infections and malignant diseases (cancers) to which they would normally be resistant. When patients become immunodeficient in this way from HIV infection they are said to be suffering from acquired immunodeficiency syndrome (AIDS).

HIV infection is essentially a sexually transmitted disease. *Unprotected promiscuous sexual activity always carries a risk of HIV infection.* HIV can also be transmitted by transfusion of blood and blood products that have not been properly screened; by intravenous drug abuse when needles or syringes are shared with infected people; by needlestick injuries with contaminated needles (percutaneous exposure); and across the placenta from an infected mother to her fetus. However, the virus is delicate and does not survive for long unless it is in blood or body fluids. It does not fly through the air as an aerosol and is not transmitted by biting insects, handshakes, or lavatory seats.

HIV and AIDS are increasingly prevalent throughout the developing world, particularly in sub-Saharan Africa, South Asia and Latin America. In these areas HIV is spread mainly through heterosexual activity. In many African cities more than 80% of prostitutes are infected with HIV. There has been a steep increase in the incidence of HIV infection in South-east Asian countries, such as Thailand and the Philippines, and in India.

Prevention

For expedition members the message is simple: do not have unprotected sexual intercourse. A good-quality condom must be worn by the male partner. Unprotected sex also carries the risk of acquiring potentially severe hepatitis B infection, for a high proportion of prostitutes carry this virus as well as a wide range of familiar domestic and more exotic sexually transmitted diseases, such as gonorrhoea, chancroid, non-specific urethritis and syphilis.

At present, there is no vaccine against HIV infection and no immediate prospect of one being developed. The infection remains incurable. However, the appropriate use of anti-retroviral drugs, such as zidovudine, didanosine, zalcitabine and protease inhibitors, can prolong the median survival of patients with diagnosed AIDS to almost two years. A course of triple combination antiviral treatment is recommended for people who develop an acute feverish, glandular fever-like illness with sore throat and rash a few weeks after acquiring the infection. A 4-week course of antiviral drugs is recommended for those who have suffered an injury with a needle contaminated with HIV positive blood and may also be considered after unprotected sexual intercourse with someone proved or highly likely to be infected with HIV. In these cases treatment should start as soon as possible. If there is concern about a possible exposure to HIV infection, expert advice should be sought as a matter or urgency.

Avoiding contaminated needles and transfused blood in developing countries

Many infectious diseases can be spread in infected blood from person to person through the use of non-sterile needles and unscreened transfused blood. Some of the most important are HIV and other retroviruses, hepatitis B and other hepatitis viruses, malaria, relapsing fevers, South American trypanosomiasis (Chagas' disease) and haemorrhagic fever viruses. Intravenous drug abusers (main liners) are at particularly high risk. Of course, drugs of addiction have no place on an expedition for, apart from any long-term damaging effects on health, they will dangerously impair the competence and judgement of expedition members.

Earlier in this book it was pointed out that an accident is the greatest hazard facing all expeditions. It can be small, such as a cut that needs suturing or a cut that has become infected and needs injection of an antibiotic. Lone travellers and small expeditions must take with them a small kit of sterile medical equipment (see Chapter 3, page 27) and insist that the contents be used for any injections or suturing that may be necessary. For larger expeditions a more elaborate kit, containing "giving sets", plasma expanders, and so on, is now essential (see Chapter 3, page 27). It is wise for every traveller to have his or her blood group determined before departure. It may be that two or more members of an expedition have compatible blood. If it has been screened in a blood transfusion centre in the UK, it will automatically have been screened for HIV. Find out in advance where you can get access in the host country to screened blood supplies. It may also be possible to obtain cover from the Blood Care Foundation, a registered charity that arranges supplies of compatible blood for transfusion to be sent by courier in the event of an emergency, in return for a nominal fee paid in advance. Cover can be arranged through most travel clinics.

15 MALARIA AND OTHER TROPICAL DISEASES

David A. Warrell

MALARIA

Malaria is endemic in almost all parts of the tropical world as far north as southern Turkey, as far south as north-eastern South Africa, as far west as Mexico and as far east as Vanuatu in the western Pacific (Figure 15.2). The females of certain species of mosquito (genus *Anopheles*), which nearly always bite between dusk and dawn, transmit malaria (Figure 15.1). Four different species of malarial parasites commonly infect humans: life-threatening *Plasmodium falciparum* and the three so-called benign malarias, *P. vivax, P. ovale* and *P. malariae. Falciparum* malaria kills 1–2 million people each year and is particularly dangerous to those who have not acquired immunity to it by growing up in a malarious part of the world. About 2,000 cases of imported malaria are reported in the UK each year, but over the last few years the proportion of dangerous *P. falciparum* cases has increased to over 60%. Each year, a few people die of imported malaria in the UK and an unknown number die abroad. Most of these deaths could have been prevented by better education of the travellers, use of approved methods of prevention and prompt medical attention when a person falls ill.

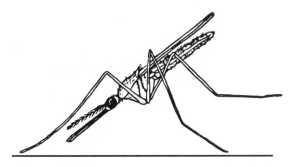

Figure 15.1   *An anopheles mosquito*

Prevention

TABLE 15.1 **PRINCIPLES OF PERSONAL PROTECTION AGAINST MALARIA**
1. **Awareness of risk:** vulnerable individuals, such as pregnant women, infants or immunocompromised people, should avoid entering a malarious area.
2. **Anti-mosquito measures:** kill, exclude, repel and avoid mosquitoes. • Sensible clothing (long sleeves, long trousers) between dusk and dawn. • Diethyltoluamide (DEET) – containing insect repellent applied to exposed skin. • Insecticide (pyrethroid) – impregnated mosquito bed net or screened accommodation sprayed with insecticide each evening. • Vaporising insecticide in the sleeping quarters (electrical, mosquito coil, knock-down insecticide).
3. **Chemoprophylaxis:** standard "safe" regimen – proguanil (Paludrine) plus chloroquine (other less safe drugs justified in some areas).
4. **Standby treatment:** Fansidar, mefloquine, quinine.
5. **In case of feverish illness within a few months of return: see a doctor and mention malaria.**

Assessing the risk

Within malarious countries, the areas of malaria transmission may be patchy, depending on environmental factors such as temperature, altitude and vegetation as well as the season. Thus there is no malarial transmission in some African capital cities that are at a comparatively high altitude, such as Addis Ababa and Nairobi, and in other areas malaria transmission occurs only during a brief rainy season. If possible, reliable local advice should be obtained about the status of malaria transmission in the area where, and at the time when, the expedition is to take place. Even within a transmission area, the risk of being bitten by an infected mosquito can vary from less than once per year to more than once per night. The chances of catching malaria during a two-week visit, while taking no protection at all, has been estimated at about 0.2% in Kenya and 1% in West Africa.

People who are especially vulnerable to malaria should seriously consider whether they need to enter the malarious area at all. These include pregnant women, infants and young children, and those who have had their spleens removed or are otherwise immunosuppressed.

Anti-mosquito measures

Since most malaria-transmitting mosquitoes bite in or near human dwellings during

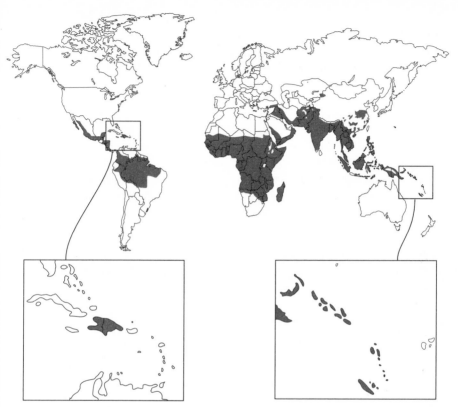

Figure 15.2   *World distribution of malaria, 1996*

the hours of darkness, the risk of infection can be reduced by insect-proofing sleeping quarters or by sleeping under a mosquito net. Individual, lightweight, self-supporting mosquito nets are available. Protection against mosquitoes and other biting invertebrates (sandflies, lice, fleas, bed bugs, and so on) is greatly enhanced by soaking the net in a pyrethroid insecticide such as permethrin (0.2g per sq metre of material every six months). Screens and curtains can also be impregnated with insecticide. In addition, bedrooms should be sprayed in the evening with a knockdown insecticide to kill any mosquitoes that may have entered the room during the day. Mosquitoes may also be killed or repelled by vaporising synthetic pyrethroids (Bioallethrin 4.2% w/w) on electrical heating devices (such as No Bite and Buzz Off) where electricity is available or over a methylated spirit burner (Travel Accessories UK Ltd, PO Box 10, Lutterworth, Leicester LE17 4FB). Burning cones or coils of mosquito repellent "incense" may also be effective. To avoid bites by any flying insect, light-coloured long-sleeved shirts and long trousers are preferable to vests and shorts. To avoid malaria-transmitting mosquito bites, this sensible clothing should be worn particularly after dark. Exposed areas of skin should be rubbed or sprayed with repellents containing N-N-diethyl-m-toluamide (DEET). Insecticide-containing soaps and suntan oil are available and clothes can be soaked in repellent solution.

Anti-malarial chemoprophylaxis

At one time comparatively harmless drugs, such as chloroquine (Nivaquine), pyrimethamine (Daraprim) and proguanil (Paludrine), gave a high degree of protection against malaria parasites. However, the rapid emergence of resistant strains of *P. falciparum* has made chemoprophylaxis much more difficult. In particular, chloroquine resistant strains of *P. falciparum* now predominate in most parts of the tropics except in Mexico and Central America, north-west of the Panama Canal, Haiti, parts of West Africa and the Middle East. The failure of travellers to take their antimalarial tablets regularly, and in particular to continue taking them for four weeks after leaving the malarious area, also reduces the effectiveness of chemoprophylaxis. During bouts of vomiting and diarrhoea (traveller's diarrhoea), these drugs may not be adequately absorbed. In choosing chemoprophylaxis, the risk of contracting malaria should be balanced against the risk of side-effects from the drug. This is illustrated by the case of mefloquine (Lariam) which has recently excited a heated debate. Although mefloquine is probably twice as effective as the chloroquine plus proguanil combination in preventing malaria in Africa, the incidence and severity of side-effects, especially in young women, is greater with mefloquine.

Chemoprophylactic drugs and combinations

1. Proguanil (Paludrine) and chloroquine (Nivaquine)

The combination of proguanil – 2 tablets (each of 100mg) every day – and chloroquine – 2 tablets (each of 150mg base) once a week – is the standard and most widely used prophylactic regimen in areas where *P. falciparum* is chloroquine resistant. It is safe in pregnancy and (in a lower dose) in children. The only side-effects are rare mouth ulcers, mild indigestion and hair loss. Chloroquine is still used because resistance is only relative and chloroquine still protects against the benign malarias in most parts of the world (see page 154). The combination is not completely effective and it should be pointed out to travellers that despite taking antimalarials they may still develop malaria. However, if they are on antimalarials they are unlikely to become seriously ill with malaria, but *they must seek medical treatment if they get a fever, especially during the first few months after returning from the malarious area.*

There is no evidence that chloroquine, taken in the doses recommended for prophylaxis against malaria, ever causes damage to the eyes in people who take the drug continuously for 5–6 years. Checks after chloroquine prophylaxis are therefore unnecessary, unless the individual has taken the drug for a very long time (more than 6 years continuously) and the total cumulative dose approaches 100g.

2. Mefloquine (Lariam)

This drug is effective against some multiresistant *P. falciparum* strains. It has some unpleasant side-effects: nausea, stomach ache and diarrhoea in 10–15% of people who take it; insomnia and nightmares; giddiness and ataxia (unsteadiness and inco-ordination) in some; and, much more serious, a rare "acute brain syndrome" consist-ing of psychological changes and in very rare cases generalised convulsions (epileptic attacks). For these reasons it is recommended for use only in areas with a high risk of resistant malaria (such as some parts of Africa, the Amazon region and South-east Asia). The dose is 1 tablet (of 250mg) a week.

3. Maloprim, Deltaprim

This is a combination of dapsone 100mg and pyrimethamine 12.5mg. When used, 1 tablet a week (for example, every Sunday), no more, no less, should be taken. Unfor-tunately, a few people are sensitive to this combination (although many have taken large amounts of dapsone on its own in the treatment of leprosy without coming to any harm). Twenty well-documented cases of aplastic anaemia or agranulocytosis have been recorded when patients were taking 2 tablets a week. More recently two further cases have been found where only 1 tablet a week of Maloprim produced sim-ilar side-effects. Although the chance of producing this unusual side-effect is remote, it can no longer be ignored. Over 20 million tablets have been consumed, so the risk is small. Recently, a few cases of severe, progressive, eosinophilic pneumonitis have been reported, caused by the standard dose of Maloprim. It can be said with some confidence that if people have been taking Maloprim in the past for 6 weeks or more, they are unlikely to develop side-effects and they can be given Maloprim with im-punity in the future.

In areas where *vivax* malaria is endemic 2 tablets of chloroquine should be taken every week as well because some strains of *vivax* malaria are insensitive to Maloprim. It is a good plan to check blood counts a fortnight after starting Maloprim for the first time, before travel. If the count is normal all is likely to be well (no drop in platelets, no marked rise in the MCV and no eosinophilia); the presence of eosinophilia is perhaps a warning that the patient may be allergic to the drug. If an individual's fingernails and lips turn blue a few hours after taking the first dose of Maloprim an alternative drug should be found. It might be wise to advise the trav-eller not to take cotrimoxazole (Septrin, Bactrim) while on Maloprim, for the sulphonamide component added to the Maloprim might give toxic side-effects. Antimicrobials without sulpha (such as trimethoprim) are preferable.

4. Doxycycline (Vibramycin)

This tetracycline antibiotic has proved useful for prophylaxis in areas where meflo-quine resistance is prevalent, such as the Thai-Cambodian border region. It gives some protection against other travellers' diseases such as typhus, leptospirosis and some types of traveller's diarrhoea. One 100mg tablet a day should be taken. Side-effects include photosensitive rashes, skin irritation, diarrhoea and oral/oesophageal or vaginal thrush. It should not be used by pregnant women and young children.

Choice of prophylactic drug/combination in different geographical areas

- Middle East, West Asia, Indian subcontinent, Africa (except high-risk areas), parts of South America (except Amazon region of Brazil), China: use proguanil plus chloroquine.
- Mexico, Central America, Haiti, Dominican Republic, parts of South America (except Amazon region of Brazil): use chloroquine.
- High-risk areas of Africa (for example, West Kenya by Lake Victoria), Amazon region of Brazil, South-east Asia (except Thai-Cambodian border region): use mefloquine.
- West Pacific, New Guinea: use Maloprim plus chloroquine, or doxycycline.
- Thai-Cambodian border region: use doxycycline.
- Turkey, Egypt, Mauritius (rural, seasonal only): use chloroquine or proguanil.

During pregnancy it is vital for the expectant mother to take antimalarials or, preferably, to avoid entering a malarious area. The hazards of getting malaria, particularly falciparum malaria, during pregnancy are great. The remote hazard of adverse effects on the baby of the antimalarial drugs is far outweighed by the advantages. Chloroquine plus proguanil as outlined above should be used. Maloprim and other pyrimethamine containing drugs should be avoided during pregnancy and lactation for fear of damage to the fetus and the newborn child.

All medication must be started the Sunday before leaving for the malarious area (unless you are going on a Monday, in which case start the previous Sunday) and continued for 4 weeks after return (2 weeks for mefloquine).

Please remember that no antimalarial drug is perfect. Much depends on whether it is taken regularly. If you are ill at all after your return you should consult your doctor and *mention the possibility of malaria*. If there is *any doubt* you should be referred to an infectious disease unit for exclusion of malaria. Please remember that if you have been taking an antimalarial it may be difficult to find the parasites and yet you may be quite ill.

Standby treatment for malaria in high-risk areas

In some parts of Indo-China, such as the Thai borders with Burma, Cambodia and Laos, in parts of tropical East and Central Africa and the Amazon region, *falciparum malaria* may break through prophylaxis. If you are going to these areas you would be wise to take a supply of *quinine*, 600mg to be taken 8 hourly for 7 days if you get a fever. *Mefloquine*, 2 tablets (each of 250mg) repeated after 8 hours (1,000mg total for an adult, 20mg/kg for children), is an alternative unless that is the drug you have been taking for prophylaxis. *Fansidar*, 3 tablets at once, is also a useful standby treatment in Africa.

Prevention of the "benign" malarias (*vivax*, *ovale* and *malariae*)

Weekly chloroquine or mefloquine will usually prevent *vivax*, *ovale* and *malariae* malarias. However, *P. vivax* and *P. ovale* can establish themselves in the liver despite chloroquine prophylaxis and may re-emerge to cause relapsing infections months or years later. *Primaquine*, 15mg a day for 2 weeks, will usually eradicate the liver cycle and should be given to travellers who have spent more than a few months in areas where these species are endemic. In parts of Indonesia, particularly Irian Jaya, and in Papua New Guinea, Thailand, the Philippines and Solomon Islands, *vivax* malaria may not be eradicated by the usual 2-week course of primaquine. In these cases a 4-week course of 22.5mg of primaquine each day should be given after the person returns home.

In New Guinea and adjacent areas of Indonesia (for example, Lombok), *vivax* malaria has become resistant to chloroquine. A double dose of chloroquine or mefloquine followed by high-dose primaquine can be used to treat such resistant infections. **Advice on malarial prophylaxis can be obtained from the following Tropical Medicine Units.**

Malaria Reference Laboratory
Office hours: +44 171 6367921
24-hour helpline: +44 891 600350

Hospital for Tropical Diseases
Tel. +44 839 337733

London School of Tropical Medicine
Tel. +44 171 6368636

Liverpool School of Tropical Medicine
Tel. +44 151 7089393

Oxford University Centre for Tropical Medicine
Tel. +44 1865 220968/220970

Birmingham Heartlands Hospital, Department of Infection and Tropical Medicine
Tel. +44 121 7666611

OTHER TROPICAL DISEASES

Bilharzia (schistosomiasis)

This fluke infection occurs in Africa, the Middle East, eastern South America, China and South-east Asia (Figure 15.3). Infection is acquired through contact with fresh water from lakes and sluggish rivers, usually by bathing or washing with water taken from these sources. Infected humans contaminate the lake by defaecating or urinating into it and infect, in turn, the intermediate snail hosts. Snails release tiny cercariae into the water which burrow through the skin of bathers. The earliest symptom of possible infection is "swimmer's itch", experienced soon after contact with infected water. Some people develop an acute feverish illness associated with an urticarial rash and blood eosinophilia a few weeks after infection. Later symptoms include passage of cloudy or frankly bloodstained urine or dysentery and, rarely, ascending paralysis and loss of sensation in the lower limbs.

Travellers usually get worried about bilharzia when they get back from their trip and remember bathing in forbidden lakes or hear that another member of the party has been diagnosed as having schistosomiasis. Diagnosis is confirmed by finding ova in stool, urine or rectal biopsies, or by a blood test. Treatment is fairly simple with 1–2 doses of praziquantel (Biltricide).

Prevent bilharzia by not bathing in sluggish fresh water sources in endemic areas. Local advice may be misleading. Lake Malawi, officially declared free of bilharzia, has been the source of many imported cases of bilharzia in the UK over the last few years.

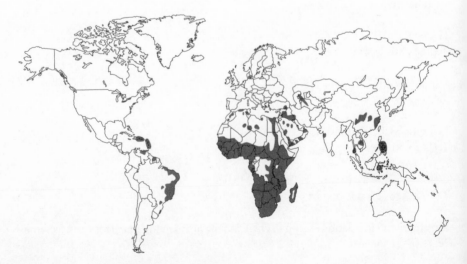

Figure 15.3 *World distribution of bilharzia*

River blindness (onchocerciasis)

In parts of East, West, Central and Southern Africa, Mexico and Central America and north-eastern South America (Figure 15.4), pernicious little black flies (for example, *Simulium damnosum*) transmit this infection from human to human in the vicinity of fast-flowing rivers and streams. The adult filarial worms live in subcutaneous nodules, especially around the waist. They produce enormous numbers of microfilariae which cause irritation and changes in the pigmentation and texture of the skin and damage the eyes, eventually causing river blindness. Foreign travellers have contracted onchocerciasis after only brief stops in the transmission zone.

Diagnosis is supported by finding blood eosinophilia and is confirmed by microscopical detection of wriggling microfilariae in skin snips taken in affected areas. There is also a blood test of moderate specificity.

Treatment with ivermectin is effective, but may cause a temporary but damaging exacerbation of lesions in the eye and skin and should therefore be supervised in a hospital.

Prevent infection by wearing light-coloured clothing (long sleeves and long trousers) and applying DEET-containing repellents to exposed areas of skin.

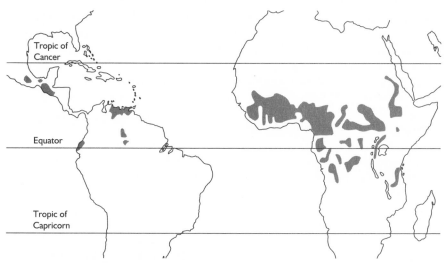

Figure 15.4   *World distribution of onchocerciasis*

Sleeping sickness (African trypanosomiasis)

Tsetse flies (*Glossina*) transmit trypanosomes (*Trypanosoma brucei gambiense*) between humans and *T.b. rhodesiense* between humans and animal reservoir hosts in a number of smallish areas scattered throughout West, Central, East and Southern Africa (Figure 15.5). A small ulcer with a scab may appear at the site of the infected

157

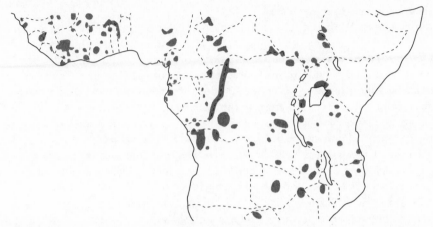

Figure 15.5   *African trypanosomiasis (sleeping sickness): distribution of infection in man*

tsetse fly bite and, within the next few days, intermittent fever begins associated with headache, loss of appetite and enlargement of lymph glands, especially in the posterior triangle of the neck. Eventually, there is invasion of the central nervous system and patients become apathetic, sleepy and eventually comatose.

The diagnosis is confirmed by finding motile trypanosomes in lymph node aspirates, blood or cerebrospinal fluid. Treatment is difficult, especially after invasion of the central nervous system. Foreign travellers, especially to the game parks of Eastern and Southern Africa, have been infected with sleeping sickness.

Dengue fever (Break bone fever)

Mosquitoes such as *Aedes aegypti and A. albopictus* transmit dengue viruses from human to human in almost every part of the tropics, notably in South-east Asia and the Caribbean, and increasingly in urban areas (Figure 15.6). In most foreign travellers, dengue causes an acute fever associated with headache, backache and pains in the muscles and joints ("break bone" fever). The most obvious reddish blotchy rash often appears after a temporary lull in the fever. Petechial haemorrhages may be found in the skin and conjunctivae. The blood count usually shows leucopenia with relative lymphocytosis and thrombocytopenia. The diagnosis can be confirmed by testing two blood samples, one taken immediately and the other 2 weeks after the acute illness.

Severe, life-threatening forms of dengue (dengue haemorrhagic fever and dengue shock syndrome) occur almost exclusively in children who have been brought up in endemic areas and are suffering their second dengue infection.

Treatment of dengue fever is symptomatic (bed rest, control of fever and paracetamol).

Prevention is by wearing sensible clothing (see above) during the daytime biting period and applying DEET-containing repellents to exposed skin surfaces.

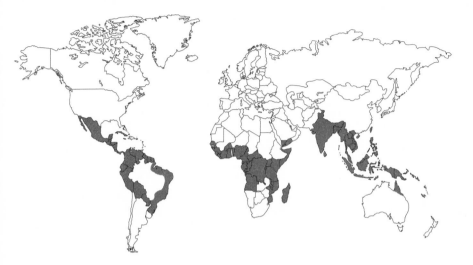

Figure 15.6   *World distribution of dengue virus since 1960*

Rabies

Rabies or hydrophobia (literally fear of water) is a virus disease of mammals which is usually transmitted to man by a dog bite. Although dogs are the most important source of human rabies worldwide, some countries have other vector species, such as cats, wolves, foxes, jackals, skunks, mongooses, racoons, vampire bats (Caribbean and Latin America only) and insectivorous bats. Rabies occurs in almost every country (see Figure 2.7, page 15); the fortunate exceptions include Antarctica, Australia, Scandinavian countries (except Greenland and Svalbard), Malaysia, New Guinea, New Zealand, Japan, the UK and some smaller islands. It is especially common in parts of Latin America, the Indian subcontinent, Vietnam, Thailand and the Philippines. The disease probably causes around 50,000 human deaths each year.

Rabies virus can enter the body in a number of ways. Virus in an animal's saliva can penetrate skin that has been broken by a bite or graze; and can invade unbroken mucous membranes, such as those covering the eye and lining the mouth and nose. Very rarely, the virus has been inhaled, for example, from the atmosphere of caves infested with insectivorous bats. Transmission of rabies from human to human must be excessively rare, but at least eight patients are known to have developed rabies after receiving infected corneal grafts. After the virus has entered the body, one of two things may happen. The virus may be killed by antiseptics or immune mechanisms before it does any harm; or it may spread along the nerves to reach the brain where it

159

multiplies and causes inflammation (encephalitis) which is almost invariably fatal. The incubation period (the interval between the bite and the first symptoms of encephalitis) is usually about 2 months but can vary from 4 days to many years. The earliest symptom is itching or tingling at the site of the healed bite. Later the patient may develop headache, fever, confusion, hallucinations and hydrophobia. Attempts to drink water induce spasm of the muscles of breathing and swallowing associated with an indescribable terror. Death supervenes after a few days of these terrible symptoms. In a form of rabies which is less often recognised there is spreading paralysis without excitement or hydrophobia. There have been only six known survivors from rabies encephalitis: they were treated with intensive care.

Prevention
Details of pre-exposure immunisation are given in Chapter 2 (see Table 2.1, page 8).

Stroking stray dogs and apparently tame wild animals, keeping carnivores as pets and other unnecessary contact with mammals should be avoided in areas where rabies is endemic. Irrespective of the risk of rabies, mammal (including human) bites and scratches and licks on mucous membranes or broken skin should be cleaned immediately.

First, scrub with soap and water under a running tap if possible, or else in sterilised water, for at least 5 minutes. The best virucidal agents are 40–70% alcohol (gin and whisky contain more than 40% alcohol) and povidone iodine. Mammal bites are frequently contaminated by a variety of micro-organisms other than rabies virus, so a doctor or the expedition nurse should be consulted. Immediate thorough cleaning of the wound is of the utmost importance in preventing infection.

Second, rabies should be considered if it is known to occur in the area. The decision whether or not to give post-exposure vaccination and rabies immune serum is made by a doctor. Ideally, it is based on examination of the biting animal; but usually this is not possible. The species of animal, its behaviour, the circumstances of the bite and, in the case of a domestic animal, when it was last vaccinated, are useful pieces of information. The decision must be made as soon as possible by a doctor working in the area where the bite occurred. On no account should it be delayed until patients return to their own country. *If in doubt, vaccinate.* Modern vaccines such as HDCV, PVRV, PCEC and PDEV are potent and safe. They require fewer injections than the older type of nervous tissue vaccine which was given on at least 21 consecutive days under the skin of the abdomen. The old Semple vaccine deserved its reputation for being dangerous; the tissue culture vaccines are safe. Timely cleaning of the bite wound combined with vaccination and use of immune serum has proved very effective in preventing rabies.If someone who has received pre-exposure immunisation is later bitten by a suspected rabid animal, immunity must be boosted with 2 injections of vaccine on days 0 and 7.

If the bitten person has not previously been immunised, a full course of post-exposure vaccination is required. The conventional course, using modern vaccines (detailed above), involves intramuscular injections of 1 whole vial (0.5ml or 1ml of reconstituted vaccine) intramuscularly on days 0, 3, 7, 14 and 30. These individuals should also receive a dose of rabies immune globulin. Half is infiltrated around the bite wound and the rest given intramuscularly into the front of the thigh. The dose of equine rabies immune globulin is 40iu/kg body weight; the dose of human rabies immune globulin is 20iu/kg body weight.

If rapid induction of active immunity is required and there is a shortage of vaccine, modern vaccines can be used effectively and economically by employing an alternative *multiple* site intradermal regimen. On day 0, 1 ampoule of vaccine is divided between eight different sites (both deltoids, both thighs, both sides of the umbilicus and above both shoulder blades at the back). At each site 0.1ml (in the case of 1ml ampoules of vaccine) or 0.05ml (in the case of 0.5ml ampoules of vaccine) is injected intradermally (so that it raises a small *peau d'orange* papule). On day 7, 4 intradermal injections are given (both deltoids and both thighs) and single intradermal injections are given on days 30 and 90.

It is essential to take rabies seriously and minimise the risk of infection by avoiding potentially rabid animals. If bitten by a suspected rabid animal and no suitable vaccine is available, the individual should be repatriated without delay so as to start post-exposure prophylaxis as soon as possible.

For dog bite/rabies queries contact:

Public Health Laboratory Health Centre
Virus Reference Laboratory
Tel. +44 181 2004400 ext. 324

16 VENOMOUS AND POISONOUS ANIMALS

David A. Warrell

ATTACKS BY LARGE ANIMALS

Large animals, wild and domestic, should be treated with respect; they may not be as tame as they appear. Lions, leopards, hyenas, domestic dogs, jackals, wolves, elephants, hippopotamuses, buffaloes, domestic cattle, domestic and wild pigs, ostriches and even rams have been responsible for occasional human deaths. Sharks kill about 50 people each year. Crocodiles (Figure 16.1) claim many human lives. It is extremely foolhardy for travellers to bathe in rivers regarded as dangerous by the local inhabitants. A Peace Corps worker in Ethiopia did this in 1967 and was promptly killed and eaten by the resident crocodile. More recently, an 18-year-old Scottish girl was killed by a crocodile while working in Tanzania.

Figure 16.1   *The Nile crocodile* Crocodilus niloticus – *a threat to human lives (D.A. Warrell)*

VENOMOUS ANIMALS

Travellers in tropical countries usually have an exaggerated fear of snakes, scorpions and other venomous animals. Most parts of the world, especially the tropical regions, harbour animals with potentially lethal venoms, but local farmers and children, rather than travellers, suffer. Thus snake bite is a major cause of death among some tribes of the Ecuadorian and Brazilian jungles, and among the inhabitants of some parts of Burma, Nigeria and Sri Lanka; and many children die of scorpion stings in parts of Mexico and North Africa. Yet the author knows of no recent case of a European traveller being killed by a venomous bite or sting.

Before travelling to a tropical country it is worth finding out about local venomous species and trying to discover if there is a national centre for antivenom production, supply and treatment. The use of antivenom (also called antivenin, antivenene or anti-snake-bite serum) requires medical training. If an expedition is going to an extremely remote and snake-infested area it might be wise to collect some antivenom from the regional centre and to ensure that there is someone in the party who has been trained to use it safely. Otherwise, rely on local medical services, but enquire about them in advance. Before buying antivenoms manufactured in Europe, seek expert advice about their effectiveness against the venoms of the species which are important causes of bites or stings in the area of your expedition.

Snake bite
Prevention
Snakes never attack humans without provocation and so the risk of snake bite can be reduced as follows. Avoid snakes and snake charmers. Do not disturb, corner or attack snakes and never handle them, even if they are said to be harmless or appear to be dead. Even a severed head can bite. If you corner a snake by mistake, keep absolutely still until it has slithered away (this demands enormous *sang froid*), because snakes strike only at moving objects. Never walk in undergrowth or deep sand without boots, socks and long trousers; and at night always carry a light. Never collect firewood or dislodge logs and boulders with your bare hands and never put your hand or push sticks into burrows or holes. Avoid climbing trees or rocks which are covered with dense foliage, and do not put your hands on sunbaked ledges you cannot see when climbing. Never swim in rivers matted with vegetation or in muddy estuaries where there are likely to be sea snakes.

Figure 16.2   *Venom apparatus of the tropical rattlesnake* Crotalus durissus terrificus
(D.A. Warrell)

Treatment of snake bite

TABLE 16.1   **TREATMENT OF SNAKE BITE**
1. Reassure the bitten patient. 2. Cover the bite with a clean dressing. 3. Immobilise the bitten limb and stop the patient exercising. 4. Treat pain with paracetamol tablets. 5. Transport patient immediately to hospital. 6. DO NOT attempt to catch or kill the snake. 7. Avoid traditional remedies.

First aid treatment of snake bite should be given by the person on the spot.

First, reassure the patient, who may be terrified by the thought of sudden death. The grounds for reassurance are that only a small minority of snake species are dangerously venomous to man and even the most notorious species, such as cobras, often bite without injecting enough venom to be harmful. The risk and rapidity of death from snake bite has been greatly exaggerated. Lethal doses of venom usually take hours (cobras, mambas, sea snakes, and so on) or days (vipers, rattlesnakes and other pit vipers, and so on) to kill a man, not seconds or minutes as is commonly believed. *Correct treatment is very effective.*

Second, cover the site of the bite with a clean dressing.

Third, immobilise the bitten limb with a splint or sling and arrange immediate transport to a hospital, a dispensary or to the expedition medical officer. The patient must avoid exercising the bitten limb.

Do not attempt to catch or kill the snake, but if it has been killed already take it with you; it is useful clinical evidence. *However, it must not be handled with bare hands even if it appears to be dead.*

Avoid traditional remedies (incisions, suction, tourniquets, electric shock, snake stone, and so on) which do more harm than good. For example:

- Do not apply a tourniquet (ligature or tight band) unless you are absolutely certain that it is one whose venom contains a dangerous neurotoxin (for example, cobra, krait, mamba, sea snake, Australian tiger snake, taipan, etc). If a tourniquet is used it must be tightly applied above the bite – around the upper arm or thigh. To avoid gangrene it must be released after 30 minutes. A much safer and less painful method of reducing absorption of the injected venom is to bind the whole of the bitten limb as tightly as you would a sprained ankle, starting around the fingers or toes, using a long stretchy crepe bandage (10cm wide, 4.5m long) and incorporating a splint (Figure 16.3).

These methods should not be used after bites by snakes whose venoms cause a lot of local swelling and gangrene (for example, most vipers and some cobras).

- Do not suck at the wound, cut it with a razor blade, introduce potassium permanganate crystals, apply ice or electric shocks, or interfere in any other way.
- Do not give aspirin which may cause bleeding.
- Do not give antivenom which can be dangerous and should be administered only by a doctor, nurse or dispenser who has emergency drugs (epinephrine/

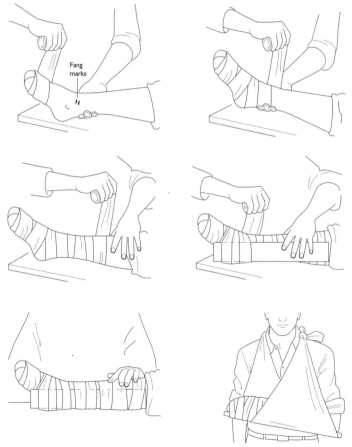

Figure 16.3   *Compression/immobilisation method for the treatment of snake bite on the leg or arm (Courtesy of Australian Venom Research Unit, University of Melbourne)*

adrenaline, antihistamine and corticosteroid) to deal with antivenom reactions should they occur. If you have your own supply of antivenom take it with you to hospital where the doctor or other trained staff can administer it.

Advice for the expedition medical officer
Absence of local swelling 4 hours after a bite by a viper, rattlesnake or other pit viper suggests that no venom was injected and that no further treatment is necessary. However, bites by some snakes with neurotoxic venoms (mambas, kraits, cobras, and so on) may not cause any local swelling, but may lead to more systemic effects.

Indications for antivenom treatment
1. Bleeding from gums, nose, gastrointestinal tract or any other site distant from the bite itself, which started spontaneously after the bite, and persistent bleeding from wounds (such as venepuncture sites).
2. Failure of the patient's blood to clot if placed in a new, clean, dry glass tube and left undisturbed for 20 minutes.
3. Signs of nervous system involvement such as drooping eyelids, difficulty in swallowing and breathing, pain, stiffness and paralysis of skeletal muscles, and extreme drowsiness or unconsciousness.
4. Passage of dark red, brown or black urine (haemoglobinuria or myoglobinuria).
5. Signs of heart involvement such as low or falling blood pressure, unusually slow pulse rate or irregular rhythm.
6. Swelling of more than half the bitten limb, swelling after bites on the fingers and toes, or swelling after bites by snakes whose venom is known to cause gangrene (for example, most vipers and rattlesnakes, some cobras).

Note: antivenom should never be given unless at least one of these six signs is definitely present.

Slight local swelling alone is not an indication for antivenom. Never give antivenom unless you have epinephrine (adrenaline) available to treat severe reactions to the antivenom. The adult dose of epinephrine (adrenaline) is 0.5ml of a 1 in 1,000 solution (1mg/ml) given intramuscularly.

Choice of appropriate antivenom
Before giving antivenom make sure that its range of specificity includes the snake that has bitten your patient. Some knowledge of Latin scientific names is useful, for example: *Naja*, cobra; *Dendroaspis*, mamba; *Bungarus*, krait; *Micrurus*, coral snake; *Bitis*, African puff adder and relatives; *Echis*, carpet viper; *Bothrops*, fer de lance; *Trimeresurus*, pit vipers; *Crotalus*, rattlesnake. It may have been possible to identify the biting snake; or its venom may have produced a diagnostic clinical sign, such as incoagulable blood caused by the carpet viper in the northern half of Africa. Other-

wise, a polyspecific antivenom with activity against the principal venomous species of the region is used.

Caution: do not give antivenom which is opaque. The change from a clear to cloudy solution indicates loss of activity and increased danger of reactions. Expiry dates can be ignored provided that the solution is crystal clear. Manufacturers' instructions included in packs of antivenom may be misleading.

How to give antivenom
For maximum effect, antivenom should be given directly into a vein, by slow intravenous injection (2ml per minute) or slow intravenous infusion of antivenom diluted approximately 50:50 in sterile isotonic saline. The initial dose depends on the type of antivenom, species of snake involved and severity of symptoms, but a typical starting dose is 4–5 10ml ampoules. This is repeated after a few hours if the life-threatening condition such as bleeding or weakness of the breathing muscles is not cured, or if the blood remains incoagulable after 6 hours. The patient should be watched for signs of an antivenom reaction, namely: fever, itching, rash, vomiting, breathlessness and wheezing, increase in pulse rate and fall in blood pressure. If this happens, give a 0.5ml injection of 1 in 1,000 epinephrine (adrenaline) solution intramuscularly; this can be repeated after 10 minutes if it is not effective. Reactions are likely to be severe in those who suffer from asthma, eczema and other allergic disorders.

Only in an extreme emergency should medically unqualified people give antivenom; for example, the victim is many hours away from medical care, has signs of severe envenoming (see above) and seems to be getting worse. Deep intramuscular injections at multiple sites into the front and side of the thighs (*not the buttocks*) can then be used. The sites should be massaged to increase absorption of antivenom and firm pressure then applied to injection sites to prevent bleeding.

Treatment of complications
1. Massive external bleeding or leakage of blood and tissue fluid into a swollen limb may leave the patient with an inadequate circulating volume. Transfusion with blood products or plasma expanders may be needed.
2. Respiratory paralysis may require mouth-to-mouth or more sophisticated forms of artificial ventilation. Neurotoxic envenoming by some species (such as cobras, Australasian death adders) responds dramatically to anticholinesterase drugs such as edrophonium, neostigmine or physostigmine. The test dose is 10mg of edrophonium (Tensilon) by slow iv injection after 0.6mg of atropine (*adult doses*). If there is an improvement in muscle power within the next 20 minutes, continue treatment with neostigmine sc.
3. Secondary infection may be introduced by the snake's fangs or local surgery at

the bite site. Patients with infected wounds and those with local gangrene should be treated with antibiotics and a tetanus toxoid booster. Gangrenous tissue should be excised surgically and the skin defect covered immediately with split skin grafts.

Note on spitting cobras
In Africa and parts of South-east Asia there are populations of cobras which can spray their venom forward from the fang tips for a distance of more than a metre towards the glint of the eyes of an aggressor. This is a defensive reaction. Venom entering the eyes or landing on other mucous membranes causes severe local pain and watering and can result in ulceration of the cornea. Treatment is the same as for any chemical injury to the eye. The eye should be irrigated with generous volumes of any bland fluid available (water, milk or even urine). Pain-killing drugs such as paracetamol can be given by mouth. 1% adrenaline (epinephrine) eye drops are said to relieve pain dramatically. Ideally, the eye should be examined by a doctor for evidence of corneal abrasion. If in doubt, antibiotics such as chloramphenicol or tetracycline eye ointment should be applied for several days.

VENOMOUS MARINE ANIMALS

Sea snakes
These are encountered mainly by fishermen in the tropical waters of the Indo-Pacific region. The principal symptoms of envenoming are drooping eyelids, lockjaw, pains, stiffness, tenderness and paralysis of skeletal muscles, passing of dark (Coca-Cola coloured) urine (myoglobinuria) and cardiac complications related to hyperkalaemia. Treatment is as described above.

Venomous fish
Many species of marine and freshwater fish have venomous spines on their gills, fins or tail. Stings occur when the fish are handled by fishermen or are trodden on by bathers. Some species attack swimmers and scuba divers around coral reefs. There is immediate excruciating pain and swelling at the site of the sting. Severe systemic effects may follow. These include vomiting, diarrhoea, sweating, irregular heart beat, fall in blood pressure, spasm or paralysis of muscles including respiratory muscles, and fits.

Treatment
Forewarned is forearmed. If your expedition has an extensive programme, say on coral reefs, try to get maximum information about dangerous species locally. The venomous spine of stingrays, which is often barbed, should be removed. Local symptoms are rapidly relieved by immersing the stung limb in hot but not scalding water. Test the

temperature with your own elbow. If you have a thermometer, the temperature should not exceed 45°C. Alternatively, 1% lignocaine or some other local anaesthetic can be injected, for example, as a ring block in the case of stung digits. Specific antivenom for some of the most dangerous species (such as stone fish, genus *Synanceja*) is available in some parts of the world. Patients may require mouth-to-mouth respiration and external cardiac massage. Atropine (0.6mg by subcutaneous injection for adults) should be given if there is a very slow pulse rate and low blood pressure.

Stingrays
The stingray attacks only when frightened and usually only when trodden upon. If it is known that there are stingrays about, it is wise to shuffle your feet or prod the ocean floor with a stick to make your presence known. Spines may be large enough to cause serious mechanical injury and are often left embedded in the wound together with the covering membrane. These foreign bodies are bound to cause infection if they are not removed. The stingray produces a heat labile venom so immersion of the stung part in hot but not scolding water (not more than 45°C) will destroy the toxin and relieve the pain.

Jellyfish, Portuguese man o'war and other coelenterates
Contact with the tentacles produces lines of very painful blisters. The venom of some species, such as the notorious box jellyfish (*Chironex, Chiropsalmus*) of tropical waters, can cause severe systemic effects, including cardiorespiratory arrest.

Treatment
Adherent fragments of tentacles must be removed (but *not* with your fingers) before more of their venomous nematocysts can discharge. Vinegar or dilute acetic acid effectively inactivates the penetrating nematocyst of box jellyfish, but many of the remedies that have been recommended in the past, such as methylated spirits, other alcohols and sunburn lotions, will stimulate massive discharge of nematocysts embedded in the patient. Antivenom is available in some of the worst-affected areas such as northern Australia. Severe cases may require mouth-to-mouth respiration and cardiac massage.

Sea urchins
The venomous spines and grapples of some sea urchins may become deeply embedded in the skin, usually of the sole of the foot when the animal has been trodden upon. Soften the skin with salicylic acid ointment and then pare down the epidermis to a depth at which the spines can be removed with forceps. Ordinary sea urchin prickles are absorbed quite rapidly provided they are broken into small pieces in the skin. Only if they have penetrated into a joint or if there is evidence of infection is surgical removal necessary.

Molluscs: octopuses and cone shells

Two species of small blue- and black-ringed octopuses of the Indo-Australasian region can cause fatal envenoming by biting. There are many species of beautiful cone shells in tropical waters. These sting by harpooning and implanting a venom-charged arrowhead. Beware of handling these attractive animals. Deaths have occurred but no antivenoms are available.

Poisoning from ingestion of fish and shellfish

Extensive feelings of pins and needles, paralysis, itching, diarrhoea, vomiting and shock can follow a few minutes or hours after eating various molluscs and fish. A large number of species in many parts of the world can cause these symptoms at various seasons of the year. Famous examples are pufferfish, red snapper, barracuda, tuna and mackerel. Treatment attempts to eliminate the toxic materials from the gut by promoting vomiting and diarrhoea with emetics and purges. Some symptoms may respond to antihistamine drugs and bronchodilators, but in severe cases assisted ventilation will be required until paralysis of the breathing muscles has worn off. Prevent these poisonings by taking local advice. "Red tides" may warn of shellfish poisoning. Avoid eating very large fish, all parts of the fish other than the flesh (muscle) and some notorious species (such as Moray eels).

VENOMOUS ARTHROPODS

Stings by bees, wasps and hornets (*Hymenoptera*)

In normal people many stings, probably hundreds, would be required to introduce enough venom to kill. A man in Zimbabwe survived more than 2,000 stings. But a small number of people have acquired hypersensitivity and could be killed by a single sting. Systemic symptoms suggest hypersensitivity: generalised tingling with rashes (urticaria, weals, nettle-rash or hives), swelling of the lips, tongue and throat, flushing, dizziness, collapse, wheezing, loss of control of bowels and bladder and unconsciousness within half an hour of the sting.

Prevention and treatment

It is possible to confirm hypersensitivity by blood or skin tests and to desensitise the patient using purified venom, but this takes a long time. People who know or suspect that they are hypersensitive should be taught how to give themselves a subcutaneous injection of 0.3ml or 0.5ml of 1 in 1,000 or 0.1% epinephrine (adrenaline – adult dose) and should carry this with them on the expedition (Epilen, Ana-Pen or Min-i-Jet self-injectable adrenaline kits with a ¼ inch long 25 gauge needle). They should wear a Medic-Alert tag in case they are found unconscious (Medic-Alert Foundation International, 12 Bridge Wharf, 156 Caledonian Road, London N1 9UU, tel. +44 171 8333034).

In tropical countries, especially Africa and Mexico, Central and South America, rock climbers and other travellers have occasionally been attacked by large swarms of angry bees, and some fatal falls have resulted. Some of these accidents could have been prevented if local advice had been sought. Thundery weather is known to upset bees. In the face of an attack, the best tried methods of evasion seem to be to run very fast or to immerse yourself in water. The climber should appreciate that a fall is probably the greatest danger. After securing himself he will have to rely on protection afforded by anorak, rucksack or tent. In South America about 100 people die each year after being attacked by furious swarms of Africanised honey bees. The principal effects of multiple stings in the non-hypersensitive subject are haemolysis, rhabdomyolysis (breakdown of skeletal muscle), bronchospasm, pneumonitis and kidney failure. No antivenom is available.

Stings by ants, beetles, moths and caterpillars
These insects, in particular the brightly coloured, hairy caterpillars, can cause severe problems: local pain, inflammation, nettle-rash, blistering and arthritis on contact and, in Venezuela and Brazil, systemic bleeding and incoagulable blood.

Figure 16.4 *Brazilian "armed" spider* Phoneutria nigriventer *in threatening posture (D.A. Warrell)*

Spider bites
Dangerous spiders occur mainly in the Americas, Southern Africa, the Mediterranean region and Australia. The most notorious genera are *Latrodectus* (black

widow spiders), *Phoneutria* (Latin American armed or banana spiders, Figure 16.4), *Atrax* (Sydney funnel web spider) and *Loxosceles* (brown recluse spiders). *Latrodectus, Phoneutria* and *Atrax* venoms affect the nerves, muscles and heart, producing cramping pains, muscle spasms, weakness, sweating, salivation, gooseflesh, fever, nausea, vomiting, alterations in pulse rate and blood pressure, and convulsions. *Loxosceles* bites cause severe local necrosis, a generalised red rash, fever, dark urine (haemoglobinuria), blood clotting disturbances and kidney failure. Deaths are unusual except among children. Bites usually occur when the victim brushes against a spider which has crept into clothes or bedding. Antivenoms are manufactured in countries such as South Africa, Australia and Brazil, where spider bite is an important medical problem.

Scorpion stings

Dangerous scorpions (Figure 16.5) occur particularly in North and South Africa, the Middle East, the United States, Mexico, South America and India. The fatal cases are usually children. Most stings are not life-threatening but cause excruciating local pain with little swelling. Symptoms reflect initial release of acetylcholine neurotransmitter (causing vomiting, abdominal pain, bradycardia, sweating, salivation, and so on) followed by release of catecholamines (causing hypertension, tachycardia,

Figure 16.5   *Dangerous scorpion* Leiurus quinquestriatus *of North Africa and the Middle East*

pulmonary oedema, ECG abnormalities). The severe local pain is treated by injecting 1–2% lignocaine, but a powerful analgesic such as tramadol injections may be required. Severe systemic symptoms should be treated with appropriate pharmacological agents (such as vasodilator drugs) and antivenom. Atropine, betablockers and digoxin are not generally recommended.

Prevention is better than cure
When establishing a base camp in a scorpion-infested area, first dig out the scorpions. Their oval-shaped entry holes are usually easily recognisable. A thin twig should be used to guide the digging as the tunnel often changes direction. Always suspect there may be a scorpion under cases, logs, and so on. *Always* shake your boots and shoes out before putting them on. *Always* look where you put your bare feet. The RGS Kora 1983 expedition dug out 180 scorpions in the base camp site.

OTHER VENOMOUS INVERTEBRATES
Bites by some tropical centipedes can be dangerous as well as painful, and some millipedes can squirt irritating defensive secretions. There is no specific treatment for either of these menaces. Many species of ticks can inject a paralysing toxin while they suck your blood. If a member of your party becomes progressively weak, it is important to search for the tick in hairy areas and to detach it as soon as possible. The symptoms should then subside.

Invasive arthropods
Various tropical arthropods have larvae which invade human tissue or are merely blood sucking.

Congo floor maggot (*Auchmeronyia luteola*)
The larvae live in the floors of huts. They attack humans who sleep on the ground and suck their blood, causing local swelling and itching. Fumigate the hut and treat the bites symptomatically, making sure that no secondary infection is introduced (wipe the skin with tincture of iodine, give systemic antimicrobials if there are signs of infection).

Tumbu fly, putsi fly, ver du cayor (*Cordylobia anthropophaga*)
This fly is common in sub-Saharan Africa. It lays its eggs on clothes and, if they are not ironed, the eggs will hatch and burrow into your skin. Do not spread your clothing on the ground to dry. A small boil develops with something moving in the middle; this is the posterior segment with the respiratory spiracles. There is a sensation of movement in these lesions.

Treatment

Cover with paraffin (Vaseline) and grasp the maggot, which will stick out its "head" to get air, or do a proper surgical excision.

Ver macaque, human botfly, Berne, El Torsalo, beefworm *(Dermatobia hominis)*

This fly is widely distributed in Central and South America from Mexico to Argentina and Chile. It lays its eggs on other insects. They hitchhike to the human skin and penetrate quickly. To begin with the maggot is bottle-shaped and, although paraffin may cause the creature breathing difficulties, in the early stages you are likely to pull off the "neck" (actually the posterior segment with the spiracles) if you attempt to extract it. Wait until it is further developed, and you may succeed as with the tumbu fly. Otherwise make a cross incision to pull the maggot out, taking care not to cut it. An alternative is to cover the lesion with candle wax. The maggot will burrow its way into the candle wax, and you have got it.

Figure 16.6   *Two human botfly larvae extracted from "boils" acquired by a traveller in Costa Rica (D.A. Warrell)*

Creeping eruptions *(larvae migrans)*

The track made under the skin is caused by the larvae of animal nematodes, such as *Ancylostoma braziliense*, *Uncinaria stenocephala* and *Ancylostoma caninum*, the hookworms of cats and dogs. The larva moves day by day. The best treatment is thiabendazole taken orally or applied topically.

Jigger fleas (*Tunga penetrans*)
After fertilisation the female of this little flea jumps (feebly) and burrows alongside the nailfold or into the skin of the groin, loses her legs and produces eggs each night. These must be curetted out and iodine applied. Jiggers and other unpleasant creatures can be avoided if you do not walk around barefoot.

Source of antivenom in the UK
Pasteur-Mérieux-Connaught, UK
Tel. +44 1628 785291, fax +44 1628 71722

Advice on venomous bites and stings

National Poisons Centre
Tel. +44 171 639694

Centre for Tropical Medicine, University of Oxford
Tel. +44 1865 220968/741166

17 PSYCHOLOGICAL PROBLEMS ON EXPEDITIONS

Michael Phelan

"God knows it is just about as much as I can stand at times, and there is absolutely no escape. I have never had my temper so tried as it is everyday now," wrote Edward Wilson, a Polar explorer, in 1902. You do not have to spend the winter in the Antarctic to share some of the frustrations and annoyances that Wilson was describing to his wife. All expeditions are stressful and inevitably cause psychological difficulties for those involved. Before organising or joining an expedition it is essential to be as aware of the potential psychological complications as of the many physical conditions described elsewhere in this book. This chapter will outline some steps that can be taken at the planning stage to reduce psychological problems, and will then describe more common difficulties that may occur and the best way to manage them.

PLANNING STAGES

Start planning for an expedition at least a year before the anticipated departure date. Having decided the main aims and objectives, select a clearly defined leader. Ideally, he or she will have had experience of leading similar expeditions, but obviously this will not always be possible. Enthusiasm, maturity and hard work will compensate for lack of experience, but a clear understanding of the responsibilities of leadership is vital. There are different styles of leadership. Successful leaders understand their own strengths and weaknesses, and do not try to emulate someone else. Lack of confidence frequently results in excessive authoritarianism and subsequent resentment from team members. Confident leaders are able to accept that they are not always right and listen to the views of others, but at the same time make decisions, even if unpopular, when required. Any expedition leader should read a wide range of books about expeditions to develop a sense of the strains that will be imposed on them. The author would also recommend studying a short paperback on management skills, before departure. Leaders of any expedition, however small, must appreciate that their lives will be dominated for months, and that their preoccupation will be a trial for people close to them.

Selecting the right team

This is the most vital factor in determining the eventual success of an expedition. The leader must be closely involved in selection. A formal interview process with the involvement of the leader helps to establish his or her authority from the outset. There are no hard and fast rules for picking the right team and instinct should not be ignored; it is often right. However, some principles should be borne in mind.

- **Background.** Past behaviour predicts future behaviour. Therefore, give more importance to what people have done than to what they say they are going to do. Find out about previous expedition experience, and any other relevant experience. Follow up references, and when possible speak to referees, as they may mention things that they have not put down on paper.
- **Motivation.** Enthusiasm is a vital characteristic in any potential candidate. Look out for people who appear to be enthusiastic about life in general, not just about the proposed expedition. Discuss in detail with people why they want to go on your expedition, and what they are expecting. Ask them what they anticipate finding difficult about the trip, and also what they will do if they do not get selected. Many candidates may have negative reasons for escaping from their normal life, such as leaving a boring job, or getting over a bereavement. Such reasons are not an absolute contraindication for selection, but they need to be discussed frankly.
- **Personality.** If there is any such thing as a normal person, they certainly do not go on expeditions. Equally, the perfect expedition person does not exist, and the happiest expeditions are those with a real mixture of characters on them. However, try and select people who have an open and friendly manner, and who are sensitive to others. Self-reliance is another vital characteristic, along with an ability to admit to failings and weaknesses with a smile. The psychological profile of the expedition members needs to be assessed, not so much by a qualified psychologist, but by the expedition leader and co-organisers with common sense and an understanding of human nature. A good psychological balance is what is needed.
- **Mental health.** Lastly, it is essential to ask about any mental health problems. If in any doubt do not hesitate to obtain a medical report from their GP (this will require their written permission). Expeditions are not suitable for people convalescing from any mental illness.

Having made your final selection make sure that the group, at the very least, spends a weekend together in the vacation preceding the expedition. This will begin the team building that is vital for a successful expedition.

Personnel selection is only one aspect of the overall planning , albeit an important one. Attention to detail is needed in all other areas. Conflict and resentment will be reduced by ensuring that everyone has adequate equipment, and good-quality food is always a great boost to morale. However, the best made plans may have to be changed at the last moment, and a degree of flexibility must be kept to cope with the unexpected.

OUT IN THE OPEN

Psychological problems which occur on expeditions can broadly be considered as those that affect the group as a whole and those that primarily affect individual members. These are described separately, but in reality there will always be some overlap.

Group problems

Humans are social animals, and are instinctively drawn to form groups with others. This behaviour is accentuated by the isolation and alien environment of most expeditions. As groups of people become more familiar with each other, individual members develop social roles within the group, such as being the joker who lifts morale, or the spokesperson who says what others are thinking. At the same time strong friendships are formed and members develop an intense sense of belonging to the group. This process is helped by joint decision-making and responsibility, as well as symbolic aspects such as expedition T-shirts.

Although being a member of a group is largely a positive experience it does have disadvantages. Intrusion into privacy and personal space can be overbearing, and there can be pressure to behave in a way that makes people feel uncomfortable. Scapegoating is a common phenomenon among any group of people. It can become a serious problem if not dealt with quickly. The leader needs to recognise when it is happening, and step in early to reinstate the excluded member. This can be done effectively by changing their role or giving them an essential task in order to increase the group's respect and sense of need for them.

A couple may have a particular problem in a group setting. The bond between them may be resented by other members and result in scapegoating of the couple. Alternatively, one of the couple may get on well with the rest of the group but leave their partner feeling rejected and isolated. The author's experience of couples on expeditions is limited to three male-dominated expeditions; however, on each occasion the women were left isolated while their male partners integrated with the rest of the group. Anyone selecting a couple for an expedition must be ready for such problems, and the couple themselves need to understand the inevitable stress on their relationship.

Most expeditions have periods of general low morale, and these will be testing times for the leader. If they persist without obvious reason one member may be responsible for transmitting their own unhappiness to the entire group. Having one person going around saying "I'm really fed up with this aren't you?" can have a devastating effect on a previously happy expedition. The leader needs to detect if this is happening and try and help the person concerned.

An important role for any leader is to facilitate communication among the team. A formal structure should be in place for information to be shared and complaints to be aired early. This may be in the form of a daily meeting, or may involve maintaining regular radio contact on a more dispersed expedition. Good leaders appreciate the importance of listening, and realise that being seen to understand the problems of others is often the only action that is required.

Individual problems

A range of psychological and psychiatric problems can affect individuals. If there is a previous history of any such problem it is essential that an expert opinion is sought, and advice taken, before departure.

Panic attacks

These can affect anyone. They may occur spontaneously but are often precipitated by a feared situation. Attacks are characterised by extreme panic, and at times people describe a feeling of impending death. The panic is accompanied by physical symptoms such as chest pain, blurred vision, dizziness and tingling of the fingers and toes. Often the person feels extremely breathless and will hyperventilate. Bystanders who have not seen an attack before will be alarmed, and this only makes the sufferer worse. The correct immediate treatment for a panic attack is calm reassurance, and to get the person to breathe in and out of a paper or plastic bag held over their nose and mouth (if a plastic bag is used it must never be put over the head). In the longer term panic attacks usually become less frequent and less severe. If they persist an expert opinion should be sought, and medication and/or specific psychological therapies will be prescribed.

Depression

Everyone becomes miserable from time to time, and this is quite normal on an expedition. Occasionally, someone may develop a depressive illness, which is quantitatively different. It may follow an infective illness or some other clear trigger, such as bad news from home, but the cause may not be immediately obvious to others, or indeed to the person himself. As well as a depressed mood and a lack of energy, other characteristic features include:

- poor sleep, especially early morning wakening;

- loss of appetite;
- poor concentration;
- frequent tearful episodes;
- preoccupation with worries and a sense of guilt;
- thoughts of suicide or self-harm.

If all or some of these features are present then the matter must be taken seriously. The person may well get better, but if their condition deteriorates, or it is felt that they are a suicide risk, they should be evacuated home.

Acute confusional states

In contrast to panic attacks and depression, which are common, acute confusional states are rare. Characteristic features include:

- bizarre and inexplicable behaviour;
- preoccupation with strange and frequently persecutory beliefs;
- hallucinations, either visual or auditory;
- disorientation in time, place and person.

Any of these signs may be present along with fluctuations in the level of consciousness, which is a serious sign. Malaria and heat stroke are just two of the many conditions that can cause confusional states. Drugs may also be responsible. Clearly, no member of the expedition should take illicit drugs, and it is important that people do not take local drugs, herbal or otherwise. Occasionally prescribed drugs may also cause a confusional state. For instance, there are some reports of the antimalarial drug mefloquine (Lariam) causing temporary mood disturbances and confusion (this is rare and should *not* stop you taking vital prophylaxis against malaria). Confusional states may follow head injuries. The onset may be delayed by some days. This is a major emergency, and the sufferer must be evacuated immediately.

Psychiatric medication

Psychiatric drugs should not be a routine part of expedition medical kits, and should never be used by someone who is not medically qualified. However, on expeditions where immediate evacuation is not possible a doctor, experienced in their use, may consider including the following:

- Antidepressants (for example, fluoxetine 20mg), although effective in relieving the symptoms of depression in approximately 65% of cases, take at least 2 weeks to work.
- Anxiloytics/hypnotics (for example, diazepam 5mg). There may be an occasional role for such drugs in the treatment of acute anxiety or severe

stress reactions, but they are addictive and their use should be limited to a few days.

- Antipsychotics (for example, chlorpromazine 50mg) may help to settle someone in an acute confusional state, but there is a risk that their use will mask a dangerous deterioration in the patient, and extra-pyramidal side-effects may require the concurrent use of anticholinergic drugs (for example, procyclidine 5mg).

Returning home

If there has been a major disaster or near disaster on an expedition this must be given attention on returning home. During the last decade there has been an increasing recognition of the severe psychological sequelae for many people involved in accidents or near-death experiences. The term post-traumatic stress disorder describes the common symptoms of intrusive thoughts and flashbacks to the traumatic experience, nightmares, disturbed sleep and avoidance of specific situations or places which can follow any traumatic experience. If others have been killed or severely injured, survivors may feel guilty that they escaped, even if they were not responsible for what happened. If untreated these symptoms can persist for years, and result in significant disability and distress. Expert help should therefore be obtained.

Most expeditions pass without disaster. Hugh Robert Mill, once the RGS librarian, described "the fine tradition of British explorers (in) passing over ... little squabbles and jealousies", and there is no doubt that minor disagreements and personality clashes will soon be forgotten once everyone is back home. However, after the initial excitement of returning, it is common to miss the camaraderie of the expedition; a feeling of anti-climax is an inevitable consequence of a successful trip. Far more attention is given to the process of team building at the beginning of an expedition than to team separation at the end. A responsible leader will recognise that this is a painful process, and pay attention to the sense of loss felt by the team. Practical steps can include circulating a list of contact details for expedition members to help people stay in touch with each other. An organised reunion a few months after coming home may help (as well as being a chance to chase people up for their contribution to the report). However, the best solution is to start planning the next expedition.

18 EMERGENCY DENTAL TREATMENT

David Watt

Dental diseases are extremely common. Hardly anyone has a perfect mouth with no experience of decay or gingivitis.

In some countries dental treatment is difficult, or even impossible, to obtain. It is essential for the traveller to have his or her mouth put in order by their own dental surgeon before the journey. This usually keeps the traveller dentally fit for at least a year, but even with the best dental treatment problems may still occur. The more common incidents are described below.

Gingivitis

Chronic gingivitis (gum disease) is almost universal, and is minimised by effective oral hygiene. Acute conditions occasionally occur, particularly under poor living conditions. Extremely sore and ulcerated gum margins are accompanied by a fever and very bad breath. Treatment is rest, fluid supplements and antibiotic therapy. The first choice of antibiotics is metronidazole.

Oral ulceration

Oral ulcers can be painful and widespread. In the absence of a fever, these will usually be aphthous ulcers, which although very sore, will heal in about 7 days. Hot saline mouth baths (1 teaspoon of salt in a mug of boiled hot water, used quite hot) have a soothing effect. Many young people are prone to mouth ulcers, and will have found a favourite remedy at their usual chemist; it is wise to carry an ample supply.

Toothache

The first stage of toothache is represented by a complaint of pain when cold foods such as ice cream are taken. The cause is the pulp, the living interior part of the tooth composed of soft tissue, becoming inflamed. The condition is called pulpitis.

It is a characteristic of pulpitis that the pain will wake the patient from slumber. Pulpitis can sometimes be reversed by the placement of a sedative filling of dental

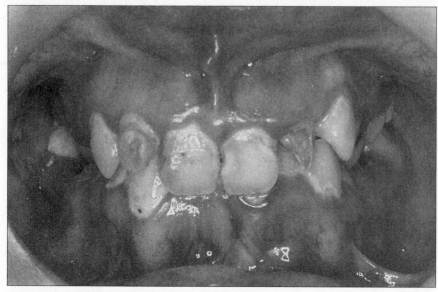

Figure 18.1   *Extensive gum disease (D. Watt)*

cement in the tooth cavity. When irreversible, the tooth may often be saved by the procedure of root filling. This procedure must be carried out by a dentist.

As a temporary measure, pain-relieving drugs may be prescribed, but pulpitis does not respond to antibiotic therapy. Pulpitis may progress to pulp death, and paradoxically the pain may subside. The relief may be short-lived, because a dead pulp is a focus of infection. A dental abscess is the natural consequence of pulp death, and may be relieved by extraction of the tooth, or by root filling, as described in *Emergency Dentistry* (see References, Appendix 3).

Impacted wisdom teeth

Wisdom teeth which are short of space are a common cause of trouble. X-ray pictures will help assess the likelihood of problems, and also the difficulty of removing a tooth. Usually, teeth which are completely buried can be left alone. Wisdom teeth which are partly erupted can be a nuisance and should be carefully assessed by a dentist – and not at the last minute before travelling.

Once part of the wisdom tooth has erupted, the tissue space surrounding the crown of the tooth is open to infection by micro-organisms from the mouth, and a chronic inflammation develops. Acute episodes occur at approximately 6-monthly intervals. More than a single acute episode is a definite indication for removal of the tooth or teeth, to prevent a recurrence of pain and swelling. Should pain from an impacted wisdom tooth develop, it can be treated temporarily by antibiotic therapy.

Metronidazole over 3 days is usually effective.

A longer-term concern is that decay can develop, either in the impacted tooth, or in the tooth immediately in front of it. Removal of impacted wisdom teeth, if shown to be necessary, should be carried out at least a month before departure.

Lost filling or crown

Sometimes a corner of an unfilled decayed tooth may break away, leaving a jagged hole, but it is more common for an old filling to fall out because further decay has occurred under it. A temporary dental cement (such as the Dentanurse kit, see page 188) is a helpful remedy. A putty-like paste is squeezed from a tube, rolled between the fingers into a little ball, and pressed into the cavity. It is helpful first to dry the cavity with cotton wool twisted around the end of a match.

Artificial crowns come in two versions, the jacket crown and the post crown. If a jacket crown is lost, a peg of tooth tissue remains, and the crown can be refixed temporarily with dental cement. When a post crown is lost, the metal post, which is a little larger than a drawing pin, can be refixed in a similar manner.

The traveller should be watchful for soreness developing around the root of the tooth, as this may indicate a dental abscess. Should one form, the first step should be to remove the temporary filling or crown, as drainage of the abscess can often occur through the root. Antibiotic therapy, such as Augmentin or metronidazole, will control spreading infection, and it may not be necessary to remove the tooth.

Dental abscess

The end result of both of the common dental diseases, gingivitis and decay, is the appearance of a swelling as a result of pus forming in the tissues. The swelling may spread to the soft tissues of the cheek and face. This may be accompanied by fever and toothache. Antibiotic therapy, such as Augmentin or metronidazole, should be prescribed, and if the swelling does not diminish it should be lanced, within the mouth if possible.

The causative tooth may be tender to touch, or there may have been a previous episode of tenderness on touching or biting. If in doubt, percussion of the teeth by tapping them with a small instrument will usually identify the troublesome tooth. When the acute symptoms have subsided, consideration should be given to root filling or to dental extraction.

Dental extraction

Removal of molar teeth (the large teeth towards the back of the jaw) can be difficult, particularly in young men, because these teeth are multirooted, and the supporting bone is usually unyielding. No attempt should be made to remove a back tooth unless proper dental extraction forceps are available. The anterior teeth are single rooted, and their removal is somewhat easier. However, *removal of teeth should be very much the last resort* for the traveller; it is usually possible to relieve the problem temporarily by prescribing pain-relieving drugs and antibiotics.

A further problem encountered is that teeth whose surrounding tissues are inflamed and tender are difficult to anaesthetise with local analgesic drugs. The prospect of tooth removal by an inexperienced operator using a local anaesthetic which does not work well in the presence of infection is not a happy one for the patient. In dire emergency, a loose tooth, or a single-rooted anterior tooth, could be removed with a pair of pliers enclosing a piece of dry linen to give a better grip.

Trauma to teeth and jaws

A broken tooth will often expose the pulp, a pink or bleeding area of soft tissue in the central part of the root. This area is exquisitely painful and local remedies are not helpful, although oil of cloves or topical anaesthetic paste may give some relief. A dentist should remove the exposed pulp prior to root filling.

People engaged in contact sports wear mouth guards, and consideration should be given to their use by travellers engaged in a hazardous activity.

The front teeth can be loosened by a blow, and if markedly displaced can usually be manipulated into their correct position by firm pressure from the fingers. If this is done immediately after the incident it is not particularly painful.

More severe trauma may result in broken facial bones, and specialist treatment in a hospital equipped for the purpose is essential. A simple fracture of the lower jaw can be stabilised by wrapping the head and jaw with a 3 inch crepe bandage. If more severe fractures of upper and/or lower jaws have occurred so that the airway is partially obstructed, the patient should be transported lying face down with the mouth turned to one side in order to free the airway.

Summary

Travellers are reminded that dental problems are common. Every effort should be made before departure to see a dentist and eliminate minor problems that could develop into more major ones, and to prepare appropriate measures to cope with dental incidents that may occur in spite of adequate preparation.

Note. David Watt is author of *Emergency Dentistry* (see Appendix 3); current price £12.50 plus p&p. Dentanurse kits and emergency dental kits can be made and supplied to order. All requests for the book or equipment to: Dental Practice, 23 Market Square, Kirkby Stephen, Cumbria CA17 4QT, tel. & fax +44 17683 71250.

SECTION 3

MEDICAL PROBLEMS OF ENVIRONMENTAL EXTREMES

19 TROPICAL AND DESERT EXPEDITIONS

Matthew Dryden

The human body is probably better adapted to heat than to cold, and this may reflect our evolutionary origins. The body nurtured in temperate zones is quite capable of acclimatising to hot conditions, but this process takes time. Warmth and sunshine seem to have a beneficial effect on the mind if not necessarily on the body. After all, millions of people head for warmer climes on package tours each year, and it is the sun rather than the culture that they are after. The same migration does not happen in reverse.

Figure 19.1   *Working with the Bedu in the Wahiba Sands, Sultanate of Oman (R. Turpin/RGS)*

It is much easier to lose heat than to conserve it. Unlike cold conditions, even the most intense climatic heat by itself cannot kill, providing certain precautions are observed. Although "sunstroke" was a well-recognised cause of death among British armies in the tropics, this was probably not so much the climate itself, but inadequate thermoregulation and dehydration from over-exertion, and carrying heavy clothes and equipment in high temperatures. Soldiers died from their inability to lose sufficient heat and dehydration. They were not killed by the rays of the sun.

Many of the health problems associated with being in tropical climates such as infectious diseases and animal bites and stings are dealt with in Chapters 15 and 16. The purpose of this chapter is to give an overview of medical problems in the tropics and to deal with a selection of specific points.

THE CLIMATE

The desert: hot and dry

Deserts and semi-arid land surround the wetter equatorial regions. They are characterised by sand, gravel, rock or mountains; high day-time temperatures, particularly in the summer months; low night-time temperatures, especially in winter; little surface water, poor or absent vegetation, cloudless sky, variable wind speed and sparse human population.

Figure 19.2   *Route finding in the Wahiba Sand Sea, Sultanate of Oman (R. Turpin/RGS)*

The humid tropics: hot and wet

The humid equatorial regions are likely to cause greater initial discomfort to unacclimatised travellers than the dry heat of the desert. It is harder to get cool when sweat will not evaporate and temperatures vary little during a 24-hour period, so that there is little respite at night. Any breeze is welcome. There is generally no lack of water, but the quality will be variable. The human population density is usually higher.

Preparation

Good preparation for expeditions cannot be over-emphasised. This is particularly the case in deserts, which apart from the polar regions are the least accessible and most inhospitable regions in the world. Most deaths and serious illness on expeditions result from accidents, many of which cannot be predicted or prevented and are therefore just bad luck. However, in deserts travellers have the potential to kill themselves quite easily through bad planning, and this is a wasteful way to go. In the hot and humid tropics expeditions may also find themselves in inaccessible spots, but in general the essentials of life can be found. Water is in abundance; food may be found in the jungle when desperate; and usually human habitation is not too far away.

For a long and remote desert journey the reliability of the means of transport is essential. If it is mechanised there should be at least two vehicles. Skilled and resourceful mechanics should be part of the team. Sufficient spare parts need to be taken, but as not everything can be carried it is necessary to be selective. If animal transport is to be used, consider where and how the animals will be acquired and who will manage them. Will you have radio back-up for disasters? If so, who is going to listen at the other end, and even if there is someone to listen, who will come and rescue you? Radio communication is generally not practicable for all but the largest and extensively sponsored expeditions. Others have to be prepared to deal with all disasters themselves. Evacuation in case of injury or illness may be difficult if not impossible in extremely remote locations. If the expedition is on foot, the health and mobility of its members are of prime importance. Delays even over short distances can be crucial when rare water sources in desert, scrub or bush are relied upon for resupply.

Think carefully about the logistics: fuel, water, food. Plan these for the expected duration of the journey plus a generous contingency, which should be greater in deserts than in jungles. Delays and breakdowns can stretch supplies; conditions may have increased fuel expenditure; and water sources may have dried up or become salinated. Decide on a form of navigation and train sufficient members of the expedition in these methods well beforehand, ensuring that the techniques and equipment are well tried at home. To die because the expedition is lost or poorly supplied is pure carelessness.

The expedition members need to be chosen carefully and the group should be well tested before departure, preferably in conditions that are less than comfortable. Ideally, all members should be fit and healthy. Most expeditions are physically strenuous to some degree and a good level of fitness will speed the rate of acclimatisation in the tropics.

Clothing, footwear and shelter

In deserts *light, loose-fitting clothes* made of natural materials covering the body and a *hat*, scarf or khaffieh covering the head provide protection from the sun and allow air to circulate and so evaporate sweat. Shorts and T-shirts are also convenient and generally perfectly adequate, but it is important to use *sun block* on exposed skin. The colour of clothes is not of great importance. In direct sunlight white will reflect heat, black will absorb it. Logically, lighter-coloured clothes should be cooler; in practice clothing, whatever its colour, that is loose-fitting and light will be most comfortable. It is also important to be aware of, and polite to comply with, local dress customs. If the exposure of limbs or display of the female figure and face in public is taboo, it is hardly surprising that if you do so you may be leered at, sneered at or even stoned. *Sunglasses* and goggles are essential for desert travel.

In hot and humid climates the ideal dress is wearing nothing at all. However, this gives the thorns, insects and leeches unimpeded access. The best compromise is loose-fitting cotton shorts and a shirt, but where the vegetation and insect population are particularly predatory long-sleeved garments and trousers are necessary. The latter are particularly important in areas of high malarial transmission, especially at dawn and dusk.

Footwear needs to be light, comfortable and tough. Shoes, trainers and boots all have disadvantages. Feet in footwear in hot climates become sweaty, smelly, soft, wrinkled and often infested with fungi. Footwear fills with sand, mud and water. The author's personal preference for footwear in warm climates is none at all but it is difficult to justify this view on health grounds. The disadvantage of bare feet or flip-flops is the lack of protection from the heat of the ground, from rocks or thorns or occasionally snakes and parasitic infections. The choice must depend on the conditions. For sand and gravel deserts go for walking sandals, trainers or desert boots; rock and volcanic larva may require heavier foot attire. The author prefers light footwear in jungles; others go for boots and gaiters. In particularly muddy and wet conditions short rubber boots are ideal. They can be slipped on easily over bare feet, they are comfortable to walk in, and they provide good protection against thorns and snakes. Whatever you choose, make sure you care for your feet. Treat blisters early and take every opportunity to allow your feet to air and dry.

It is possible to travel for months in desert, scrub and bush land without the need of shelter. A camp bed off the ground as protection against snakes, scorpions and spiders makes a perfect bed, but remember to shake out your shoes in the morning. A tent will protect you from flies and the unwanted attention of domestic dogs near human habitation. A tent and a decent camp fire will provide a reasonable sense of security against hyena and lion for those dubious about the protection of fire alone.

Where large animals and domestic dogs are present, keep food in a secure position away from you, preferably in a locked vehicle. If there is wind or a sandstorm a bivouac against the natural shelter of rocks or, failing that, staying within a vehicle provides protection. Beware of making camp in wadis or dry river courses. Flooding from rain many miles away can be very rapid, and if not lethal, it will be inconvenient. In jungles shelter is required against downpours. Tents are fine, but they have to be carried and get very hot to sleep in. The author's preference is for a string hammock. These take a bit of getting used to but once this has been achieved they are extremely comfortable and can be put up anywhere. An insect net can be designed for hammock use, and if necessary a shelter can be rigged up over the hammock when it is likely to be wet.

Camp hygiene and clean water supplies are particularly important in the tropics (see Chapters 8 and 9).

Acclimatisation

Direct travel from a temperate to a tropical climate can be a shock, both physically and mentally. Walking out of the aircraft can literally take your breath away, and it is not uncommon to feel totally drained of energy for the first few days. Slower travel to the tropics by boat or vehicle allows plenty of time for acclimatisation, but for most expeditions time is at a premium. The body is capable of acclimatisation but this may take from one to several weeks. During this time it is important to reduce heat stress by keeping exertion to a minimum and avoiding direct sunlight. Do not spend the acclimatisation period in air-conditioned rooms. Hot and humid conditions are likely to be more uncomfortable because of the low rate of heat loss through evaporation. You will feel sweaty day and night. In deserts you feel drier and the night brings some relief.

MEDICAL PROBLEMS SPECIFIC TO HOT CLIMATES

Heat control

The body maintains its temperature at about 37°C (98.6°F). Heat is generated in the body by the metabolism of food and by exercise (80% of exercise energy is released as heat). In addition, the body temperature is influenced by the environmental temperature. The body controls this by detecting the temperature at the skin via the free nerve endings, feeding this information back to a part of the brain called the hypothalamus, which can also directly measure the temperature of the blood, and then initiating any corrective measures if necessary. It is rather like a central heating control system. If it is cold, heat-laden blood is diverted away from the skin (vasoconstriction) and heat is generated by muscle activity (shivering). If it is too hot, the superficial blood vessels dilate allowing radiation of heat, and increased sweating permits further heat loss through evaporation. We also feel hot or cold and this allows us to take avoidance action: head for the shade, or put on more clothing.

These mechanisms work well in hot climates providing certain rules are obeyed. These are to maintain hydration and reduce heat gain. It is possible to lose up to 12 litres of sweat a day in the desert. By comparison, a marathon runner in temperate climates may lose 8–11 litres in the course of the race. In very strenuous exercise the sweating rate may increase to 4 litres an hour, but this rate cannot be maintained for long. The fluid, and the salt that goes with it, need to be replaced. The normal fluid intake of an adult is 2–2.5 litres a day, so it can be appreciated that in hot climates considerably greater volumes will need to be consumed. In hot climates drink several litres of fluid a day, although this should not consist solely of tea, coffee and alcohol. The colour of urine is a rough guide to hydration and it should be pale.

An average 65kg man contains about 40 litres of water. The sensation of thirst comes into operation with a loss of 0.5–1 litres (1–2% dehydration). If you can spit, you will be less than 5% dehydrated. After losing 1.5–2 litres (3–5% dehydration) there is considerable loss of strength and endurance, and confusion may occur. Death will occur with a loss of 6–8 litres (15–20% dehydration). So the message is drink plenty or, if you cannot do this, conserve body water by keeping as cool as possible: keep in the shade and travel at night. In humid climates there should be no lack of water, although it may be contaminated with micro-organisms. Adequate disinfection of water supplies is important (see Chapter 9). In deserts water supplies may taste unpleasant and saline. If the saline content is well below 2g/100ml the water will save lives. You will not know what the concentration is in such situations, but if the water comes from a well it should be drinkable, although it may be contaminated with germs.

The salt lost in sweating also needs to be replaced. Take salt regularly and in reasonable quantity on your food. Do not take salt tablets.

In hot climates heat is gained directly from radiation from the sun's rays and from the surrounding terrain. If the air temperature is higher than that of the skin, heat will be gained, unless the evaporation of sweat can reduce the skin temperature. If in addition the body increases heat production by exercising, the body temperature may rise to dangerous levels (>39°C). It is most important to avoid this. The message again is keep to the shade and do not over-exercise when it is very hot.

When someone is unable to produce saliva to spit, or if they stop sweating when hot, they need urgent rehydration and cooling. Heat-related illness starts with muscle cramps, headache, nausea, vomiting and increased heart rate. There may be irritability, anxiety or confusion. Coma may then develop, and death is likely to occur if the body is not rapidly cooled. With heat exhaustion, the patient should ideally be placed in an iced bath, or ice packs should be placed over the major veins (neck and groin). However, these are unlikely to be available to most expeditions. Lie the patient down, keeping their legs up. Spray the patient with cool water (urine is better than nothing if there is no water) and fan the body. Coma is a bad sign. The more prolonged it is the greater is the likelihood of death.

Sunburn

The solution to sunburn is obvious – do not let it happen. Avoid direct sunlight, wear protective clothing, cover exposed skin with sun block. By doing this you will also reduce the long-term chances of developing skin cancer, and will prevent early ageing of the skin.

Eyes

In deserts eyes need protection from the sun, glare and sand. Sunglasses are essential in desert travel, and goggles should be worn in windy conditions or where there is dust or sand being blown around. A sand-filled eye can be cleared by bathing the open eye in water.

Diarrhoea

Gastroenteritis can be a problem in hot climates as it can be in travel to any part of the world. To avoid it a general rule of thumb is that if you cannot cook it, boil it or peel it, do not eat it. This subject is dealt with in Chapter 14, but as diarrhoea leads to rapid loss of water and electrolytes, and if the climatic heat is also taking its toll on the body's precious water and salt resources, it is important to remember that adequate replacement is essential.

Infected wounds

Desert climates are fairly aseptic and conducive to the healing of scratches and cuts, providing flies are kept away from the wound. The same cannot be said of humid environments, where minor wounds may rapidly become septic. This leads to uncomfortable and unsightly suppurating lesions which eventually heal and scar or which may lead to more life-threatening conditions such as rapidly spreading infection of the soft tissue (cellulitis), abscess formation, or in extreme cases septicaemia. It is best to prevent this happening by careful dressing of minor wounds. Wash your hands thoroughly with soap and water before touching the wound. Wash the wound and dry it with gauze. Add a topical antiseptic cream and cover with a plaster or gauze bandage.

SUMMARY

Plan your travels in desert or jungle carefully, paying particular attention to the mode of transport and other logistics. Have generous contingency supplies of fuel and water. In remote areas have plans for evacuation should disaster strike. There is nowhere on earth where the climatic heat in itself is sufficient to kill, providing you avoid the worst of the heat by keeping to shade, avoid over-exertion and maintain adequate hydration.

20 POLAR EXPEDITIONS

Chris Johnson

The polar explorer will encounter meteorological extremes. Strong winds and low temperatures combine to create conditions similar to a blast-freezer and a calm summer's day brings the risks of heat exhaustion, sunburn and snowblindness. Katabatic winds, whiteout, shifting sea-ice and crevassed glacier ice are further hazards. It is difficult, dangerous and expensive to evacuate casualties and storms may make evacuation impossible, so independent groups should have enough medical equipment and expertise to be able to care for a sick or injured person for several days.

Figure 20.1   *A dog ambulance approaches Finse in Norway (C. Johnson)*

PREPARATION

All expedition members should be instructed in basic first aid, personal hygiene and the hazards of the area they are to visit. Before departure, the expedition medical officer (MO) should contact the emergency services, if any, in the area to be visited and find out how they can be contacted and how to evacuate a casualty. Satellite beacons (emergency position indicating beacons – EPIRBs) may be worth taking if there are sophisticated emergency services in the area you plan to visit. Avalanche transceivers are desirable if you intend to travel in mountainous areas. You must have adequate medical insurance and some countries demand that expeditions hold search-and-rescue insurance.

To reiterate previous chapters, all travellers should have medical and dental examinations well before the date of departure so that any necessary treatments can be completed. Conditions such as toothache and piles that are merely a nuisance at home can become a serious problem on an expedition. People with a stable medical condition such as well-controlled hypertension, diabetes or epilepsy can take part in expeditions, but the expedition leader and the MO should be aware of their condition as worsening of the disease could cause problems to everyone. Several separate sets of their usual drugs should be carried in case some are lost. People with unstable medical conditions, for example those prone to hypoglycaemic attacks, grand-mal epilepsy or inflammatory bowel disease, should not travel to remote areas unless comprehensive medical support is available nearby. The condition may worsen under stress and the infirmity of one expedition member may threaten the lives of all. People with poor peripheral circulation in the cold (Raynaud's disease) are more likely to suffer from cold injuries in severe conditions.

Eyes

Anyone whose vision is so poor that they always need to wear glasses or contact lenses must plan to avoid the difficulties that might arise from loss or breakage; as a minimum, a spare pair should be taken. When the air temperature is below –20°C glasses invariably mist over. Metal-rimmed spectacle frames can become very cold and cause frostbite; plastic-framed glasses or snow goggles are preferable. For the same reason, rings and earrings should not be worn in extreme conditions.

Infectious diseases

These are uncommon in polar areas. However, some sledge dogs carry rabies and a course of rabies inoculations is advisable if the expedition is likely to work with these animals. Other immunisations may be needed for the journey to and from the expedition base. It is always sensible to ensure that you are covered against tetanus.

Medical supplies

These must be compatible with the potential needs of the party. Drugs and dressings are both bulky and expensive, and over-enthusiastic ordering of medical supplies may deprive the team of funds better spent elsewhere. Some aqueous drugs crystallise and degrade in the cold; therefore powdered preparations and plastic containers should be selected whenever possible. Careful packing is essential to prevent breakages. Most medical supplies will be stored together, but a standby kit should be available in case the bulk of the supplies are lost in an accident. Suggestions for basic medical supplies are given in Chapter 3. The firm of L E West & Co, Beeby Road, London E16 1QJ (tel. +44 171 4761644) has supplied the British Antarctic Survey for many years and is happy to offer advice on suitable drugs and equipment.

FIELD ARRANGEMENTS

At base camp the MO should be responsible for supervising the water supply and sanitary arrangements (see Chapter 8). Fresh water can usually be obtained by melting snow, and this is safe to drink unless it comes from an area frequented by animals or birds. Deer and beaver live near to many apparently pristine melt streams. They can contaminate the water with giardia spores which, if drunk, cause chronic diarrhoea and crampy abdominal pain. If in doubt boil the water or use sterilising tablets. Beware of glacier outwash streams which contain fine, highly abrasive rock dust in suspension (see B. Dawson in References, Appendix 3); this is a powerful laxative. Bathing in cold climates is a masochistic pastime, but both people and clothes must be washed whenever possible as skin infections are common among sweaty, unwashed individuals.

Toilet facilities and rubbish dumps should be well demarcated and sited downwind and downstream of the camp site and water supply. In cold climates waste matter and materials break down very slowly and are your gift to future generations. As far as possible all waste should be removed from the area you visit. It may be hidden by a covering of snow during winter and spring, but it will be horribly visible at the end of the summer melt. There is now evidence that exposing excrement to direct sunlight results in less environmental pollution than hiding it away, as UV light sterilises harmful bacteria. Some North American National Parks are now recommending smearing rather than digging for small groups in remote areas, but a properly designed field latrine is necessary whenever groups are bigger and stay longer.

Food

Food is a much discussed topic on any expedition. It is necessary to balance variety with the need to obtain sufficient energy. While at base camp energy requirements will be similar to those of an outdoor worker in the UK (2,500–3,000 Kcals/day); however, manhauling is an extremely energetic pastime requiring two or even three times this energy intake. In cold climates a greater proportion of the diet is likely to be made up of fatty foods. In the past polar expeditions have lived off the land, but many animal and bird species are now protected and permission must be obtained before they are killed. The internal organs of many polar animals contain toxic amounts of vitamin A and must be discarded; they are in any case not a gastronomic treat.

Dehydration

Because polar air is very dry, sweat evaporates quickly and it is easy to underestimate the amount of fluid that is lost. Dehydration is common during the first days of the expedition, and everyone should be encouraged to drink a lot even if they do not feel thirsty. A combination of malaise, headache and raised body temperature is common when parties first begin work on the ice, and this may be a mild form of heat exhaustion.

MEDICAL PROBLEMS SPECIFIC TO POLAR REGIONS

The tents and clothing that the expedition takes should be designed to cope with severe weather. Cold injury is more likely to develop in windy conditions at low air temperatures and the degree of risk may be assessed using the wind chill scale. Conditions which exceed 20/20, that is −20°C with a 20 knot wind, are potentially dangerous. Prevention of cold injury requires constant vigilance on the part of expedition members, who should be paired off in the buddy system to check each

Wind speed		Ambient temperature °C							
mph	kph	−40	−30	−20	−10	−5	0	+5	+10
		Equivalent temperatures °C and danger of hypothermia for a fully clothed person							
		GREAT (exposed flesh may freeze)			INCREASING			SMALL	
46	74	−87	−71	−54	−38	−29	−21	−13	−4
35	56	−84	−68	−52	−36	−28	−20	−12	−3
23	38	−77	−62	−49	−31	−24	−16	−9	−1
12	20	−62	−49	−36	−23	−16	−10	−3	+2
6	10	−48	−37	−26	−15	−9	−3	+1	+7
0	0	−40	−30	−20	−10	−5	0	+5	+10

Figure 20.2   *Wind Chill Index*

other regularly for the tell-tale signs. Peripheral parts of the body such as fingers, toes and ears may become chilled causing frostnip or frostbite or, far more seriously, the victim may be unable to maintain their body temperature and become hypothermic.

Hypothermia

Hypothermia is a fall of the victim's core temperature below 35°C (normal is 37°C). It is uncommon in a properly clothed fit person, but occurs if someone is injured or if clothing is inadequate or wet. It usually develops insidiously over several hours, although it can happen within minutes if someone falls into cold water. The symptoms are similar to drunkenness; the victim is poorly co-ordinated, falls over, is confused and shivers uncontrollably. They may vehemently deny that anything is wrong and refuse help. Untreated, they will eventually become comatose and die.

TABLE 20.1	**FEATURES OF HYPOTHERMIA**
Body core temperature (°C)	Associated symptoms
37	Normal body temperature
36	
35	Judgement may be affected; poor decision-making
	Feels cold, looks cold, shivering
34	Change of personality, usually withdrawn – "switches off/doesn't care"
	Inappropriate behaviour – may shed clothing
	Stumbling, falling, confused
33	Consciousness clouded, incoherent
	Shivering stops
32	Serious risk of cardiac arrest
	Body cannot restore temperature without help
	Limbs stiffen
31	Unconscious
30	Pulse and breathing undetectable
29	
28	Pupils of eye become fixed and dilated
27	
26	
25	
24	Few victims recover from this temperature
23	
22	
21	
20	
19	
18	Lowest recorded temperature of survival

Experts have disagreed about the best treatment for severe hypothermia and this has led to conflicting advice in textbooks. However, the controversies are irrelevant to most expeditions which will not have the type of advanced resuscitation equipment that some mountain rescue groups now carry. The aim of treatment is to restore the body heat of the victim.

Shelter must be sought. Damp outer clothing should be removed and the casualty wrapped in additional dry insulation such as a sleeping bag. Body heat can be restored by warm drinks, warming the air with a stove and sharing the body heat of an unaffected rescuer. Chemical heat pads can be helpful if they are available, but ensure that they do not cause burns. Do not give alcohol. Even after body temperature has been restored the casualty may remain confused; they must rest and be closely supervised for at least 24 hours. Additional information on the treatment of accidental hypothermia is given in *Kurafid* (see References, Appendix 3).

Frostnip

In contrast to hypothermia, which usually develops quite slowly, peripheral cold injury can develop within seconds. The earliest change is termed frostnip and is a numb, waxy, white patch of skin most commonly seen on the earlobe or over the cheekbone. It is painless and its onset is usually unnoticed, although some experienced polar travellers may detect a sudden burning "ping" as it develops. The lesion may be treated by rewarming the part by covering it with a gloved hand or blowing warm exhaled air over the skin. *Do not rub nipped skin.* No permanent injury is done if skin is nipped and quickly rewarmed, although redness and swelling may persist for a day or two.

Frostbite

Frostbite – freezing of the underlying tissue – is the progression of the superficial injury of frostnip if it is left untreated. A frostbitten part should be thawed only if the victim can rest for a prolonged period afterwards. Although it is desirable to protect a damaged limb, it is possible for the victim to walk to safety on a frostbitten foot, but once thawed the limb will be useless. The affected part can be rewarmed by putting it in water which is then warmed slowly up to a maximum of 40°C. The treatment will hurt and strong painkillers should be given. After circulation has been restored the affected part will look red, blistered and severely swollen. Once treatment has begun, the damaged part must be protected against all forms of pressure and must not be allowed to refreeze. Raw areas should be covered by sterile dressings and these will need to be changed regularly. The tops should be taken off white blisters, but blood blisters should be left alone (see P.S. Auerbach, *Wilderness Medicine*). The victim should take penicillin and regular painkillers, for instance, ibuprofen (Nurofen). Severe frostbite takes months to heal, and the patient should be evacuated to a hospital that is used to dealing with the problem. Most doctors have seen dry gangrene associated with poor circulation; this causes death of the digit or limb from the inside. Frostbite injuries look similar, but are less serious as they are generally associated with superficial damage and the core of the limb is healthy. Amputation should be undertaken only when a line of demarcation between healthy and dead tissue has become obvious.

Sunburn

Solar energy is intense in polar areas with strong reflection off the snow, and the radiation levels may exceed those in equatorial regions. Sunburn is common and is particularly uncomfortable when rays reflected upwards off the snow burn the eyelids and underside of the chin and nostrils. The medical significance of the spring thinning of the ozone layer in polar areas is not yet clear, but it makes sense to take precautions and ensure that all exposed skin is protected by a sunscreen offering protection (factor 15 or above).

Snowblindness

This is the term given to sunburn of the membrane that covers the front of the eye – the conjunctiva. The eyelids swell up and cannot open (hence the term blindness; the eye itself is unaffected). The sensation is similar to having sand ground into the eyeball. The victim will be incapacitated for several days and should rest in a darkened room or tent. One dose of local anaesthetic eyedrops (for example, amethocaine) relieves the initial discomfort, but further painkilling tablets will be required. Eyedrops that prevent spasm of the ciliary muscles of the pupil (for example, homatropine) can help, but repeated use of the local anaesthetic drug is no longer recommended. The eyes should be lightly bandaged until they have fully recovered. Ultraviolet light can penetrate cloud and snowblindness may develop even on overcast days. Expedition personnel should wear goggles or dark glasses with side protectors whenever they are working in bright conditions. If sunglasses are lost or damaged, an eye covering fashioned by making a couple of small slits in a sheet of card will provide an effective emergency alternative. Some experienced polar travellers have found that they are almost immune to snowblindness, but their apparent resistance should not entice newcomers to discard their eye protection.

Other hazards

Other polar hazards include the risk of suffocation or *carbon monoxide poisoning* in snowed-in tents and snow-holes. Ventilation holes must be checked regularly to ensure that they are not blocked by crystals of water vapour. Some polar expeditions climb high enough for *mountain sickness* to be a problem (this topic is covered in Chapter 21). Although *wildlife* in the southern hemisphere is usually friendly, the same cannot be said of polar bears, which may take an unwanted interest in your presence; seek local advice and, if recommended, take a firearm.

Many aspects of medicine and physiology have been studied by medical personnel attached to government polar research groups, but the results of their investigations may be difficult to obtain as they are published in specialist professional journals. It is difficult to conduct field research in extreme conditions, but there remain opportunities for an enthusiastic MO to undertake a small research project. *Man in the Antarctic* (see References, Appendix 3) is a good place to start reading about polar medical research.

The major hazard of the polar environment lies in its unfamiliarity. Once the hazards have been realised and guarded against, the cleanliness, beauty and remoteness of the polar wilderness provide inexhaustible pleasure for those fortunate enough to venture into it.

Figure 20.3   *Party arriving on Tasman Glacier in New Zealand (C. Johnson)*

21 HIGH-ALTITUDE AND MOUNTAINEERING EXPEDITIONS

Charles Clarke

A number of related medical conditions develop when people travel to altitudes above 3,500m (11,500ft). There is a wide variation in both the speed of onset and severity of symptoms and also at the height at which they develop. The problems are caused by lack of oxygen.

In Nepal, the country with most high-altitude visitors (probably over 50,000 per year), the mortality rate of trekkers is believed to be around seven per year, with a quarter of the deaths due to altitude-related illness. In other words, several people die each year. On high-altitude climbing expeditions to peaks over 7,000m death rates are much higher, at around 4%. It is difficult to ascertain the importance of altitude illness compared with accident. In practical terms, for the expedition organiser or doctor, on a trip to heights over 5,000m, illness due to lack of oxygen demands recognition, chiefly as an unpleasant hindrance, but also, rarely, as a cause of very serious illness.

MEDICAL PROBLEMS SPECIFIC TO HIGH ALTITUDE

Acute mountain sickness

Most people feel unwell if they drive, fly or travel by train from sea level to 3,500m. Headache, fatigue, undue breathlessness on exertion, the sensation of the heart beating forcibly, loss of appetite, nausea, vomiting, dizziness, difficulty sleeping and irregular breathing during sleep are the common complaints. Shivering and feeling the cold are also common. These are symptoms of acute mountain sickness (AMS) which usually develop during the first 36 hours at altitude and not immediately on arrival. The symptoms pass off in several days.

Well over 50% of travellers develop some form of AMS at 3,500m, but almost all do so if they ascend rapidly to 5,000m (16,400ft).

Figure 21.1   *Sepu Kangri, 4,700m, Eastern Tibet, May 1997. Serious altitude sickness is*
a problem at these altitudes, despite the gentle terrain of base camp
(C. Bonington, Chris Bonington Picture Library)

Acclimatisation and suggested rate of height gain

Acclimatisation, that is feeling well again, takes place over several days. Once acclimatised in this way, further gradual height gain can take place although symptoms may recur.

The question "How high, how fast?" has no absolute answer because of individual variation, but it is reasonable for healthy people of any age to travel rapidly to 3,500m (Lhasa, for example, is 3,620m), although many will develop AMS after arrival. It is unwise to travel much above 3,500m immediately from sea level.

Above 3,500m the speed of further height gain should be gradual and it is advisable to spend a week above 3,500m before sleeping at 5,000m. The highest altitude where humans live permanently is about 5,500m (18,000ft), but on mountaineering expeditions or treks, residence for several weeks around 6,000m (20,000ft) is quite possible. At these altitudes people who are acclimatised should feel entirely well, being limited only by breathlessness on exertion. It is often impossible (for example, on the Tibetan plateau) to keep to this counsel of perfection.

Prediction and prevention of AMS

There is unfortunately no way of predicting who will be seriously troubled by AMS and who will escape it. It is tempting to suppose that being physically fit and avoiding smoking would help in prevention, but unfortunately this is not so. Strenuous exercise at altitude, whether or not the subject is fit, makes AMS worse. Undue exertion and carrying heavy loads should therefore be avoided until acclimatised.

Patients with heart or lung disease or high blood pressure should seek specialist advice before travelling above 4,000m.

Prevention of AMS

- Graded ascent (see above).
- Consider acetazolamide (Diamox) 250mg tablets twice a day.

Graded ascent is the best preventer of AMS. However, there has been much research on acetazolamide (Diamox), a drug used to reduce fluid retention (it makes you urinate) and in the treatment of glaucoma. There is no doubt that Diamox is genuinely useful in the prevention of AMS if taken for several days before ascent. If Diamox is being used, one 250mg tablet should be given twice daily for 3 days before 3,500–5,000 metres is reached. Exactly how Diamox works is unknown, but its effect on breathing (making breathing faster and deeper in sleep) may be more important than its direct effect on the output of urine.

Travellers who take Diamox should be aware of its unwanted effects (all drugs have their dangers). Diamox makes some people feel nauseated and generally unwell and quite commonly causes tingling of the fingers. These cease when the drug is stopped. More unusual reported side-effects include flushing, rashes, thirst, drowsiness or excitement. I suggest a trial of Diamox at sea level for 2 days, so that its effects are known to the individual. I do not recommend the drug routinely, and do not take it myself.

Treatment of AMS

It is important to emphasise that AMS, although unpleasant, is usually a self-limiting condition without serious sequelae. Principles of treatment include:

- Rest days, relaxation, descent?
- Simple analgesia for headache: aspirin, paracetamol.
- Consider dexamethasone 4mg every 4 hours (3 doses).
- Consider hyperbaric chamber (portable pressure bag).

I use no drugs unless really necessary because the symptoms usually resolve; the only real cure is to become acclimatised to the lack of oxygen. The most important treatment is not to go higher if symptoms occur and to consider losing altitude if recovery does not take place within several days and certainly if the symptoms worsen.

Pulmonary and cerebral oedema: severe forms of AMS

In less than 2% of travellers AMS occurs in several serious forms at 4,000–5,000m and occasionally lower.

High-altitude pulmonary oedema

This is a condition in which fluid accumulates in the lung causing severe illness (which may come on in minutes). It is characterised by breathlessness and frothy phlegm. Early pulmonary oedema should be suspected if breathlessness at rest occurs or if someone has what appears to be a persistent dry cough or chest infection causing breathlessness. Pulmonary oedema may be preceded by AMS.

Prevention of high-altitude pulmonary oedema

- Ascend slowly, avoiding heavy loads.
- Do not climb with a chest infection.

Treatment of high-altitude pulmonary oedema

Patients with pulmonary oedema are dangerously ill and should be evacuated to a lower altitude as an emergency. Frequently, a descent of only 500m (1,500ft) is sufficient to improve the situation dramatically. Principles of treatment include:

- DESCENT, evacuation, oxygen.
- Nifedipine (Adalat) 20mg by mouth every 6 hours.
- Hyperbaric chamber (portable pressure bag).

Cerebral oedema

Cerebral oedema is another form of AMS. It is usually preceded by AMS and it is due to fluid collecting within the brain. Patients become headachy, irrational, drowsy and confused over a period of hours and their walking becomes unsteady. Double vision may occur. The condition is a serious one and evacuation to lower altitudes is mandatory. Principles of treatment include:

- DESCENT, evacuation, oxygen.
- Dexamethasone 8mg by mouth, followed by 4mg every 4 hours for 24 hours.
- Hyperbaric chamber (portable pressure bag).

In both pulmonary and cerebral oedema medical advice is desirable, although it may not be available. Those who are suspected of having pulmonary or cerebral oedema should be evacuated to lower altitude promptly and should certainly not go high again until they have been seen by a doctor. Complete recovery is usual in both if patients have been treated early and appropriately.

Treatment of severe altitude sickness, type unknown

- DESCENT, evacuation, oxygen.
- Dexamethasone as above.
- Nifedipine as above.
- Hyperbaric chamber.

Peripheral oedema and retinal haemorrhages

Fluid retention causing swelling of an arm, a leg or the face is sometimes noticed on waking or after a long march. This is peripheral oedema. It usually subsides over several days and does not herald pulmonary or cerebral oedema.

Haemorrhages into the retina (minute blood blisters in the back of the eye) are known to occur quite commonly around 5,000m but rarely cause any problems, being unnoticed by the subject and visible only to a trained observer with specialist equipment (an ophthalmoscope). Very occasionally these tiny haemorrhages interfere with vision (causing a "hole" in the vision); descent is advised and complete recovery is usual.

Other problems

Cold and frostbite and their prevention and treatment are dealt with in Chapter 20.

Prevention of sunburn is essential. Although many proprietary creams and blocks are available, RoC Creme Ecran Total Protection Extreme – SPF 25, and Uvistat are particularly recommended. Simply covering exposed parts with silk or cotton masks is equally effective.

Snowblindness is a severe conjunctivitis (inflammation of the white of the eye) and keratitis (inflammation of the cornea) caused by exposure to UV light reflected off snow. This can happen in a matter of hours. Spare sunglasses should always be carried, and if these are not available a simple mask of cardboard or material with a thin slit to peer through can be used. Snowblindness is recognised by intensely red painful eyes. Treat it with rest, lying in a dark tent, and chloramphenicol (antibiotic) and betamethasone (steroid) eye drops.

Summary

AMS is a common and minor, although debilitating, problem of high altitude. Rarely it leads to two, potentially fatal conditions – pulmonary and cerebral oedema – both of which are medical emergencies.

In giving advice about travel to high altitudes it must be stressed that the simple adage of travelling slowly and descending if you are ill – advice known for generations in all high-altitude countries – cannot be bettered.

ADDITIONAL SUPPLIES FOR HIGH-ALTITUDE EXPEDITIONS

Medication
1. Acetazolamide (Diamox) 250mg by mouth twice daily for 5 days.
2. Dexamethasone 4mg tablets. Take 8mg at once and 4mg every 4 hours for up to 2 days.
3. Nifedipine (Adalat) 20mg by mouth at once and every 6 hours for 2 days.
4. Oxygen by mask, if available.
5. Portable hyperbaric chamber.

Pressure bags
Portable pressure chambers, which are bags inflated by a foot pump, can be life-saving and are easy to use. The patient is placed in a sleeping bag and the chamber zipped up. A simulated descent of 500 metres or more can be achieved in less than 15 minutes. Any expedition to altitudes of over 5,000 metres should consider carrying a pressure bag. They weigh less than 10kg.

Pressure bag suppliers

GAMOW Bag
Hyperbaric Technologies Inc
PO Box 69, Amsterdam
NY 12010, USA
Tel. +1 800 382 2491, fax +1 800 842 1031

CERTEC Bag
CERTEC
Sourcieux-les-Mines
69210 France
Tel. +33 74703982

Portable Altitude Chamber
CE Bartlett Pty Ltd
PO Box 49, Wendouree
VIC 3355, Australia
Tel. +61 3 53393103, fax +61 3 53381241

Each of these systems is effective and reliable. The Portable Altitude Chamber is the cheapest at present. Offers are sometimes made by the manufacturers, and it may be possible to borrow or hire equipment in Kathmandu (try Himalayan Rescue Association, PO Box 4044 Thamel, Kathmandu) and other centres.

Figure 21.2   *Testing a portable pressure chamber at high altitude – Sepu Kangri Base Camp, 4,700m, Eastern Tibet*
(C. Bonington, Chris Bonington Picture Library)

UIAA Mountain Medicine Centre at the British Mountaineering Council

For further information contact the Mountain Medicine Centre, which aims to advise climbers and mountain travellers. Eleven Information Sheets are produced for climbers and trekkers:

1. Mountain Sickness, Oedemas and Travel to High Altitude
2. Climbing at Extreme Altitudes above 7,000m
3. Diamox, Decadron and Nifedipine at High Altitudes
4. Portable Compression Chamber in Acute Mountain Sickness
5. First Aid Kits
6. Sunscreens and Altitude
7. International Transport of Drugs and Oxygen from Britain
8. Oxygen Systems Available for Use at High Altitudes
9. Causes of Death at Extreme Altitude
10. Frostbite – Practical Suggestions
11. The Oral Contraceptive Pill and High Altitudes

These are available from:
British Mountaineering Council (BMC)
177–179 Burton Road
West Didsbury
Manchester M20 2BB
Tel. +44 161 4454747, fax +44 161 4454500
E-mail: info@thebmc.co.uk

Expedition Advisory Centre
Royal Geographical Society
1 Kensington Gore
London SW7 2AR
Tel. +44 171 5913030, fax +44 171 5913031
E-mail: eac@rgs.org

22 UNDERWATER EXPEDITIONS

Victor de Lima and Bobby Forbes

Increasing interest in the exploration and conservation of the underwater world for scientific and recreational purposes has produced a dramatic increase in the use of diving as a means to achieve these goals. Study of the physiological stresses during and after increased pressure exposures has resulted in the development of the specialist field of hyperbaric medicine. This chapter presents general guidelines which may assist those involved in organising the medical care of diving expeditions. Inevitably, detailed consideration of the syndromes specific to diving pathology and their treatment is beyond the scope of this book and the reader is referred to the texts listed in the References (Appendix 3).

The vast majority of diving expeditions proceed smoothly as a result of meticulous preparation. Accident statistics from the Scientific Diving Supervisory Committee database show an incidence rate of approximately 0.2%. Table 22.1 gives an indication of the types of incidents that have been reported. It should be noted that a significant number of these have not resulted in injury to the diver. This excellent safety record may be attributed to precise planning, rigorous standards for diver selection, diver training and equipment design as well as careful pre-dive planning and adherence to established diving codes of practice. The member of the expedition designated as medical officer (MO) should ideally have a medical or nursing qualification and an interest in diving medicine, or be a diver with paramedic training.

PREPARATION
Diver selection
Divers on an expedition should have been examined medically by a physician with an interest in diving medicine to assess their fitness to dive. Physical requirements vary considerably and are reflected in the format of the medical examinations. For instance, the current recreational medical is a routine physical examination, with a chest X-ray where clinically indicated. In contrast, the medical examination carried

Figure 22.1   *Blue Holes Project, Caribbean (C. Howes)*

TABLE 22.1 ACCIDENT STATISTICS

1992 incidents

15	Free flow DVs (Antarctica)
1	Shared air ascent (failure to monitor air supply)
1	Concussion (hit by support boat)
1	Decompression illness

Incident rate 0.23%

1993 incidents

9	Free flow DVs
1	Burst HP hose
1	Burst LP hose
1	Mask
1	Outboard breakdown (requiring RNLI assistance)
1	Rapid ascent
2	Dangerous animals (Antarctica)
3	Slip on rock prior to dive
1	Decompression illness

Incidence rate 0.20%
(DCI rate 1 in 11,341)

out on working divers in the UK includes, in addition to the detailed physical check, routine haematology, blood grouping, sickle cell checks, chest X-ray where appropriate, electrocardiography, audiometry, obesity assessment and an exercise tolerance test. The current recommendations for medical examinations for fitness to dive can be found in the Code of Practice for Scientific Diving.

Absolute contraindications to scuba diving include the following:

- People subject to spontaneous pneumothorax.
- People subject to epileptic seizures or syncopal attacks.
- Lung cysts or definite air trapping lesions on chest X-ray.
- Perforated eardrum.
- Active asthma.
- Drug addiction.
- Unstable diabetes mellitus.
- Ear surgery involving a prosthesis in the air conduction chain.

Relative contraindications, subject to other considerations, include the following:

- Decrease of pulmonary reserve from any cause.
- Pregnancy.
- Obesity (body weight more than 20% above mean).
- History of thoracotomy.
- Myocardial infarction (if less than one year previously and if cardiac sequelae are present).
- Psychiatric or personality problems.

Conditions that may necessitate temporary disqualification from diving (and which may develop during the course of the expedition) include the following:

- Allergy resulting in sinus or middle ear congestion.
- Acute upper or lower respiratory tract infection.
- Alcoholic intoxication.
- Drugs that may interfere with normal diving – of particular relevance are anti-emetics, decongestants and hypnotics.

Diver training

Self Contained Underwater Breathing Apparatus (SCUBA), introduced by the late Jacques Cousteau, is the predominant diving technique employed by scientists. Training standards adopted by both recreational and professional diving federations are structured in such a way that students are initially taught fundamental diving skills, then progress to more demanding skills and tasks during their training period. All federations are structured on a tier certification system with an initial basic diving qualification progressing through a number of levels to an advanced qualification. In the UK the minimum qualification required by working scientists under the Code of Practice for Scientific Diving is Confédération Mondiale des Subaquatiques (CMAS) 3 Star. Divers qualified to this level possess a good theoretical and practical knowledge of basic diving techniques and have also received training in basic first aid, cardiopulmonary resuscitation (CPR) and diver rescue techniques.

One of the key contributing factors in diving accidents is the failure of divers to respond quickly and appropriately in an emergency situation as a result of the deterioration of basic skills since training. It is therefore advisable to assemble team members prior to the expedition to carry out a series of work-up dives to refresh basic emergency procedures and allow team members who may not have dived together before to become familiar with the diving procedures to be adopted on the expedition.

Equipment selection

As already mentioned SCUBA is the predominant technique used by the scientific diving community, although both surface supplied and saturation techniques have been used. In recent years there have been several developments in SCUBA to extend both depth and duration of the dive over conventional air SCUBA procedures. Notable among these is the use of decompression computers to give real-time decompression schedules and the increasing popularity of Enriched Air Nitrox (EANx) and rebreather systems. All of these advanced SCUBA techniques can considerably increase the safety of diving operations but require specialist training to prevent their misuse.

Medical supplies

The medical kit required by a diving expedition is unlikely to vary greatly from that of a non-diving expedition to the same geographical region (see Chapter 3). The expedition MO will find it useful to designate two kits: a major kit at base camp (which may or may not be at the site of the therapeutic chamber) which will have supplies of IV fluids and second-line drugs; and a minor kit at the immediate dive site, with a suitable portable oxygen set. Please refer to the end of this chapter for suggestions on the make-up of such kits.

In the initial planning stages of the expedition it will have been decided how, if necessary, the recompression of a diver will be carried out, either by on-site arrangements or by rapid evacuation to the nearest recompression facility. Regardless of which option is chosen, suitable quantities of oxygen must be available to cover the likely transit time. If the transit time from base camp to the nearest facility is likely to be of long duration then consideration should be given to carrying a monoplace chamber. It must be borne in mind, however, that should the casualty's condition worsen it is impossible to render effective treatment with such a unit.

MEDICAL PROBLEMS SPECIFIC TO DIVING EXPEDITIONS

The causes of incidents that may require treatment during a diving expedition can be categorised in three broad groups:

- General hazards
- Diving problems not requiring therapeutic recompression
- Diving problems requiring therapeutic recompression

General hazards

Under this heading fall a number of illnesses that are not necessarily specific to diving expeditions.

Sea sickness

Although not related to diving *per se*, this condition can have serious implications in diving operations. Medication for sea sickness should have been tried before the person embarks on diving, since the sedative effect of these drugs may increase nitrogen narcosis. However, if judiciously used they may lessen the risk of accidents caused by the distraction of motion sickness, as well as the possibility of disorientation underwater as a result of the associated vertigo. The drug most commonly used to combat sea sickness is cinnarizine: 30mg taken orally 2 hours prior to travel and then 15mg every 8 hours during sea travel.

Trauma

Minor lacerations and abrasions can become rapidly infected in the damp conditions encountered during diving and should be treated by the usual application of sterile dressings. Fortunately, major lacerations from propeller injuries and animal attacks are rare, but should they occur they require standard first aid management to prevent further blood loss.

Infections, envenoming and poisoning

The dangers posed by venomous marine animals are of specific relevance and are covered by David Warrell in Chapter 16. Superficial infections such as infected coral abrasions or of the external ear are common and generally respond to topical antiseptic/antibiotic preparations. Respiratory infections pose specific problems to the diver and should be treated with systemic (oral) antibiotics as well as systemic and/or local decongestants. Although decongestants have dangers, as they may wear off during a dive, their judicious use may make a probable dive definite as the diver begins to recover from an infection, and they considerably reduce the risk of ear barotrauma.

Diving problems not requiring therapeutic recompression

Carbon monoxide poisoning

Carbon monoxide may accidentally contaminate a diver's air supply because exhaust fumes from a petrol or diesel engine have been drawn into the compressor air intake while cylinders were being filled. Smokers have a higher concentration of carboxyhaemoglobin in the blood making them more sensitive to this condition. Toxic levels are achieved at depth because of the increased inspired partial pressure of the gas.

Symptoms range from dizziness, headache, fatigue and flushed lips and cheeks in mild cases to nausea, vomiting, unconsciousness and death.

Treatment includes immediate administration of 100% oxygen, preferably under

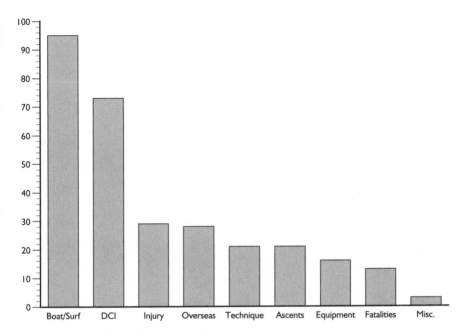

Figure 22.2 *Diving incidents by major category*
Source: BSAC Incident Report, 1996.

pressure to wash out the carbon monoxide from the blood. Hyperbaric schedules exist for therapeutic administration of oxygen for this purpose.

Nitrogen narcosis
Nitrogen toxicity is generally associated with breathing compressed air at a depth of around 30 metres; however, there is tremendous variability between and within individuals on a day-to-day basis. This effect may be aggravated by other factors including heavy exercise and carbon dioxide retention, cold, apprehension, alcohol hangover and poor physical condition.

Symptoms are similar to alcohol toxicity and include personality changes, impaired thinking ability, dizziness, loss of co-ordination and amnesia.

Treatment. As this condition is purely related to the partial pressure of nitrogen in the breathing gas the symptoms are alleviated by reducing the pressure, leaving no after-effects.

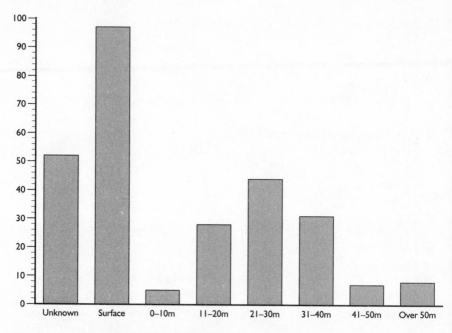

Figure 22.3   *Diving incidents – depth range*
          Source: BSAC Incident Report, 1996.

Oxygen toxicity

Oxygen toxicity exists in two forms: *pulmonary (chronic) toxicity*, which occurs when breathing elevated partial pressures of oxygen (0.5–1.4 bars) over extended periods of time; and *CNS (acute) toxicity*, when breathing partial pressures in excess of approximately 1.6 bars for much shorter periods. In terms of conventional air SCUBA, partial pressures and durations are neither high enough, at the depths used, nor long enough, because of limited gas supply, to be considered a problem. However, with the use of Nitrox and rebreather becoming more likely in the near future, oxygen toxicity poses a real danger if the established guidelines are not adhered to.

1. Pulmonary (chronic) oxygen toxicity

This results from breathing slightly elevated levels of oxygen over extended periods of time. The problems associated with this form of oxygen toxicity are well understood and guidelines for both daily and multiday exposure limits have been established through the National Oceanographic and Atmospheric Administration (NOAA) diving programme.

Symptoms. Sore chest, dry cough and reduced vital capacity.

Treatment. Prevent further exposure to elevated oxygen levels.

2. Central nervous system (acute) oxygen toxicity

This results from breathing oxygen at partial pressures of around 1.6 bars and above. However, individual variations in susceptibility mean that the condition may be present at lower thresholds; this is likely in cold conditions or during heavy exercise.

Symptoms include twitching of the limbs and other facial muscles, dizziness, nausea, disturbance of breathing rhythm, euphoria, tunnel vision and, most dramatically, convulsions similar to an epileptic fit followed by unconsciousness. Breath-holding during this condition means that care must be taken in recovering a diver from depth during an incident to prevent the possibility of pulmonary barotrauma.

Treatment involves returning the casualty to air breathing, and general supportive measures including observation of the casualty in the recovery position or resuscitation if appropriate. Once the diver is returned to air breathing they should recover consciousness in 5–30 minutes, but during this period there may be further convulsions. Following recovery the diver will be amnesic for the event, and should be observed for associated problems of musculo-skeletal injury resulting from the convulsion or pulmonary barotrauma resulting from breath-holding in the course of a convulsion during ascent.

Carbon dioxide poisoning (hypercapnia)

Normally, carbon dioxide should be removed by breathing out, so the factors resulting in a raised CO_2 blood level include those which reduce normal breathing efficiency in the diver or his apparatus. These may include an inefficient demand valve, a large dead space in the breathing circuit, restrictive clothing, an inefficient or exhausted CO_2 scrubber in a rebreather system, inappropriate flow rates with free-flow helmets and overexertion.

Symptoms. Levels of CO_2 in excess of 0.05 bars will cause breathlessness with an increased rate of breathing, and a progressive rise in CO_2 pressure will result in headaches, confusion, convulsions, unconsciousness and death.

Treatment. Once CO_2 toxicity is recognised the diver should stop physical exertion, relax and try to remain calm, concentrate on developing a controlled breathing rate, flush the mask or helmet with air, and breath deeply rather than in rapid shallow breaths before attempting to ascend. As CO_2 is a metabolic by-product, output is constant regardless of depth. Should the diver ascend on initial recognition of CO_2 toxicity there will be a rapid increase in the percentage of CO_2, resulting in a *shallow water blackout* and possible drowning. If the diver is on a closed or semi-closed breathing set he should change to open circuit as soon as possible.

Barotrauma

Pressure induced injuries (barotrauma) may affect any gas-filled space such as the lungs, ear (external, middle or inner), sinuses and dental cavities, as well as dry suit, mask or helmet spaces. These lesser forms of barotrauma may occur on descent ("squeeze") or ascent and should generally be avoidable by routine pressure equalisation techniques.

Sinus barotrauma of descent is associated with diving with a respiratory tract infection. During descent pain is usually felt in the frontal sinuses, but this may be noticed only as momentary discomfort as a result of bleeding into the sinus allowing equalisation. During ascent the expanding gas may explosively clear the sinus ducts causing blood release into the nasal passage. Antibiotic treatment may be necessary.

Ear barotrauma is by far the most common problem associated with diving as the pressure to complete survey work often overrides the rationale of not diving with a cold. This condition has several forms.

1. *Middle ear barotrauma of descent* arises because of failure to equalise middle ear air pressure with that of the environment as a result of inflammation of the Eustachian tube. There are varying degrees of damage caused by this condition ranging from slight haemorrhaging of the eardrum to blood observed behind the eardrum to the most severe case of a perforated eardrum. Symptoms range from pain in mild cases to reduced or loss of hearing in more severe conditions. In cold water conditions the diver may suffer from transient vertigo as water enters the middle ear. Treatment is to avoid further diving until recovery and the use of antibiotics (Augmentin) may be necessary. The length of recovery will vary from several days in the case of slight haemorrhaging to several weeks in the case of a ruptured eardrum.

2. *Middle ear barotrauma of ascent (reversed ear)* arises where the diver has managed to equalise during the descent, albeit with some degree of difficulty, but during ascent the expanding gas in the middle ear can no longer escape through the Eustachian tube. The trapped gas causes the eardrum to be displaced outwards again causing pain, haemorrhaging and in severe cases rupture of the eardrum. Treatment is as for barotrauma of descent.

3. *Inner ear barotrauma of descent* is potentially the most severe of the three and is usually associated with a sudden and violent equalisation causing displacement of the round window of the inner ear. Symptoms first manifest as tinnitus and may not appear until reaching the bottom or during ascent. On surfacing the diver may then

display signs of nausea and vertigo and be unco-ordinated. These symptoms are similar to those of a neurological decompression incident but in the case of inner ear barotrauma are transitory. A careful history of the dive should be taken in order to eliminate the possibility of decompression illness, as further subjection to pressure will increase the damage in a barotrauma incident. Treatment usually comprises rest and not being subjected to any further pressure changes or loud noise in less severe cases, or surgery if there is extensive damage.

Pulmonary barotrauma (burst lung) is usually caused by breath-holding on ascent and is particularly likely if the diver runs out of air and returns to the surface by free uncontrolled ascent. It will take one of two forms:

1. *Interstitial emphysema.* The gas may escape into the subcutaneous tissues in the chest and neck, with some discomfort and a feeling of fullness in the neck area and a crackling sensation of the skin. The condition is likely to resolve spontaneously without any need for recompression therapy. The gas may, however, track into the mediastinal cavity, the region between the lungs, causing cardiac distress. This is a potentially life-threatening condition and may require rapid recompression.

2. *Pneumothorax.* Escape of gas into the space between the lung and chest wall (pleural cavity) causing collapse of the lung will manifest as shortness of breath, chest pain, coughing of bloody, frothy sputum and swelling of the neck veins with an irregular pulse. Most divers with pneumothorax will respond to breathing 100% oxygen, and cannulation is only indicated if more than 40% of the lung has collapsed (as determined by chest X-ray), or if there is hypoxia or a coincident need for recompression.

Diving problems that require recompression

Arterial gas embolism (AGE)
A significant percentage of cases of pulmonary barotrauma involve a degree of entry of gas from the burst lung into the bloodstream (pulmonary veins) from where the bubbles find their way into the arterial circulation. They may then cause a blockage through gas embolism or plugging of the cerebral arteries to the brain or occasionally the coronary arteries to the heart. Because of cerebral involvement a wide variety of neurological symptoms may be present and the diver may become unconscious at the surface, often within a few minutes of resurfacing. Any diver having made a rapid ascent and becoming unconscious on reaching the surface should be assumed to be suffering from a cerebral air gas embolism (CAGE).

Treatment. This is EXTREMELY URGENT and IMMEDIATE RECOMPRESSION in

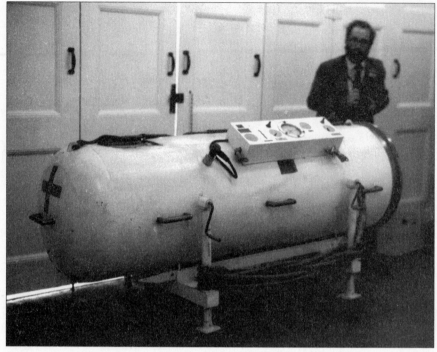

Figure 22.4   *Monoplace decompression chamber (V. de Lima/B. Forbes)*

a chamber should be undertaken following therapeutic flow charts and decompression tables. As victims are often also likely to have suffered drowning, cardio-pulmonary resuscitation may have to be initiated.

Decompression illness (DCI)

Decompression illness occurs when inert gases in the tissues come out of solution to form tissue bubbles causing localised symptoms, or bloodstream bubbles causing circulatory blockage with resulting tissue hypoxia.

Symptoms. Classically, decompression illness is divided into two types:

- Type I (mild). Symptoms may be skin bends with pain and itching of the skin or a blotchy mottled rash, joint pains and fatigue.
- Type II (serious). There may be a variety of symptoms including shock, nausea, hearing and speech difficulty, abnormal "girdle pains", chest pain, shortness of breath (chokes), weakness, numbness or paralysis of the limbs, involuntary flickering of the eye (nystagmus) and loss of consciousness.

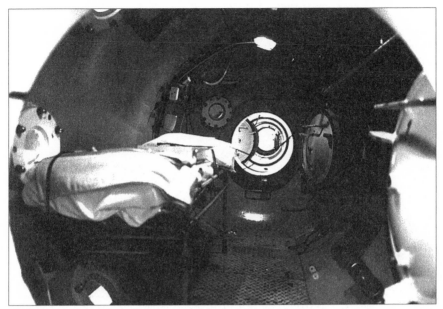

Figure 22.5   *Therapeutic decompression chamber (V. de Lima/B. Forbes)*

The symptoms of DCI usually have a latent period of at least 5 minutes after surfacing from a dive but may occur many hours after the dive has ended and may be progressive with mild symptoms developing to a more serious presentation. This latent period is the main diagnostic criterion in distinguishing between serious neurological DCI and a CAGE.

Treatment. If there is no recompression (hyperbaric) chamber on site a diver with suspected Type I DCI should be observed carefully. In the event of progressive symptoms, or with Type II DCI, the diver should be given 100% oxygen via a face mask, and intravenous fluid (arbitrarily 1 litre of crystalloid solution every 2–4 hours, assuming there is no evidence of brain and/or pulmonary oedema). The diver should be transferred immediately to the nearest recompression chamber and compressed on oxygen. Further therapeutic treatment will depend on response to initial recompression. The consensus of opinion is that the head down position is of transient benefit for those with arterial bubbles, and that injured divers are better nursed in the supine position unless unconscious or vomiting, in which case they should be nursed on their side. Particularly if neurological symptoms are present, divers should not be allowed to sit up until inside a recompression chamber.

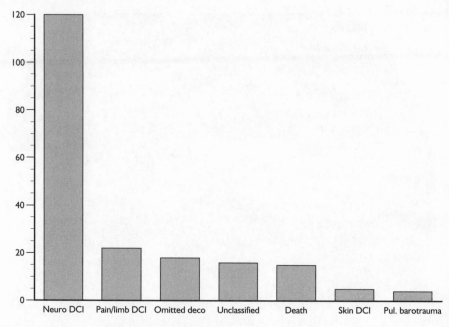

Figure 22.6   *Decompression illness by type*
            Source: BSAC Incident Report, 1996.

Advice about the management of diving accidents is available continuously by telephone from the International Divers' Alert Network (DAN)

United States: +1 191 6848111
Europe (Italy): +39 821 64026
Australasia: 008 088 200 (within Australia); +61 82232855 (outside Australia)

Within the UK the Royal Navy provides an additional service:
Superintendent of Diving at HMS Vernon (Portsmouth)
Tel. +44 1705 822351 ext. 872375 (during the day); ext. 872417/4/5 at other times

ADDITIONAL MEDICAL SUPPLIES FOR DIVING EXPEDITIONS

Base camp medical kit

Additional items to those listed in Chapter 3:

Oxygen with mask and tubing
Normal saline 500ml × 4
Intravenous fluid infusion sets
Intravenous cannulae 18g × 4 (eg Venflon)
Inflatable splints
Plaster of Paris bandage
Velband
Chest drains, tubing and Heimlich valves
Urinary catheter and drainage bag
Laryngoscope and batteries
Endotracheal tubes
Airways
Artery forceps
Suction catheter and apparatus
Syringes 10ml, 20ml and 50ml
Naso-gastric tube
Aneroid sphygmomanometer and BP cuff
50% dextrose injection
Ventolin inhaler and spacer device
Diazepam injection
Ketamine injection

Dive site/mobile camp medical kit

Additional items to those listed in Chapter 3, Table 3.2:

Auroscope
Stethoscope
Sleek adhesive tape (2 rolls)
Sutures:
    0-0 Black silk on hand needle
    3-0 Dexon
    5-0 Nylon
Syringes 2ml and 5ml
Injection needles and cannulae (assorted)
Sofratulle – dressing for a wide range of infected lesions
Fusidic acid cream 30g – topical antibacterial cream for skin infections

Miconazole cream 30g – topical antifungal cream for feet infections
Betnovate cream 30g
Neutrogena hand cream
Antacid tablets (eg Alcin)
Cinnarizine tablets 15mg – anti-sea sickness medication
Buccastem 3mg – anti-sea sickness medication
Glyceryl trinitrate spray
Lip salve
Calamine cream
Space blanket

Emergency injections box
Adrenaline 1 in 1,000 solution
Atropine 600mcg/ml
Dexamethasone 4mg/ml; 20mg/ml
Benzyl penicillin 600mg vial
Hydrocortisone 100mg/2ml vial
Metoclopramide 5mg/ml
Chlorpheniramine 10mg/ml

Note. Figures 22.2, 22.3 and 22.6 are reproduced from the BSAC Incident Report 1996, by kind permission of Brian Cumming, Safety Adviser, British Sub-Aqua Club.

23 CAVING EXPEDITIONS

Jon Buchan

Caving expeditions are exciting. The great majority take place without accidents or mishaps, and for the medical officer (MO) many of the medical problems seen are similar to any other expedition.

THE RISKS

Bryan Ellis of the British Cave Research Association (BCRA) has kindly supplied the following figures culled from insurance claims by expedition members for the past five years. The author is grateful to him for his help.

TABLE 23.1	INSURANCE CLAIMS BY EXPEDITION MEMBERS, 1992–97	
Year	People insured	Medical incidents resulting in claims
1992–93	754	3
1993–94	629	No claims made
1994–95	581	2
1995–96	707	1
1996–97	517	2

Note. The figures include four fatalities.

There are risks, but these must be put into perspective and it is for expedition members to decide for themselves what is an acceptable risk. Most cavers would prefer to risk their lives exploring some unknown caving system abroad rather than remaining in the UK. It is a matter of priorities.

PREPARATION

Knowledge of the area

The first task is to learn as much as possible about the expedition area. The BCRA library in Matlock is a good starting point. There is an index of BCRA reports which is currently being prepared for publication. There are not many recent British papers on caving medical problems because the trend seems to be towards smaller expeditions which manage their medical affairs without difficulty. Small expeditions do not produce medical reports as such and it may be necessary to make personal contact to find out if there were any problems, what they were, what the conditions were like and how the MO coped. It is far more important to know what the conditions were like than what went on during the expedition.

Attitudes and commitment

Cave exploration pushes people to the limits of their strength and endurance; this is all part of the fun. The problem is that, at those limits, quite a small loss of function can have a profound effect on performance. One of the hardest jobs for an MO is to stop someone going underground for health reasons, perhaps just when something exciting is found. People need to be well; exploration depends on it. As MO you will need to think about whether or not you are going to become involved. You may find yourself asked a range of questions which reflect more the anxiety of the expedition member than a strictly medical problem. Is this aspect of the work something you

Figure 23.1   *River cave passage, Mulu, Sarawak (A. Eavis/RGS)*

can handle? Are you going to give advice or not? There may be no right answer, it depends on the individual, but it is best to be clear in your own mind at the outset how you are going to react and cope with this.

Figure 23.2   *Moulin Rouge Passage, Mulu, Sarawak (A. Eavis/RGS)*

MEDICAL PROBLEMS SPECIFIC TO CAVING EXPEDITIONS

Flooding
The utmost vigilance is needed when exploring a new system that is liable to flood. The problem is particularly acute in tropical regions where there can be really sudden, heavy rain. One expedition was seriously thwarted by a complete flood of the system it was meant to explore. Despite the greatest possible care it is not uncommon for explorers to be trapped by rising water. They can then opt to sit it out, dive out or find a dry way back. Medically, there should not be a problem; the worst hazard would be for the MO to be one of those trapped when there was an incident somewhere else.

Hypothermia
Cavers should be well aware of this hazard. Whether or not it is relevant to your expedition depends on where you are going. Not just the MO but all members of the team must prepare for possible exposure/exhaustion and take all necessary steps to

avoid it. The experience of expedition members should make hypothermia unlikely unless there has been an unavoidable mishap. (See Chapter 20.)

Histoplasmosis

The curse of Tutankhamen is said to be histoplasma infection. The disease is found in guano caves. It was responsible for some serious sickness in Mexico in the early 1980s but it is treatable. Most cavers with tropical experience have been exposed to the illness without realising it. They have had a subclinical infection. There is a comprehensive list of infected caves in the American literature.

Leptospirosis

This infection is rare and only occasionally seen in the UK among sewerage workers. Some caves have drainage that puts them almost into the category of a sewer, and there have been cases of Weil's disease, the most severe form of leptospirosis.

Other strains of leptospira have caused feverish illnesses in explorers and it has been a particular problem in Mulu, Sarawak. Leptospirosis can be a hazard to cave explorers but it is treatable. The subject has been well reviewed by Self *et al.* (see References, Appendix 3).

Rabies

Bats carry rabies and there is evidence that the disease can be transmitted to humans. Those who explore bat infested caves would probably be wise to be protected against rabies in addition to the routine inoculations recommended in Chapter 2. It is not treatable and prevention is the only option.

Radon gas

Some caves have quite high concentrations of radioactive radon. Most expeditions do not measure radioactivity so the extent of the hazard, if any, is not known. Perhaps one day the Geiger counter will become as much part of caving expeditions as the tape and compass but, for the moment, exploration can continue untrammelled by fears of imperceptible and therefore doubly sinister hazards.

Trauma

This is not peculiar to caving. You will need to consider injuries underground and how they are to be managed. The helicopter is useless as a get-me-home-quick device so it will be all improvisation and muscles.

All the British-based rescue organisations say that the majority of call-outs are to novice cavers who have done something that has got them into trouble. This should not be a problem. No one will get stuck on a rope or fail to climb a pitch because of a grazed hand. Nevertheless, some caving accidents cannot be foreseen and, after one of these, a rescue may be inevitable. The team as a whole will be responsible for organising the rescue, but prior to the expedition the expedition leader will have given considerable thought as to how it is to be managed. The skill and experience of the expedition members are likely to mean that the problem is resolved quickly. As MO you should consider your role. Normally, it will be to care for the victim to the exclusion of all else. Your place is at the side of the casualty to make sure nothing happens, such as a boot in the face, and you should also advise your rescuing colleagues of any change in the casualty's condition. Deterioration may mean more urgency, but improvement may allow a more sophisticated rescue technique which is less demanding of the rescuers.

Falls

Even expert cavers sometimes make mistakes and this must be accepted. Falls come in all grades of severity from the immediately fatal, for example, when a caver abseiled off the wrong rope, to the spectacularly trivial, when a well-known expedition leader was filmed disappearing down a pitch only to land safely on a soft colleague below.

Rock falls

These, again, can be of all degrees of severity from a dislodged rock landing on a colleague's head and damaging only the video camera he was carrying in his helmet to the immediate and unremarked death of a young man in the Gouffre Berger. Explorers are always on the lookout for instability and generally try to avoid obvious traps. A rock fall has, nevertheless, been the cause of at least one expedition rescue and was responsible for a spectacular near miss when a boulder and a tape recorder went plummeting down a shaft. A caver dangling on a rope in the shaft heard the shout just in time to pendulum out of the way. It is this kind of skill and experience that helps expeditions stay out of serious trouble.

SUMMARY

Caving expeditions are exciting. For the MO many of the medical problems encountered are the same as for any other expedition. Negotiating skills are important for the MO to make sure that whoever has responsibility takes into account the medical dimension. The same applies to transport and evacuation routes. A helicopter pad may seem a luxury until you have to fly out a sick explorer. The MO is usually not the decision-maker in any of these cases and it is important to know who is. A good team will find the right solution with the minimum of fuss and a good team is what every expedition aspires to be.

24 CANOE, KAYAK AND RAFT EXPEDITIONS

Andy Watt

DEFINITIONS

Kayaks are usually single-seat, decked craft powered by double-bladed paddles; canoes are bigger, open craft, with single-bladed paddles. Rafts are inflatable rubber craft, powered by either a guide with a set of oars mounted centrally, or by less experienced people (up to eight) using paddles and steered by a guide at the back.

Water journeys can be expeditions, where people, usually with some experience, plan and carry out their own trip, or commercial, where private companies take

Figure 24.1 *Kayaker tackling white water (A. Watt)*

clients down white-water rivers. Expeditions can be grouped into the following:

Flat water

These expeditions are undertaken for pleasure or scientific purposes, on slow-flowing rivers or lakes, in rafts, kayaks and open canoes. The terrain they pass through, such as jungle or arid areas, is often as important to the expedition members as the water they travel on (see previous chapters). This chapter is aimed at more specialist paddlers.

River

These expeditions are undertaken by white-water kayakers to whom the terrain is often less important than the rapids they seek. With the growth in popularity of destinations like Nepal and Chile, increasing numbers of paddlers with little expedition or medical experience are travelling to remote areas. In addition, the rivers are bigger, significantly faster and more powerful, they show marked seasonal variation and there is less information available on them compared with rivers at home.

Sea canoeing

People who participate in this activity are often experienced in multiday trips and in eliciting tidal and local weather information.

PREPARATION

As you will be paddling on long, multiday trips, which are more physically and mentally demanding than day trips at home, you should be fit. For cardiovascular fitness running and swimming are better than weight training, but time in a boat (especially distance paddling) is the best preparation. Anyone who has suffered from tenosynovitis (inflammation of the synovium, the sheath surrounding muscle tendons) should consider changing their paddle feather or using cranked shafts.

All the team members should review their management of a near-drowned casualty, including resuscitation. Although many practise their deep-water rescue techniques, prevention is better than cure, especially the ability to roll in agitated water.

As space is usually limited, a lot of thought has to go into deciding what medical kit is indispensable. (See Chapter 3 for further general information on medical kits.) Waterproofing the kit is essential. Put groups of items in Ziplok plastic bags; double dry bags for the whole kit would not be excessive. Also make sure that a spare kit is carried in another boat, and that each paddler takes a plastic dropper bottle for iodine. Take one bandage, but it should be a large one that can be cut to fit. A strong painkiller is essential and some thought should be given as to which one to include.

Additional medical supplies for water-based expeditions

- Iodine or povidone for cuts and water purification
- Anti-friction plaster, eg Moleskin
- Otosporin eardrops
- Sea sickness tablets, eg cinnarizine 15mg
- Ear plugs, cotton wool and Vaseline
- Neutrogena handcream
- Lipsalve
- Calamine lotion for sunburn

MEDICAL PROBLEMS SPECIFIC TO WATER-BASED EXPEDITIONS

Water quality
Iodine is the preferred option for sterilising water among experienced paddlers, with each carrying their own personal supply. Canoes do not have much space for extra fuel to boil water or for filters, although rafts may have.

The water in lakes or rivers in developing countries should always be considered unclean, but the concentration of bugs is usually low enough for your stomach acid to deal with small volumes of water (for example, from splashes).

In countries with seasonal monsoons the rivers are most dirty immediately after the rains start, when the land gets "flushed".

Dehydration
Paradoxically, despite being surrounded by water, dehydration can be a problem, especially for raft groups in hot countries or sea kayakers in semi-tropical areas, who may not realise that water intake in the sun should be about 3–4 litres a day. The early signs of dehydration are vague symptoms such as headache, light-headedness, lethargy and just feeling unwell. These are difficult to recognise unless you are on the lookout for them.

Diarrhoea
If a paddler gets diarrhoea the group should tighten up its hygiene practices. Treatment for simple diarrhoea for the first few days is fluid replacement, not medicines. If the diarrhoea is accompanied by abdominal pain, blood or fever, or persists for more than 3 days, antibiotics, such as ciprofloxacin, may be considered (see Chapter 14). Paddlers with simple diarrhoea on the harder, more exhausting rivers may consider antibiotics before 3 days have passed.

Accidents

Although many first-time paddlers are concerned about exotic diseases abroad, in fact more are killed or injured by road accidents on the way to the river, especially when driving at night. Once on the trip you are more likely to be hampered by accidents caused by foolishness or lack of foresight (campfire burns, twisted ankles because of inadequate footwear, and so on) than by natural incidents.

The most important item of equipment on the water is a lifejacket/buoyancy aid, especially for the flat-water sections, where people, particularly those on rafts, can become careless. If for any reason you end up in the water, your chances of drowning, or being seriously incapacitated, after a head injury, hypothermia, and so on, are much higher if a lifejacket/buoyancy aid is not worn.

Near drowning

This term is more accurate than drowned (someone who is dead). Near drowning ranges from a bad swim with a gasping but conscious victim to prolonged immersion with loss of consciousness. These stages can be with or without water inhalation (dry drowning is caused by the larynx or voice box closing in spasm and preventing both air and water getting to the lungs).

If the patient has suffered prolonged immersion, for example, at sea, they should be lifted out horizontally (to stop the blood pressure dropping severely) and gently, if they are hypothermic. (Rough handling can induce fatal rhythms in a hypothermic heart.)

Head injuries may be a cause of unconsciousness and are often accompanied by neck injuries. Removal of helmets should be done by two people, with one responsible for holding the head stable. If a neck injury is suspected, remember that establishing the airway means lifting the chin, in other words not bending the neck. Clearly, if you are on your own on a slippery bank such advice is hard to follow. If there is only a low suspicion of neck injury, then absent breathing demands more urgent attention. The lungs cannot be emptied of water; besides, manoeuvres to do this precipitate vomiting.

Aftercare of the near-drowned patient

Remember to place an unconscious individual in the recovery position (see page 105); and be aware that they will be quite likely to vomit immediately afterwards. Keep them warm and move them as little as possible. You should commence regular observations of respiratory rate, pulse, temperature and urine output to pick up early signs of impending trouble (see Chapter 10).

Severe respiratory illness (secondary drowning) can occur 12–24 hours after a near drowning. This is more likely if the near drowning was severe, for example with unconsciousness, or if "crackles" can be heard when you put your ear to the patient's chest. They should be evacuated to a facility that has oxygen and artificial ventilation (usually only available in cities). After a near drowning in dirty water, antibiotics (such as amoxycillin/erythromycin plus metronidazole) may be needed to prevent pneumonia.

A lot of people are aware that there are differences between fresh- and salt-water near drowning, but in practice this does not affect your management. Near-drowned people do not usually inhale enough water to cause these problems; if they do, they are likely to be extremely unwell no matter what the composition of the water.

Hypothermia

Significant hypothermia can occur in water temperatures below 20°C, which covers most waters that expeditions paddle in. It can be a big drain on the body's resources because water removes heat 25 times faster than the air trapped by our clothes. Hypothermia can be a hidden danger. Experienced paddlers will notice the subtle early signs of hypothermia in group members, especially those who have been rolling a lot or have had a swim. These include shivering, mild confusion, muscle inco-ordination and the simple statement "I'm feeling cold".

Shivering can be absent when body temperatures fall below 32°C, so you should still consider the possibility of hypothermia in someone who is very unwell but not shivering.

Muscles become weak, stiff and less responsive to commands. The resultant poor co-ordination can cause capsizes, and failure to roll and can prevent paddlers from climbing out of the water. Mental faculties become slower leading to poor judgement. This progresses to confusion and disorientation with slurred speech. Accidents then become inevitable.

The group should stop and get the person warmed up. If you are at the end of the day, close to your destination, with no ideal campsite, the temptation is to press on. But remember that the hypothermic person (and, probably, others in the group) will be markedly less competent at paddling.

Warming up should preferably be done with wet clothes off and in a sleeping bag, possibly with someone else. Insulate the person from the cold ground and cover their head. Encourage the person to drink warm fluids. Remember that the skin warms up before the inner (core) temperature, and the person feels inappropriately better. Allow plenty of time for rewarming, and up to a day for rest thereafter.

Seriously hypothermic patients should be handled carefully, as fatal heart rhythms can be precipitated. Unfortunately, in remote areas, not much more can be done to rewarm them beyond the measures mentioned above.

Resuscitation of the drowned

The management of a casualty, pulled out of the water during a remote developing world expedition, who has stopped breathing, is as follows:

- Check airway and breathing, and give a quick inflation of expired air resuscitation (EAR) if breathing is absent.
- Lift out of the water horizontally (if immersion is prolonged) and as gently as possible.
- Check circulation.

Remember that on an expedition in a developing country, starting external cardiac compression (ECC) may not be as useful as in a developed country.

If the pulse is absent

This usually means that the heart has stopped. If so, you cannot restart it with ECC. The only thing that can restart a stopped heart is a defibrillator from a reasonably good medical facility. Current advice from the Medical Commission on Accident Prevention is that this has to be within 2 hours of the drowning incident. The purpose of ECC is to keep the circulation going until a defibrillator is reached; in a developing country this is very unlikely.

However, the feeling that "you must do something" means that most people will start ECC, but they should ensure that:

- the pulse is definitely absent (the carotid pulse is the easiest to feel – just beside, and deep to, the Adam's apple);
- the victim is not significantly hypothermic (see below).

Once started, ECC has to be applied efficiently and without a break at 80–100 compressions a minute. This is clearly very difficult in the wilderness, and almost impossible in an evacuation.

Realistically, you are applying ECC in the small hope that a condition other than a stopped heart is responsible for the absent pulse. Someone with a heart that has stopped is effectively dead, and this should always be borne in mind in any resuscitation attempt.

If breathing has stopped

If breathing has stopped and you are unsure of the pulse, you should start EAR. It can provide oxygen to a heart that is beating weakly; it can stimulate breathing in the near-drowning condition of "cold shock" where the breathing stops; it is applied at a slower and less exhausting rate than ECC; and it can help a little in rewarming a body.

If the heart stops in the presence of a rescuer (a witnessed arrest) then an immediate thump to the chest can (very occasionally) restart it. This is called a pre-cordial thump. However, in the situation being discussed, this must be given within 5 minutes of immersion, and where the pulse was present as the body was pulled from the water but then stopped.

Hypothermia and drowning

If the victim is in very cold water, severe hypothermia can modify the above advice. This can be roughly assessed by feeling the armpit to see if it is marble cold.

Severe hypothermia can mimic death in that the body is cold, stiff, with white/blue skin, dilated pupils and barely detectable breathing or pulses, so your examination should be very thorough (for example, you should feel for a carotid pulse for 1 minute). If there is a chance that the victim is still alive, you should start EAR and rewarming (but not ECC – see below). If you start EAR the advice is that you cannot say the patient is dead (that is, there is no pulse, or other sign of life) until they have been rewarmed; theoretically, this means to 36°C, which may take 6 hours or more. In other words, they are not dead until they are warm and dead.

There are cases that have survived prolonged immersion (up to an hour) in very cold water, but most of them have been children who get to a high-tech medical facility).

The heart is very unstable in severe hypothermia, and thus can be easily jolted into a fatal rhythm. This means that:

- ECC probably should not be applied. If the pulse is too weak or slow to be felt, ECC may cause fatal rhythms in a heart that is beating; the heart has a slightly better chance of slowly improving by itself if only rewarming and EAR are provided;
- the body should only be moved if it is strictly necessary, and then as carefully as possible.

The above information is complex and, in reality, very few people are likely to be in this situation. However, this text aims to give you a better understanding of your options. If you are within 2 hours of a medical facility (longer if significantly hypothermic), then start resuscitation.

One of the points to be made is that you should always try, but this can be a problem in situations where the rescuers themselves are in danger or are exhausted from prolonged resuscitation. The result may be that, in the wilderness, cardiopulmonary resuscitation (CPR) of hopeless cases, in dangerous circumstances, will be halted sooner and attention turned to the next problem: the management of the tired, cold, shocked, bereaved group and the prevention of further accidents.

Shoulder injuries and dislocation

Shoulder dislocations are probably the most serious injury that canoeists will experience. Intermediate kayakers, unfamiliar with the power of big water rivers, should be especially careful. Your future in white-water canoeing is limited if you have a dislocation, as subsequent dislocations happen a lot more easily. Prevention is better than cure. When paddling, you should never let your hands rise above the level of your shoulders.

In the wilderness, it is reasonable for you to try and put back ("reduce") a dislocated shoulder. The technique is simple, you are unlikely to cause more damage than has already been caused, the healing process can start sooner, there is likely to be less damage to the shoulder in the long term, and the patient will be more comfortable during the evacuation. However, it should always be the patient's decision as to whether reduction is attempted.

Action must be swift. Relocation can more easily be done in the first few minutes, but becomes progressively more difficult during the next 2 hours as muscle spasm sets in.

If you suspect a dislocated shoulder:

- Administer your strongest painkiller and, if you have it, 5mg of valium to suck as it is absorbed faster than by swallowing (valium is a muscle as well as a brain relaxant).
- Gently remove buoyancy aid and paddle jacket and carefully examine the arm and shoulder. Check and record the pulse and that the patient can move their fingers.

The diagnosis is usually obvious and the patient realises their shoulder is "out"; the elbow will lie away from their side and they cannot move their arm. From the front, the shoulder looks abnormally square compared with the other side. The head of the upper arm bone (humerus) can usually be felt in front of the cup of the joint.

Complications are unusual but the following should be checked for:

- Fracture of the upper arm is rare and indicated by severe pain, excessive swelling and grating of the arm with movement. The elbow may touch the trunk. Do not attempt to relocate; strap up the arm and evacuate the patient.
- Common, but not serious, is numbness in the upper part of the arm (where injections are given). This indicates bruising of a small nerve close to the shoulder joint and should be noted (subsequent physiotherapy will be delayed).
- Very uncommon is paralysis of the fingers with definite numbness; this may indicate major nerve damage.

The principle of good reduction is *a very slow continuous pull* to tease out the muscle spasm. When the humerus head comes to the edge of the cup of the joint it will suddenly "clunk" into place. If you pull too hard or too sharply, muscle spasm will worsen and grip the humeral head more firmly outside the cup.

There are several techniques, but the two easiest ones are as follows:

1. Lie the victim face down on a flat boulder, rock ledge or similar with a table-like

edge, so that their arm hangs down freely. Attach a helmet or bucket to their wrist. Add a weight (eg small stones) of around 2kg (3kg for a large patient) and very slowly increase this to double; if the patient has pain then decrease the weight. Leave the patient alone; gravity does the work as the patient's muscles relax. After 5–15 minutes the patient should feel a "clunk" which will indicate relocation.

2. Lie the patient on their back and sit with your legs extended, facing the head, holding the wrist between your thighs. If the right shoulder is dislocated, place the arch of your right foot (not the toes) in the armpit and press against the chest wall. Keeping your arms straight (less tiring), very, very slowly lean back. (Do not press too hard with your foot as it is resting close to nerves in the armpit.) After 5–10 minutes a clunk will indicate relocation.

After treatment, whether relocated or not, check and record the wrist pulse again, and strap the arm to the front of the chest with the hand level with the other shoulder. (See Chapter 11 for further information.) You should consult a good physiotherapist as soon as possible, so that you can minimise long-term damage.

MISCELLANEOUS MEDICAL PROBLEMS IN CANOEISTS

Cuts
Cuts, especially on the legs, may not heal until the trip is finished. Even the smallest of cuts regularly get infected, so at the end of every day's paddling, wash the cut, apply iodine or povidone and a small plaster. So-called waterproof dressings usually are not (although some people use Opsite successfully). My preferred option is the ubiquitous duct-tape. It is not stretchy, but it does stick well and most canoeists carry some in any case for boat repair.

The best way to prevent infection is to close cuts, with Steristrips or sutures, if you have the training. On water-based trips, you may find that Steristrips do not stick well, even with the addition of sticky tincture of benzoin to the skin.

Hand blisters
These are fairly common on multiday trips, even among experienced paddlers who perhaps have not been paddling recently. If you feel a faint, early soreness it is worthwhile trying some Moleskin or second skin strapped over the friction point before a blister is formed. Blisters usually de-roof with further paddling; treat them as you would a simple cut.

Burns
Wood fires are common on river trips and burn injuries are frequent. If the burn is

Figure 24.2   *Kayaking on open sea water (A. Watt)*

severe enough to require a flamazine dressing, then keeping it dry is important, but it probably does not need to be changed unless it gets drenched (see Chapter 11).

Piles (haemorrhoids)

These are common in rafters, kayakers and mountaineers but no one knows why. Symptoms are pain, bright red bleeding on defaecation, or a lump sticking out of the anus. Treat with careful washing and application of a local anaesthetic, for example, Xyloproct ointment. Paradoxically, both diarrhoea and constipation can make haemorrhoids worse. If you do suffer from them, consider getting them treated before you go.

Colds and sore throats

These are fairly common on multiday trips. Treatment is simple, with paracetamol and plenty of fluids. If the infection moves down to your chest, a dirty spit, sometimes green, can result. Anything worse than this should probably be treated with antibiotics (such as amoxycillin or erythromycin), especially if the patient has a temperature.

Kayakers sometimes complain of "water in the ear", often when they have a cold and have been rolling. The sensation is in fact not caused by water in the external ear but by an imbalance of pressure in the inner ear caused by a blockage of the very narrow tube that joins the inner ear to the throat (Eustachian tube). This may be eased by exhaling against a closed mouth and pinched nose, or by swallowing. Inhaling steam helps. You should wait until any colds have cleared before you go back to doing Eskimo rolls.

External ear infections

To treat external ear infections, apply Otosporin eardrops (2 drops 3 times a day) and use an earplug of cotton wool in Vaseline. If you already suffer from "Surfer's Ear" (exostoses, or bony lumps caused by years of exposure to cold water), with the help of your ENT specialist you should have a plan for its treatment (including well-fitting earplugs) before you go.

Tenosynovitis (tendonitis)

This is an inflammation of the synovium, the sheath surrounding muscle tendons, usually at the wrist. There will be moderate to severe pain on slight wrist movement, sometimes with palpable creaking. One point is very tender to touch, usually on the thumb side of the back of the wrist. Point tenderness can distinguish tenosynovitis from other wrist pains.

This is an overuse injury and the only cure is complete rest, ideally in a splint. If you insist on paddling then try a wrist bandage (of neoprene, for example); think of using a paddle with a different control (feather) or with a cranked shaft; and consider an anti-inflammatory drug like ibuprofen or aspirin.

Muscle pains

Knotted muscles and stiff bodies are common on multiday trips and when moving heavy craft. If severe, especially in your neck, or between shoulder blades, these can affect your paddling. Doing warm up stretches before and after paddling is a routine worth following. Sea paddlers can get leg strains through constantly sitting in the same position.

Back trouble is common in paddlers, especially as the kayaking posture flexes the lower, lumbar spine against its natural curve. If you suffer from recurrent back trouble, the hazards of becoming disabled in a remote area should stimulate you to remember proper lifting techniques; to review flexibility exercises with a physiotherapist before you go; and to fit a proper backrest.

Sea paddling

In the tropics be aware of the glare of the sun. Take sunglasses, hats and spares and plenty of high-factor sun cream. Dry skin can be a problem, especially for hands that are constantly getting wet, so carry something like Neutrogena handcream.

In cold climates lips especially can suffer from chapping; a cap or bonnet for the head is important for hypothermia prevention.

Sea sickness can happen in experienced as well as novice paddlers, especially when staring at a compass in poor visibility. Sea-sickness medicines (for example, cinnarizine tablets) are most likely to be effective if taken before the onset of nausea.

Sore skin from friction on constantly wet skin (such as the armpits) can be prevented by Vaseline and so on.

Burn-out

If you do more than a couple of long trips your body may not recover fully before the next trip, and chronic mild exhaustion can result. Do not plan ambitious schedules, especially in developing countries, where the pace of life is slower.

COMMERCIAL WHITE-WATER RAFTING

White-water rafting is a thrilling activity, often part of a unique wilderness journey. People with no experience of rafting, or even of outdoor activities, can be guided safely down reasonably hard rapids. On the quieter sections, there is accessibility to wilderness areas, especially on multiday trips. Certain places in the world have thus experienced a massive growth in white-water rafting, for example, the Zambezi in Zimbabwe, and Nepal. At these sites, experienced river runners can use their hard-earned skills in gainful employment as raft guides.

Figure 24.3   *Transporting equipment by inflatable raft (A. Watt)*

Before going on a raft trip

You need to be reasonably fit, so simple activities like running or swimming are ideal. An ability to swim is preferable, but at least you should not be scared of water. For developing country destinations, add hepatitis A to your list of vaccinations. Clothing items will be advised by your raft company, but should include a peaked sun cap and good river sandals with buckles, or velcro with additional fastening. You should have your own small medical kit, including paracetamol, plasters, sun screen and iodine for grazes and cuts and for water sterilising.

Safety and raft companies

Although white-water rafting appears dangerous it is actually quite safe, with low accident rates, if basic safety rules are followed. You should remember this is an assumed risk adventure activity, that is, you are assuming the risk by signing on. Good companies run professional standard trips, but local competition can reduce prices to the detriment of safety. You should ask about the following:

- the experience of the guides;
- the age and serviceability of the rafts, buoyancy aids and helmets;
- whether another craft (raft or kayak) will accompany your raft.

The provision of "safety kayakers" adds to the security of the trip. There should be a safety briefing before you start that covers paddling, holding on when not paddling, and what to do if you fall in the water.

On the river in hot developing countries do not forget suntan cream and remember to drink plenty of clean water to prevent dehydration. Your buoyancy aid is vital if you fall in the water for any reason, and it should therefore be worn when manoeuvring on flowing water, or if any white water is encountered.

Newcomers to foreign parts worry about exotic tropical diseases, but in fact the biggest threat to your health will come from factors that you control:

- prevention of accidents (especially around the fireplace);
- hygiene, especially handwashing before meals.

The river guides will explain water sterilisation procedures. Enjoy it – white-water rafting is a great experience.

Water-based trips are an enjoyable and rewarding way to travel when abroad. However, do not neglect your preparation and make sure you are fit before you go.

Note. The author would like to thank Surgeon Rear Admiral F. St. C. Golden, P. Knowles, K. Trotter, Doctors J. Bevan, E. Lloyd, P. Lyne and C. Sladden for their help and advice.

AUTHOR BIOGRAPHIES AND ACKNOWLEDGEMENTS

Sarah R. Anderson, MA MB BChir MRCP (Ireland) MRCGP DTM&H

Sarah trained as a doctor in both Cambridge and London. While at Cambridge she organised an expedition to Uganda to assess the knowledge, attitudes and awareness of HIV and AIDS. She has a Diploma in Tropical Medicine and Hygiene and has worked in hospitals in Uganda, Zimbabwe and also Kenya, where she acted as a flying doctor with AMREF. Through the RGS Medical Cell and as honorary medical officer to the Expeditions Fieldwork Division, Sarah continues to be actively involved with the Royal Geographical Society.

Clive Barrow

Clive has led or participated in 16 expeditions in developing countries since 1983, including Chile, Guyana, Venezuela, Ecuador, Canada, Morocco, Kenya, Tanzania, Namibia, Zimbabwe, Pakistan, Papua New Guinea, Australia and New Zealand. He most recently led an expedition to Poland conducting community tasks and treks in the High Tatras for Endeavour Training. Clive was field director for Operation Raleigh 1985–89, operations director for World Challenge Expeditions 1989–96, and is currently running ITEC, an independent expedition consultancy including a recruitment service for expedition staff and leaders. He is a YET trustee and a member of the John Hunt Exploration Group Executive Committee.

Hokey Bennett-Jones

Hokey trained at Westminster Hospital, London, and attended an external course at the London School of Tropical Medicine; she did midwifery in Edinburgh and a family planning course at Kings College Hospital, London. Her jobs have included general medical ward and outpatient work, oncology, nuclear medicine and anaesthetics. She has travelled in North and East Africa, Australia and the Caribbean, and was expedition nurse on Royal Geographical Society research projects in Mulu (Sarawak), Kora (Kenya) and Wahiba Sands (Sultanate of Oman). Hokey is now a full-time housewife and mother.

Jon Buchan, MA BM BCh MRCGP

Jon was born in Sheffield, educated at the local grammar school and trained in medicine at Oxford University and Westminster Hospital. In 1967 he moved to the West Riding of Yorkshire and discovered caving. He signed up as medical officer on an expedition to Papua New Guinea in 1975, a trip that was repeated in 1978. He went on two further trips to Mulu (Sarawak) and one to China before becoming a medical civil servant. In 1994 he retrained, moved to Orkney, and is currently the sole GP on the remote island of Stronsay.

Charles Clarke, MA MB BChir FRCP

Charlie is a consultant neurologist who has been climbing for 36 years and has visited the Himalayas on more than ten occasions. He was expedition doctor with Chris Bonington on the ascent of the south-west face of Everest in 1975; on Kongur in 1981; on the north-east ridge of Everest in 1982; and more recently in Tibet on the Sepu Kangri expedition in 1997. He is the founder of the UIAA Mountain Medicine Data Centre, now administered by the British Mountaineering Council.

Jon Dallimore, MRCGP DCH DRCOG

Jon is a general practitioner in Chepstow, South Wales. He has acted as doctor or leader on 14 expeditions in South America, Africa and Asia, particularly to Nepal. His experience varies from jungle-based trips to high-altitude mountaineering and camel trekking in the desert. For the last six years Jon has developed and taught courses about expedition medicine to lay people and has formed Wilderness Medical Training, an organisation designed to give medical advice and to prepare people for travel to remote areas of the world. He is a member of the British Association for Immediate Care, and has a particular interest in the management of injuries, undertaking regular sessions as a part-time medical officer at the Bristol Royal Infirmary.

Tom Davies, MD (Cantab) FFPHM

Tom worked with the British Antarctic Survey which included a year in the Antarctic. He then joined the Factory Inspectorate, London, after completing his MD thesis on the environment and blood pressure. He spent two years in the Solomon Islands as district medical officer, and on his return to the UK in 1974 did general medicine for a year before resuming public health. Tom was appointed a university lecturer at Cambridge in 1977 and since then has run the Cambridge Expeditions Medical Advisory Service.

Richard Dawood, MD DTM&H

Richard has travelled to 80 countries. Having worked in the NHS for 16 years, he has recently opened a new, independent travel clinic in Fleet Street, London. He is the editor of *Travellers' Health: how to stay healthy abroad* (OUP) and writes for travel magazines in the UK and United States.

Dr Victor R.F. de Lima, MB ChB MRCGP AFOM (RCP)

Born in Kenya and now living in Scotland, Victor is a graduate of the University of Edinburgh Medical School. He is a general practitioner and occupational physician and has been physician-in-charge at Heriot-Watt University, Edinburgh, since 1984. In this capacity he has advised university staff and students undertaking various expeditions. Diving medicine is one of his interests. He is a member of the European Undersea Biomedical Society and an HSE approved doctor for professional diving.

Matthew S. Dryden, MA MBBS MSc MD MRCPath

Matthew has travelled widely, often in a medical capacity. He has been an expedition doctor on several occasions, usually in jungle and desert environments including South America, the Sahara, Kenya, Botswana, Costa Rica, Sudan, Australia and Papua New Guinea. Matthew is currently working at the Royal Hampshire County Hospital as a specialist in microbiology and infectious diseases.

Bobby Forbes, BSc

Bobby is university diving officer at Heriot-Watt University. Based at the university's diving facility in Orkney, he is responsible for all diving activities at the International Centre for Island Technology, Stromness. Bobby has dived in many parts of the world, and is also a qualified life-support technician and diver medical officer. He is currently involved in several scientific groups, including the HSE Training Standards Working Group, the UK Scientific Diving Supervisory Committee and the RGS Shoals of Capricorn Programme.

Larry Goodyer, BPharm MPharm PhD MRPharmS

Larry is a lecturer in clinical pharmacy at the Department of Pharmacy, King's College, London. Apart from travel medicine, his research interests include clinical trials on OTC medicines and multimedia computer presentation systems. In 1990 he helped set up and become a director of the Nomad Travel Pharmacy, which specialises in medical provision for people travelling overseas, from large sponsored expeditions to private individuals.

Paul Goodyer

Paul is the managing director of Nomad Traveller's Store and Medical Centre. He has travelled for the last 20 years and visited among other areas Africa, South America, the Middle East and South-east Asia. In his early travelling days he contracted infections such as dysentery through drinking contaminated water. He knows the secrets of staying healthy while travelling and passes this information on via his own travel store so that new travellers can avoid the pitfalls he has experienced.

Beverley Holt, MA MRCS MRCP FFARCS

Bev is a mountaineering doctor with extensive expedition experience. As an anaesthetist and director of an intensive care unit, he developed an interest in hypoxia and high-altitude medicine. This led to several Himalayan expeditions, including the 1986 British K2 Expedition. He also has experience of the Arctic as well as the Andes and Mongolia. He spent 11 years in Africa and eight in Canada with the Grenfell Mission, and is one-time officer in charge of an RAF mountain rescue unit and ex-outward bound instructor.

Robin Illingworth, MA BM BCh FRCP FFAEM

Robin is a consultant in accident and emergency medicine at St James's University Hospital, Leeds. From 1974 to 1990 he was honorary medical adviser to the Brathay Exploration Group, which is based at Ambleside, Cumbria, and organises many expeditions. Robin has been on expeditions to Iceland, Greenland, Alaska, Morocco, Nepal and Borneo and has visited several other countries. He is the author of *Expedition Medicine*, a planning guide (3rd edition, 1984) and has edited books on accident and emergency medicine.

Chris Johnson, MA MD, FRCA

Chris was medical officer to the British Antarctic Survey at Halley Bay during 1979/80. On his return to the UK he worked at the Institute of Environmental and Offshore Medicine in Aberdeen where he completed his PhD on the effects of cold on peripheral circulation. Chris has also been involved with epidemiological work on expedition medical problems. He is currently a consultant anaesthetist at Southmead Hospital, Bristol, but regularly goes cross-country skiing in Norway and the Canadian Rockies.

Michael Phelan, BSc MB BS MRC Psych

Michael is a consultant psychiatrist at Charing Cross Hospital, London. He has previously worked at the Institute of Psychiatry, London, and at Prince Alfred Hospital, Sydney, Australia. His interest in expeditions started when he was invited to join an anthropological expedition to the highlands of Papua New Guinea. Since then he has been the doctor on a three-month expedition in the Ecuadorian rainforest, where he ran out of suture material as a result of the overenthusiastic use of machetes by team members. He also has extensive experience of long-distance sailing trips, where sea sickness and complete isolation often result in even greater strains and tensions than on land-based expeditions.

Charles Siderfin MB ChB MSc MRCGP

Charles is a general practitioner currently working in the Highlands of Scotland. His particular interests are in expedition medicine and remote health care. He spent three years as a medical officer with the British Antarctic Survey, during which time he developed an integrated system of health care for expeditions. This included advanced training for non-medical personnel and 24-hour medical cover using low-technology communication systems.

Rod Stables, TD MA BM BCh MRCP

Rod is currently senior registrar in cardiology at the Royal Brompton Hospital, London. He has been involved in civilian expeditions and military operations over all types of terrain and in all climates from the Arctic Circle to the jungles of South-east Asia. He is an active mountaineer with experience in the UK, European Alps and Greater Ranges. He was the deputy of the UK Reserve Forces expeditions to Mt McKinley, Alaska, in 1991 and to Everest in winter in 1992/93.

David A. Warrell, MA DM DSc FRCP

David is professor of tropical medicine and infectious diseases and director of the Centre for Tropical Medicine, University of Oxford. He has lived and worked in Ethiopia, Nigeria, Sierra Leone, Kenya, Thailand, Burma, Sri Lanka, Papua New Guinea, Brazil and Ecuador. David is co-editor of the *Oxford Textbook of Medicine* and *Bruce Chwatt's Essential Malariology*, and author of articles on malaria, rabies, relapsing fever and venomous animals.

Andy Watt, MB ChB MRCP BSc DTMH

Andy discovered white-water canoeing at Glasgow University and spent a year kayaking and raft guiding the rivers of the Indian and Nepalese Himalayas. He was river leader and cameraman on the Disabled White Water trip to Turkey and is currently the project director for the proposed artificial white-water course in Glasgow. His hospital speciality is care of the elderly, but he has a broad range of skills derived from time spent in surgery, obstetrics and a year in an Indian mission hospital.

David Watt, BDS DPD DGDP (UK) MGDS RCPS (Glas)

David is an experienced general dental practitioner who has always worked in more or less isolated areas including Scotland, Nigeria, Zambia, Scandinavia, Cumbria and Nepal. He is also author of *Emergency Dentistry*. Dr Watt gives advice on dental kits for expeditions and makes up these kits to individual requirements.

Mark Whittingham

Mark is a chartered insurance practitioner working with Aon Risk Services, where he is currently a branch unit manager. Mark has nine years' experience advising expeditions on insurance matters.

ACKNOWLEDGEMENTS

The antecedents of this book were the five successful earlier editions of "Expedition Medicine" edited from 1986 to 1994 by Bent Juel-Jensen. Much of Bent's wisdom survives in this edition.

The editors would also like to acknowledge the assistance of the staff of the RGS Expedition Advisory Centre, especially Deborah Boys, Tim Jones and Shane Winser.

THE ROYAL GEOGRAPHICAL SOCIETY

(WITH THE INSTITUTE OF BRITISH GEOGRAPHERS)

The Royal Geographical Society (with The Institute of British Geographers) has, for over 165 years, been a national and international focus of geographical research, information and exploration. The recent merger of these two organisations has created the most vigorous geographical society in Europe.

The objectives of the Society are defined in its original Royal Charter, namely: "the advancement of geographical science and the improvement and diffusion of geographical knowledge". As part of these objectives the Society seeks to:

- Stimulate awareness, interest and enjoyment of geography and environmental matters in people of all ages and from all backgrounds.
- Act as an authoritative voice representing and promoting geography and geographers in the UK and overseas.
- Act as a focus for geographical research, and where possible fund geographical research, including field projects overseas.
- Promote and enhance the value of geography in education, with particular reference to higher education.
- Provide a national geographical information resource, and a database of geographical expertise.
- Give training and advice to those organising expeditions.

The Society serves the geographical interests of a wide range of people, including those studying geography and in geographical-related professions, as well as those with a wider interest in the human and physical environment, travel and exploration. Members do not require special qualifications and the Society welcomes all who wish to support its objectives and participate in its activities.

Conferences, meetings and information resources

Numerous lectures, conferences and meetings are convened by the Society throughout the country. Weekly popular lectures on geographical and exploratory topics are held in the Society's house, where information resources of national importance are held by the Society's library, map room, archives and picture library.

Overseas field research and expedition support

The Society is one of the largest organisers in the UK of geographical field research overseas. It runs a programme of major multi-disciplinary projects involving British researchers and those in participating countries, with programmes currently under way in Nepal, Jordan and Mauritius/Seychelles. The Society is also the country's main organisation for screening and grant-aiding small research expeditions.

Expedition Advisory Centre

The Society's internationally acclaimed Expedition Advisory Centre (EAC) provides training and advice to anyone embarking on an expedition. It is the leading such centre in the world. Each year it assists more than 500 teams, the majority of which are university-based. The EAC publishes a range of training manuals on every aspect of expeditionary research and logistics. In 1996 The EAC organised a two-day seminar on *Expedition Health and Safety: the prevention and treatment of medical problems in challenging environments*, and this book is a direct result of that meeting. The EAC also helps expeditions recruit medical personnel for expeditions through its *Register of Personnel available for Expeditions*.

Medical Cell

As part of the Society's commitment to provide support to its overseas research projects and others planning expeditions, leading doctors in the field of expedition medicine established a Medical Cell, chaired by Professor Warrell of the Centre for Tropical Medicine, University of Oxford, to provide a forum for discussion, information and advice to those operating in remote areas.

For further information on the work of the Society please contact:
Information Officer
RGS-IBG
1 Kensington Gore
London
SW7 2AR
Tel. +44 171 5913030
Fax +44 171 5913031
E-mail eac@rgs.org
Website http://www.rgs.org/eac

APPENDICES

1 PRE-EXPEDITION MEDICAL QUESTIONNAIRE

Name: **Date:**

Address:

Home telephone:
Work telephone:
Fax number:

Age: **Date of Birth:**

Passport details: Nationality:
                                   Passport number:
                                   Place of issue:
                                   Date of issue:
                                   Date of expiry:

Next of kin: Name:
                                   Address:

                                   Telephone/fax:
                                   Relationship:

GP details: Name:
                                   Address:

                                   Telephone/fax:

Current medical problems: 1.
                                   2.
                                   3.

Past medical problems:
    1.
    2.
    3.

Past psychiatric history:

Current medication:

Allergies (drugs, food, environmental):

Immunisations (with dates):

Routine:

                               Diphtheria   ....

                               Polio   ....

                               Tetanus   ....

Travel: Hepatitis A   ....

                               Gammagobulin   ....

                               Hepatitis B   ....

                               Japanese Encephalitis   ....

                               Meningoccocal Meningitis ....

                               Rabies   ....

                               Tick-borne Encephalitis   ....

                               Tuberculosis (BCG)   ....

                               Typhoid   ....

                               Yellow Fever   ....

Blood group:

Itinerary: **Country**   **Date**

Departure date: **Return date:**

Total length of trip:

2 MEDICAL ASSESSMENT QUESTIONNAIRE

(A) PATIENT DETAILS

1. Name
2. Address
3. Date of Birth
4. Age
5. Sex
6. Occupation
7. Time (at completion of form)
8. Date
9. Location of patient at present

(B) PATIENT'S MAIN COMPLAINT/COMPLAINTS

1:
2:
3:
4:

(C) A SHORT DESCRIPTIVE HISTORY OF THE ABOVE PROBLEMS IN THE ORDER THEY OCCURRED

(in the patient's own words, including how long ago the problem/s started)

(D) PAIN

1. Is there any pain   **No**   **Yes**
(If no then pass to section E)

   2. Site of the pain at onset   *Use diagram 1a (front) or 1b (back)*
      or describe in words

   3. Site of the pain now   *Use diagram 2a (front) or 2b (back)*
      or describe in words

   4. Time since pain began   hrs   mins
   5. Severity of pain now
      (mild, severe, etc)
   6. Since beginning has the pain   Got better/stayed the same/worsened
   7. What is the pain like
      (dull, hot, sharp, etc)
   8. Is the pain   Constant   Variable
   9. Does the pain go anywhere   No   Yes
 10. Did it come on during activity   No   Yes
 11. How did the pain start   Suddenly   Gradually
 12. Does anything make it better   No   Yes
      If yes, what?

 13. Does anything make it worse   No   Yes
      If yes, what?

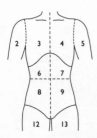 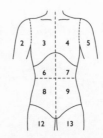 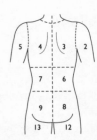

Diagram 1a and 1b   Diagram 2a and 2b
Site of pain at onset   *Site of pain now*

(E) CHEST

1. Is there any shortness of breath (SOB)	**No**	**Yes**
2. How severe is this SOB	Very slight	
A little tight chested		
Short of breath at rest		
Gasping for air		
3. How long ago did this SOB start	hrs	mins
4. Does anything make it better	No	Yes
If yes, what?		
5. Does anything make it worse	No	Yes
If yes, what?		
6. Is a cough present	**No**	**Yes**
7. Is there any phlegm/spit	**No**	**Yes**
8. Colour of phlegm/spit		
9. Is the heart pounding in the chest	**No**	**Yes**

(F) SICKNESS AND BOWELS

1. Is there any feeling of sickness	**No**	**Yes**
2. Time since this feeling began	hrs	mins
3. Has there been vomiting	**No**	**Yes**
4. Time since vomiting began	hrs	mins
5. Colour of the vomit		Food
		Yellow/green/bile
		Red/blood/other
6. Is the appetite changed	**No**	**Yes**
7. Is the bowel habit changed	**No**	**Yes, constipation**
		Yes, diarrhoea
8. Frequency of moving bowels	**Normally**	**times per day**
	Now	**times per day**
9. Is this at all painful	**No**	**Yes**
10. Colour of the bowel motion		

(G) URINE

I. Is there any pain on passing urine (PU)	**No**	**Yes**
2. Where is this pain felt		
3. Timing of pain when PU	**During**	**After**
4. Any blood seen when PU	**No**	**Yes**
5. Frequency of PU	**Normally**	**/day**
		/night
	Changed to	**/day**
		/night

(H) OTHER COMPLAINTS

I. Headache present	**No**	**Yes**
2. Severity of headache		Mild, fully active
		Moderate, non-restricting
		Severe, restricting activity
3. Blackout or collapse	**No**	**Yes**
4. Light-headed or faint	**No**	**Yes**
5. Sweating	**No**	**Yes**
6. Shaking or shivering	**No**	**Yes**
7. Feeling weak	**No**	**Yes**
8. Muscle ache	**No**	**Yes**
9. Vision blurred	**No**	**Yes**
10. Earache	**No**	**Yes**
II. Nose clear	**Yes**	**No, blocked**
		No, running
		No, bleeding
12. Sore throat	**No**	**Yes**
13. Skin rash present	**No**	**Yes, all body**
		Yes, trunk
		Yes, limbs
		Yes, head/neck
14. Is the rash itchy	No	Yes

(I)   WOMEN ONLY

1. Unusual vaginal bleeding	No	Yes, spotting
		Yes, light
		Yes, heavy
		Yes, clots
2. Is this linked to any pain	No	Yes
3. Date of last period starting		
4. Was this a "normal" period	Yes	No

(J)   PAST MEDICAL HISTORY

1. Has this occurred before	No	Yes
2. What was wrong then	Date:	
	Diagnosis:	
2. Has the patient been admitted to hospital before	No	Yes
3. For what conditions		
4. Any other significant episodes of illness or injury	No	Yes
5. Dates and conditions		

(K)   DRUG HISTORY

1. Is the patient taking any medications	No	Yes
2. Drug name	Dosage	
3. Is the patient allergic to anything	No	Yes
4. Allergies to what?		

CLINICAL EXAMINATION

(N) ALWAYS ANSWER THE FIRST 13 QUESTIONS

1. **PATIENT LOOKS**	Well	Unwell Ill Awful
2. **PATIENT APPEARS**	Awake and alert	Awake but confused Drowsy Responds to pain only Unwakable
3. **TEMPERATURE**		Centigrade
4. **PULSE (AT REST)**		beats/minute
5. **BREATHING RATE**		breaths/minute
6. **BLOOD PRESSURE**	........../............ mmHg	
7. **SKIN COLOUR**	Normal	Flushed Blue or cyanosed Pale or anaemic Yellow or jaundiced
8. **SKIN TEMPERATURE TO TOUCH**	Warm or normal	Hot or fevered Cold and dry Cold and clammy
9. **A HEAVING CHEST ON BREATHING**	No	Yes
10. **PERSPIRATION or SWEATING**	No	Yes
11. **DEHYDRATION or DRY TONGUE**	No	Yes
12. **PAIN or DISTRESS ON MOVING**	No	Yes
13. **PAIN or STIFFNESS IN THE NECK**	No	Yes

**THESE BODY DIAGRAMS MAY BE USED
FOR ILLUSTRATION IF REQUIRED**

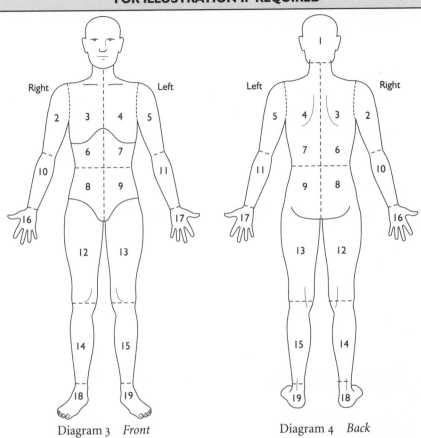

Diagram 3 *Front*   Diagram 4 *Back*

(O)   CHEST (bare all chest, front and back)

1. Signs of injury to chest	No	Yes	
2. Tender chest wall	No	Yes	
3. Position of windpipe in neck	Central	To right	To left
4. Chest movement on breathing	Relaxed	Heaving	
		Painful	
		Unequal	
5. Air entry of chest (describe the position of any abnormality):	Normal	Wheezy	
		Crackly	

(P) ABDOMEN (ABDO)

1. Abdo size	Normal	Distended
2. Abdo pain on coughing	No	Yes
3. Abdo pain on moving	No	Yes
4. Abdo pain on puffing out or sucking in tummy wall	No	Yes
5. Areas of tenderness found	No	Yes
6. Any lumps or swellings found	No	Yes
7. Bowel sounds (BS)	Normal BS	Increased BS
		Tinkling BS
		No BS heard

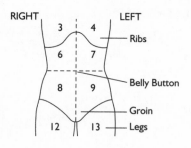

Diagram 5   *Abdomen*

(Q) GENERAL EXAMINATION

1. Glands found	No	Yes, neck	R	L
		Tender	Yes	No
		Yes, armpit	R	L
		Tender	Yes	No
		Yes, groin	R	L
		Tender	Yes	No
2. Ear discharge (If no pass to 4)	No	Yes, from	R	L
3. Colour of ear discharge		Clear		
		Pus		
		Blood		

4. Throat colour   **Normal**   **Red**
5. Tonsil size   **Normal**   **Enlarged**
6. Skin rash found   **No**   **Yes**
    7. Size of rash (in cm)
    8. Colour
    9. Surface (to touch)
  10. Where rash found

(R) ANY OTHER COMMENTS OR FINDINGS

(S) POSSIBLE DIAGNOSIS

Examiner's signature

Name (printed) and qualifications

Source: Siderfin, C., Maclean, J. and Haston, W. (1995) The Medical Assessment Questionnaire for Radio. *Journal of Telemedicine and Telecare* 1: 57–60.

3 REFERENCES AND FURTHER READING

I What is expedition medicine?

Auerbach, P.S. (1995) *Wilderness Medicine. Management of Wilderness and Environmental Emergencies.* 3rd edition. Mosby, St Louis

Robinson, W.A. and Oelz, O. (1990) *Wilderness and Environmental Medicine.* Wilderness Medical Society Periodical (001-317-6311745), PO Box 2463, Indianapolis, IN 46206

2 Immunisations

Salisbury, D.M. and Begg, N.T. (1996) *Immunisation against Infectious Disease.* HMSO, London

3 Expedition medical kits

A'Court, C.H.D., Stables, R.H. and Travis, S. (1995) Doctor on a mountaineering expedition. *British Medical Journal* 310: 1248–1252. This paper lists the medical supplies taken on the 1992 expedition to Everest in winter

Bollen, S. (1989) *First Aid on Mountains.* British Mountaineering Council, Manchester

Illingworth, R.N. (1984) *Expedition Medicine, A Planning Guide.* 3rd Edition. Blackwell Scientific Publications, Oxford

Steele, P. (1988) *Medical Handbook for Mountaineers.* Constable, London

Wilkerson, J.A. (1992) *Medicine for Mountaineering and Other Wilderness Activities.* 4th edition. The Mountaineers, Washington, Seattle

4 First aid training

American College of Surgeons (1989) *Advanced Trauma Life Support Course Manual.* American College of Surgeons, Chicago

Colquhoun, M.C. *et al.* (1995) *ABC of Resuscitation.* British Medical Journal Publications, London

Dunne, J. (ed.) (1997) *First Aid Manual. The Authorised Manual of the St. John Ambulance, St. Andrews Ambulance Association and The British Red Cross,* 7th Edition. Dorling Kindersley, London

Goth, P. and Isacc, J. (1994) *Outward Bound First Aid Handbook.* Ward Lock, London

Renouf, J. and Hulse, S. (1989) *First Aid for Hillwalkers and Climbers.* Cicerone Press, Milnthorpe, Cumbria

5 Legal liability and medical insurance

Berridge, J. (1997) *Expedition Insurance.* Expedition Advisory Centre, London

Dinnick, S. (1996) Antarctica Revisited. *Summons: The Journal for the Medical and Dental Defence Union of Scotland:* 5

6 Risk assessment and crisis management

UK Health and Safety Executive (1996) *Five steps to risk assessment Ind (G) 163L.* ISBN 0 7176 0904 9

UK Health and Safety Executive (1996) *Licensing Regulations.* Pamphlet L77. ISBN 0 7176 1160 4

Putnam, R. (1994) *Safe and Responsible Youth Expeditions.* Young Explorers' Trust, London

Young Explorers' Trust (1994) *Code of Practice for Youth Expeditions.* London

8 Base camp hygiene and health

Wilson Howarth, J. (1995) *Bugs, Bites and Bowels.* Cadogan Books, London

The Guide Association *Health and Hygiene.* Commonwealth Headquarters Shop, 17–19 Buckingham Palace Road, London SW1W oPT, tel. +44 171 8346242

10 Water purification

Epstein, O. (1993) *Clinical Examination.* Wolf Publications

Dunne, J. (ed.) (1997) *First Aid Manual. The Authorised Manual of the St. John Ambulance, St. Andrews Ambulance Association and The British Red Cross, 7th Edition.* Dorling Kindersley, London

Siderfin, C.D. (1995) Low-technology telemedicine in Antarctica. *Journal of Telemedicine and Telecare* 1: 54–60

Werner, D. (1979) *Where there is No Doctor.* Macmillan Tropical Community Health Manuals, Macmillan Press, London. Available from TALC, PO Box 49, St Albans, Herts AL1 4AX

11 First aid and management of minor injuries

American College of Surgeons (1989) *Advanced Trauma Life Support Course Manual.* American College of Surgeons, Chicago

Benner, A.G. *et al.* (1987) *Emergency Medical Procedures for the Outdoors.* Menasha Ridge Press, Birmingham

Burge, P. (1989) *Limb Injuries.* JB Lippincott Company, Raven

Dunne, J. (ed.) (1997) *First Aid Manual. The Authorised Manual of the St. John Ambulance, St. Andrews Ambulance Association and The British Red Cross, 7th Edition.* Dorling Kindersley, London

Eaton, C.J. (1995) *Essentials of Immediate Medical Care.* Churchill Livingstone

Ferguson, D.G. and Fodden, D.I. (1993) *Accident and Emergency Medicine.* Churchill Livingstone

Goth, P. and Isacc, J. (1994) *Outward Bound First Aid Handbook.* Ward Lock, London
Huckstep, R.L. and Sherry, E. (1994) *Orthopaedics and Trauma.* Churchill Livingstone
Kirby, N.G. (1985) *Field Surgery Pocket Book.* HMSO, London
Renouf, J. and Hulse, S. (1989) *First Aid for Hillwalkers and Climbers.* Cicerone Press, Milnthorpe, Cumbria
Skinner, D. *et al.* (1996) *ABC of Major Trauma.* British Medical Journal Publications, London

12 Casualty evacuation
March, B. (1973) *Modern Rope Techniques.* Cicerone Press, Milnthorpe, Cumbria

13 Medical aspects of survival
Wiseman, J. (1995) *The SAS Survival Handbook.* HarperCollins
Greenbank, A. (1976) *The Book of Survival.* Wolfe Publishing
Robertson, D. (1975) *Survive the Savage Sea.* Penguin Books, London

14 Traveller's diarrhoea and other common infections
Dawood, R. (1997) *Travellers' Health: How to stay healthy abroad.* Oxford University Press

15 Malaria and other tropical diseases
Bell, D.R. (1995) *Lecture notes on Tropical Medicine, 4th edition.* Blackwell Science, Oxford
Bradley, D.J. and Warhurst, D.C. (1997) Guidelines for the Prevention of Malaria in Travellers from the UK. *CDR Review* (PHLS, Colindale, London) Vol. 7, Review No. 10 R1–152.
British Medical Association (1995) *The BMA Guide to Rabies.* Radcliffe Medical Press
Cook, G.C. (1996) *Manson's Tropical Diseases, 20th edition.* W.B. Saunders, London
Gilles, H.M. and Warrell, D.A. (1993). *Bruce Chwatt's Essential Malariology, 3rd edition.* Edward Arnold, London
Weatherall, D.J., Ledingham, J.G.G. and Warrell, D.A. (1996) *Oxford Textbook of Medicine, 3rd edition.* Oxford University Press. Vol. I, Section 7, Infection

16 Venomous and poisonous animals
Junghanss, T. and Bodio, M. (1996) *Notfall-Handbuch Gifttiere.* Georg Thieme, Stuttgart (Rildigerstrasse 14, D-70469 Stuttgart). In German
Meier, J. and White, J. (1995) *Handbook of clinical toxicology of animal venoms and poisons.* CRC Press, Boca Raton (2000 Corporate Bvd, NW Boca Raton, FL 33431). Comprehensive and authoritative account

Warrell, D.A. (1996). Animal Toxins, in Cook, G.C. (ed.) *Manson's Tropical Diseases, 20th edition*. W.B. Saunders, London, pages 468–515

Warrell, D.A. (1996) Injuries, envenoming, poisoning and allergic reactions caused by animals, in Weatherall, D.J., Ledingham, J.G.G. and Warrell, D.A. (eds) *Oxford Textbook of Medicine, 3rd edition*. Oxford University Press, pages 1124–1151

18 Emergency dental treatment
Watt, D.G. (1975) *Emergency Dentistry*. Clausen Publications, Weybridge, Surrey

19 Tropical and desert expeditions
Chapman, R. and Jermy, C. (1993) *Tropical Forest Expeditions*. Expedition Advisory Centre, London

Melville, K.E.M. (1984) *Stay Alive in the Desert*. Roger Lascalles, London

Schroeder, D.G. (1993) *Staying Healthy in Asia, Africa and Latin America*. Moon Publications, Chicago

Sheppard, Tom (1988) *Desert Expeditions*. Expedition Advisory Centre, London

20 Polar expeditions
Adam, J.M. (1981) *Hypothermia: Ashore and Afloat*. Aberdeen University Press

Dawson, B. (1974) The removal of rock flour from glacial streams. *Island: Bulletin of the Iceland Unit, Young Explorers' Trust* 7: 7–8

Milne, A.H. and Siderfin, C.D. (1995) *Kurafid, 4th Edition*. British Antarctic Survey, Madingley Road, Cambridge. Advanced first aid for well-equipped expeditions

Rivolier, J., Goldsmith, R., Lugg, D.J. and Taylor, A.J.W. (1988) *Man in the Antarctic*. Taylor & Francis. A summary of research work in polar areas

21 High-altitude and mountaineering expeditions
Bezruchka, S. (1994) *Altitude Illness, Prevention and Treatment*. The Mountaineers, Seattle and Cordee, Leicester

Hultgren, H. (1997) *High Altitude Medicine*. Hultgren Publications. Fax +1 415 4934225

Pollard, A.J. (1997) *The High Altitude Medicine Handbook*. Radcliffe Medical Press

UIAA Mountain Medicine Data Centre leaflets. Available from the British Mountaineering Council, 177-179 Burton Road, Manchester M20 2BB. Tel. +44 161 4454747, fax +44 161 4454500

Ward, M.P., Milledge, J.S. and West, J.B, (1994). *High Altitude Medicine and Physiology*. Chapman and Hall Medical

Wilkerson, J.A. (1985) *Medicine for Mountaineering*. The Mountaineers, Seattle. Frequently re-edited; available through Cordee, 3a De Montfort Street, Leicester LE1 7HD

22 Underwater expeditions

Bennet, P.B. and Elliot, D.H. *The Physiology and Medicine of Diving, 4th Edition.* W.B. Saunders Co Ltd

British Sub-Aqua Club (1993) *Sports Diving: the BSAC Diving Manual.* British Sub Aqua Club, Telford's Quay, Ellesmere Port, Cheshire L65 4FY. Tel. +44 151 3571951, fax +44 151 3571250

Flemming, N.C. and Max, M.D. (1996) *Scientific diving: a general code of practice.* 2nd edition. UNESCO

Sisman, D. (1995) *The Professional Diver's Handbook.* Best Publishing

23 Caving expeditions

Advice for Cavers Concerning Hypothermia. *Plymouth Caving Group Newsletter and Journal* 119 (1993–94), pages 16–20

Baguley, F.S. (1994–95) Cryptosporidium in water. *Red Dragon Cambrian Caving Council Annual Journal* 21

Bailey, D. (1994) Hypothermia – When the Shivering Stops. *The Speleograph* 30: 112–113

Brocklebank, T. (1992) Falls!!! *British Caver.* Vol. 115, pages 5–7

Buchan, J. (1976) Medical report on British New Guinea Expedition. *Transactions of the British Cave Research Association.* Vol. 3, pages 238–242

Cave Rescue Association. Annual Reports.

Fogg, T. (1989) Mulu Caves 88 Expedition Report. *Cave Science* 16 No. 2, 57

Frankland, J.C. (1984) Hypothermia in Cavers. *Transactions of the British Cave Research Association.* Vol. 11, No. 3, pages 154–159

Lewis, W. (1989) Histoplasmosis: a hazard to new tropical cavers. *National Speleological Society Bulletin* (Huntsville, Alabama) 51: 52–65

Lyons, T (1984) Medical Equipment for Caving Expeditions. *Transactions of the British Cave Research Association.* Vol. 11, page 171

Self, W.I. *et al.* (1989) Leptospirosis among British Cavers. *Transactions of the British Cave Research Association.* Vol. 14, No. 3, pages 131–134

Willis, D.W. (1993) *Caving Expeditions.* 2nd edition. BCRA/Expedition Advisory Centre

24 Canoe, kayak and raft expeditions

Adam, J.M. (1981) *Hypothermia: Ashore and Afloat.* Aberdeen University Press

Medical Commission on Accident Prevention. *Hypothermia and Drowning.* Pamphlet. Lincoln's Inn Fields, London

4 USEFUL ADDRESSES

BCB International
Moorland Road, Cardiff CF2 2YL
Tel. +44 1222 464464
First Aid kits and emergency medical supplies

Blood Care Foundation
PO Box 7, Sevenoaks, Kent TN13 2SZ
Tel. +44 1732 742427
Emergency blood supplies

British Airways Travel Clinics
Information line: Tel. +44 1276 685040

British Association for Immediate Care (BASICS)
7 Black Horse Lane, Ipswich, Suffolk IP1 2EF
Tel. +44 1473 218407

British Dental Association
64 Wimpole Street, London W1M 8AL
Tel. +44 171 9350875

British Medical Association
Tavistock Square, London WC1P 9PJ
Tel. +44 171 3874499

British Red Cross Society
9 Grosvenor Gardens, London SW1X 7EJ
Tel. +44 171 2355454

Department of Health (Medicines Division)
Market Towers, 1 Nine Elms Lane, London SW1 5NQ
Tel. +44 171 7202188 ext. 3408
For UK drug export certificates

Diving Diseases Research Centre
The Hyperbaric Medical Centre, Tamar Science Park, Derriford Road,
Plymouth PL6 8BQ
Tel. +44 1752 209999

Expedition Advisory Centre
Royal Geographical Society (with the Institute of British Geographers)
1 Kensington Gore, London SW7 2AR
Tel. +44 171 5913030, fax +44 171 5913031, e-mail s.winser@rgs.org

Foreign and Commonwealth Office Travel Advice Unit
Consular Division, Foreign and Commonwealth Office
1 Palace Street, London SW1E 5HE
Tel. +44 171 2384503/4504, fax +44 171 2384545, website http://www.fco.gov.uk/

Health Projects Abroad
PO Box 24, Bakewell, Derbyshire DE45 1ZW
Tel. +44 1629 640051, fax +44 1629 640054
Recruits volunteer health workers

Health Literature Line
Tel. +44 800 555777 any time, free of charge
Orders for more than 10 copies should be placed with:
Department of Health, PO Box 410, Wetherby LS23 7LN
Health advice for travellers

Hospital for Tropical Diseases
4 St Pancras Way, London NW1 0PE
Tel. +44 171 3874411
Travel Clinic: Tel. +44 171 3889600
Health Information Line: Tel. +44 839 337733

HSE Books
PO Box 1999, Sudbury, Suffolk CO10 6FS
Tel. +44 1787 881165, fax +44 1787 313995

Independent Travel and Expedition Consultancy
Forge House, Bodsham, Ashford, Kent TN25 5JQ
Tel. +44 1233 750401
Expedition planning and risk assessment services

INTERHEALTH
157 Waterloo Road, London SE1 8US
Tel. +44 171 9029000
Long-term advice and treatment for aid workers and expatriates

International Health Exchange
8–10 Dryden Street, London WC2E 9NA
Tel. +44 171 8365833, fax +44 171 3791239
Maintains a register of health professionals wanting to work in developing countries, and runs training courses on Primary Health Care and Refugee Community Health.

John Bell and Croyden
50 Wigmore Street, London W1H 0AU
Tel. +44 171 9355555
Pharmacy and medical supplier

Lifesystems Limited
4 Mercury House, Calleva Park, Aldermaston, Berkshire RG7 4QW
Tel. +44 1734 811433, fax +44 1734 811406
First aid and emergency dental kits

Liverpool School of Tropical Medicine
Pembroke Place, Liverpool L3 5QA
Tel. +44 151 7089393

London School of Hygiene and Tropical Medicine
Keppel Street, London WC1E 7HT
Tel. +44 171 6368636

Malaria Reference Laboratory
Tel. +44 171 6367921 (office hours)
Tel. +44 891 600350 (24-hour helpline for the general public)

Medical Advisory Service for Travellers Abroad (MASTA)
51 Gower Street, London WC1E 6HU
MASTA Health Line: Tel. +44 891 224100
Other enquiries: Tel. +44 113 2391707

Medic-Alert Foundation International
12 Bridge Wharf, 156 Caledonian Road, London N1 9UU
Tel. +44 171 8333034

Nomad Traveller's Store and Medical Centre
3–4 Turnpike Lane, London N8 0PX
Tel. +44 181 8897014, fax +44 181 8899529, e-mail nomad.travstore@virgin.net

Oxford University Centre for Tropical Medicine
Nuffield Department of Clinical Medicine, John Radcliffe Hospital, Headington,
Oxford OX3 9DU
Tel. +44 1865 220968/220970/225430

Pinkerton Risk Assessment Services
220 North Glebe Road, Suite 1011, Arlington, VA 22203, USA
Tel. +1 703 5256111, fax +1 703 5252454
Security consultants; publishes *The World Status Map* based on the US Department
of State Travel advisory warnings

Public Health Laboratory Health Centres
Birmingham   Tel. +44 121 7666611
Glasgow   Tel. +44 141 9467120
Liverpool   Tel. +44 151 708393
London   Tel. +44 171 9272437
Oxford   Tel. +44 1865 225570

Royal College of Nursing
20 Cavendish Square, London W1M 0AB
Tel. +44 171 4093333

Royal Society for the Prevention of Accidents
Cannon House, The Priory, Queensways, Birmingham B4 6BS
Tel. +44 121 2482000

St Andrew's Ambulance Association
St Andrew's House, 48 Milton Street, Glasgow G4 0HR
Tel. +44 141 3324031

St John Ambulance
Edwina Mountbatten House, 63 York Street, London W1H 1PS
Tel. +44 171 235 5231
First aid courses: Tel. +44 171 2583456
First aid kits: Tel: 0171 2787888

Trailfinders Travel Clinics
Tel. +44 171 9383999 (London)
Tel. +44 141 3530066 (Glasgow)

UIAA Mountain Medicine Data Centre
c/o British Mountaineering Council, 177–179 Burton Road, Manchester M20 2BB
Tel. +44 161 4454747, fax +44 161 4454500

Wilderness Medical Training
25 Beaconsfield Street, Leamington Spa, Warwickshire CV31 1DT
Tel. & fax +44 1926 882763

World Challenge Expeditions
Black Arrow House, 2 Chandos Road, London NW10 6NF
Tel. +44 181 9611551, fax +44 181 9611122

GLOSSARY

Abdomen	Body cavity which contains the liver, spleen, kidneys and bladder
Abrasion	Superficial wound caused by damage to the outermost layers of skin or cornea
Abscess	A localised collection of pus (infection)
Airway	The passage through which air moves from the nose and mouth via the throat to the lungs
Airway, lower	Trachea, bronchi, alveoli
Airway, upper	Mouth, nose, throat
Altitude sickness (AMS or acute mountain sickness)	A condition caused by the lack of oxygen at high altitude
Alveoli	Small sacs of air in the lungs where gas is exchanged with the blood
Anaphylaxis	Severe allergic reaction involving widespread oedema and shock
Aspiration	The breathing in of foreign liquid or solid into the lungs
Basic life support (BLS)	The process of supporting a person's respiratory and circulatory function using artificial ventilation, chest compressions and bleeding control
Cardiac arrest	The loss of an effective pumping action of the heart
Cardiogenic shock	Shock caused by an inadequate pumping action of the heart
Cardiopulmonary resuscitation (CPR)	A technique using artificial respiration and chest compressions to circulate oxygenated blood in the absence of an effectively pumping heart
Capillaries	The narrowest blood vessels in the body where gases and nutrients are exchanged between circulating blood and tissue cells
Carotid pulse	The pulse felt on either side of the neck at the site of the carotid artery
Central Nervous System (CNS)	The brain and spinal cord
Cervical spine	The portion of spine in the neck between the skull base and the top of the thorax
Conjunctiva	The membrane that covers the front of the eye and the inside of the eyelids
Conjunctivitis	Inflammation (swelling and redness) of the conjunctiva due to irritation, infection or injury

Consciousness, level of	Describes the level of brain function in terms of responsivenesss to specific stimuli (the AVPU scale): A = Awake and Alert V = responds to Voice P = responds to Pain U = Unresponsive to any stimulus
Cornea	The clear part of the eye which covers the iris and the pupil
Dental abscess	Infection at the base of a tooth
Diagnosis	The specific identification of an injury or illness by name
Diaphragm	A dome-shaped muscle that separates the chest from the abdominal cavity
Discharge	Excess fluid escaping from the site of infection or inflammation
Dislocation	Disruption of a normal joint's position
Drowning, near	At least temporary survival of water inhalation. Often associated with the protective effects of hypothermia in cold water
Evacuation	The removal of a patient from the scene of injury or illness to a place of expert medical care
Extension	A movement which is the opposite of flexion
Exudate	Discharge
Femoral artery	A large artery found in the thigh alongside the femur
Femur	Long bone of the thigh
Fits	The movement of an unconscious patient as a result of unco-ordinated electrical activity in the brain
Flexion	The bending of a joint to bring the bones forming it closer together
Fracture	Broken bone or cartilage
Frostbite	Frozen tissue
Frostnip	Loss of blood flow to the skin during the early stages of tissue freezing as a result of blood vessels narrowing (vasoconstriction)
Heart attack	An episode of ischaemia or lack of oxygen to the heart muscle caused by a blood clot or spasm of the coronary arteries
Heat stroke	Severe elevation of body temperature (over 40°C)

High-altitude cerebral oedema (HACE)	The accumulation of excess fluid within the brain owing to a lack of oxygen at high altitude
Hyperextension	The extension of a joint beyond its normal range of movement
Hyperventilation syndrome	Symptoms usually associated with acute stress caused by reduced carbon dioxide in the blood as a result of overbreathing
Hypothermia	The lowering of body temperature below the normal body-core temperature (below 35°C). Can be mild (35°C) or severe (<35°C)
Infection	Invasion of body tissues by harmful organisms such as bacteria, viruses or fungi
Intracranial	Inside the skull
Intravenous (IV) fluids	Fluids given directly into the blood through a needle inserted into a vein
Ischaemia	A lack of blood flow to a part of the body
Ligament	A tough band of tissue that joins two bones across a joint
Lumbar spine	The lower portion of the spine between the thorax (chest) and the pelvis
Monitor	To regularly and repeatedly reassess a patient for the purpose of revising treatment plans as the situation changes
Neutral position	The position half-way between flexion and extension
Oedema	The accumulation of excess fluid within body tissue
Open fracture	A broken bone with an associated break in the skin
Oxygenation	To saturate the blood with oxygen. This takes place in the lungs
Patella	Knee cap
Penicillin	An antibiotic drug
Perfusion	The flow of blood through blood vessels in body tissues
Peripheral nerves	The nerves running from the central nervous system (brain and spinal cord) to the body tissues (periphery)
Pneumonia	Infection of the lungs
Pneumothorax	A collection of free air in the chest cavity, usually from a puncture to the chest wall or lung
Pulmonary oedema	The accumulation of excess fluid within the airspaces of the lung

Reduction	Restoration of a dislocated joint or a displaced fracture to normal anatomic position
Resuscitation	The process of trying to revive a person who appears to be dead
Scene survey	After an accident, this is the assessment in which you look for dangers to the rescuer and patient and assess the mechanism of injury
Sexually transmitted disease (STD)	Infection passed from person to person by sexual activity
Shock	A condition associated with inadequate blood supply leading to circulatory collapse; the patient is pale and sweaty, has a weak rapid pulse, irregular breathing and a reduced flow of urine
Sinuses	Hollow spaces in the bones of the skull
Spasm	Involuntary contraction of muscle
Spinal cord	The portion of the central nervous system running from the base of the brain to the lower spine, encased within the bones of the spinal column
Spine	The column of vertebral bones extending from the base of the skull to the pelvis
Stethoscope	An instrument used to listen to body sounds and transmit them to the ears of the examiner via rubber tubes
Survey	A systematic examination
Swelling	An excess of fluid in body tissues from bleeding or oedema
Symptoms	The problems complained of by the patient, eg pain, shortness of breath
Systemic	Involving the whole body
Thorax	The region of the body between the top of the abdomen and the base of the neck
Tourniquet	A constricting band used to restrict and prevent the flow of blood to an extremity
Traction	Tension applied along the long axis of bone
Trauma	Injury
Ventilation	The movement of air in and out of the lungs
Vertebrae	The bones of the spine
Vital signs	The measurement of body functions including pulse, blood pressure, respiration, consciousness, skin colour and temperature

INDEX

A

C

B

D